D0039392

# FAITH HILL & TIM McGRAW

# FAITH HILL & TIM M<sup>c</sup>GRAW

## *Soul 2 Soul*

Jim Brown

QUARRY MUSIC BOOKS

The publisher acknowledges the support of the Government of Canada, Department of Canadian Heritage, Book Publishing Industry Development Program.

*Faith Hill & Tim McGraw: Soul2Soul* is a serious critical and biographical study of the music and career of these artists. The quotation of lyrics from songs written or performed by Faith Hill and Tim McGraw illustrates the biographical information and critical analysis presented by the author and thus constitutes fair use under existing copyright conventions. The authors of all lyrics cited in the text are duly credited.

ISBN 1-55082-294-4

Designed and typeset by The Right Type, Kingston, Ontario.

Printed in Canada by Transcontinental.

Published by Quarry Press Inc,
P.O. Box 1061, Kingston, Ontario K7L 4Y5 Canada.

# CONTENTS

# MR & MRS COUNTRY MUSIC

Back in 1967 sweeping changes were taking place in our music culture as the new age of Aquarius was dawning. In June, the Beatles released SGT. PEPPER'S LONELY HEARTS CLUB BAND, and in California at the Monterey Pop Festival, Jimi Hendrix and Janis Joplin led a flower power revolution that set the music world ablaze during what has become known as the summer of love. The battle hymn of the republic became Jim Morrison's impassioned *Light My Fire!* But in the Deep South environs of Jackson, Mississippi and Monroe, Louisiana, where Faith Hill and Tim McGraw first saw the light of day, Elvis was still the King, George Jones was 'Mr' Country Music, and a divorced hairdresser from Birmingham, Alabama would soon become his 'Mrs' following the release of her debut single, *Your Good Girl's Gonna Go Bad.*

The King faded away during the 1970s, leaving millions of bereaved fans to mourn his passing, but George Jones and Tammy Wynette set the country music world on fire with their torrid romance and elopement, their marriage and divorce, electrifying the country music world with a string of hit duet records, and touring the nation with "Mr & Mrs Country Music" emblazoned on their bus. They had been married to others when they met, but their stolen romance caught the American fancy, expanding the audience for country music exponentially each time their private lives spilled over into the press, each time they released another song. George Jones' chart-topping records *Walk Through This World With Me* and *I'll Share My World With You* affirmed his love for Tammy. Her hit *Stand By Your Man* rose to the number one spot on country stations and crossed over to spend nine weeks in the pop Top 40. Country fans had never been happier.

During the '70s George and Tammy's on again, off again marriage continued to capture headlines, especially when producer Billy Sherrill fueled the flames of controversy and instigated rumors with cuts like *The Ceremony*, where they were married again on record; *Let's Build A World Together*, a song that envisioned a utopian life together; and during the final stages of their marriage breakdown, the hopeful *We're Gonna Hold On*. By 1975 the "first couple of country," as they were often called in the press, had divorced, but their chart-topping career together continued with number one hits like *Golden Ring* and *Near You* until the early 1980s. Long after their storybook marriage turned into a series of cheatin', hurtin', lovin', and leavin' incidents, "Mr & Mrs Country Music" continued to fascinate country fans 'round the world. Some 20 years after their divorce, George Jones reported in his autobiography *I Lived To Tell It All* that "not a week goes by that one of the Jones Boys isn't asked about Tammy and me. . . . Some folks are really out of touch." Almost 20 years after George and Tammy had divorced, his current wife Nancy answered the call of a doorbell rung long after midnight and faced an indignant fan who declared, when Nancy identified herself, "You're not Tammy Wynette."

Duet acts have always fascinated country fans. Perhaps they provide a fairy tale dream of love and happiness in a hard-scrabble world. While some country singers who recorded duets during the 1960s and '70s, such as Merle Haggard and Leona Williams, were also married, most were simply collaborators on record and on stage. Loretta Lynn and Conway Twitty were exceptionally popular as duet partners, winning most of the duet awards during the '70s, and although their romance was fictional, depicted only in song, country fans regarded them as a couple. Dolly Parton's first duet partner was Porter Wagoner, a man many years her senior and, she has always maintained, never her lover. When Dolly sang *Islands In The Stream* with Kenny Rogers, her fans at her solo concerts wondered where Kenny was. Kenny and Dottie West gave country fans hope for another real romance in the 1980s. Then George and Tammy were reunited in the studio to reprise their 1975 number one hit *Golden Ring*, making fans nostalgic for the days when the love being professed in song between the duet partners was true to the heart of the singer.

But by the beginning of the "Garth-Shania Era" in the early 1990s, all these fans had to hold on to was the rumor that Garth Brooks and his frequent singing partner, Trisha Yearwood, were carrying on a secret romance. As new country artists replaced traditional country artists on radio charts, the country world was more than ready for the appearance of a "first couple of *new* country." Thus in 1996, when it was reported in the media that emerging country superstar Tim McGraw and his opening act, Faith Hill, had begun to sing together on Tim's Spontaneous Combustion tour, country fans dared to speculate that the sparks flying between the two would flare into a full-blown romance, despite, of course, the fact that it was widely known Faith was engaged to be married to Scott Hendricks, a Nashville record label executive and her producer. As the 140-city tour progressed, night after night Faith joined Tim during his set to deliver a new power ballad called *It's Your Love*, and each night the two singers would slow dance together as the band played on, then finish with a kiss. Fifty shows and fifty kisses later, they were in love. In October, when they wed before playing Tim's annual fundraising Swampstock concert in Rayville, Louisiana, the stage was set for Faith and Tim to become a new first couple of country music.

Tim McGraw's rise to headlining stature had taken seven years from the time he first arrived in Nashville. There had been plenty of competition along the way, but Tim had the same competitive spirit that his father, major league baseball pitcher Tug McGraw, had displayed during pennant runs to three World Series championships. Tug had been one of the fiercest relief pitchers to ever take the mound. Batters did not look forward to facing his devastating screwball. Since Tim released his politically incorrect *Indian Outlaw* single, he has seldom been out of the national spotlight, right through to his highly publicized charge for assaulting a police officer while on tour with the George Strait Country Music Festival. While he remains somewhat of a renegade, Tim has become a loving husband and a devoted father of three daughters. He takes great pride in Faith's achievements, even now that she has surpassed him in total album sales. Among the dozens of awards on display in his home there is one he received simply for being America's number one dad. Tim's family values, coupled with his good looks, genuinely friendly temperament, crowd-pleasing live performances, and talent for selecting great songs to record, have made him new country's premiere act, bar none.

Neither Tim McGraw nor Faith Hill had it all that easy when they first came to Nashville during the late 1980s, before Garth Brooks and Shania Twain emerged as country artists who would finally outsell their pop counterparts for the first time in the history of the genre. Garth Brooks and Clint Black led the class of '89 into the fray, along with Travis Tritt, Doug Stone, and Alan Jackson. Clint's debut album, KILLING TIME, sold three million copies, an impressive debut in years past, but Garth's NO FENCES, propelled by his Country-meets-Kiss dynamics, would go on to sell more than 17 million. As an entire generation of so-called 'hat acts' followed in his footsteps, the Garthmeister never looked back. There were plenty of rookie male vocalists vying for air play—Collin Raye, Joe Diffie, Mark Chesnutt, Sammy Kershaw, Hal Ketchum, Billy Ray Cyrus, Neal McCoy, Clinton Gregory, Wade Hayes, Chris LeDoux, Tracy Lawrence, Tracy Byrd, and Toby Keith. At first, everyone was pleased that these young artists seemed to have learned their vocal style by studying George Jones, but after a while, both fans and critics began complaining that, with the exception of Brooks himself, there was little to distinguish one hat act from another. That is, until Tim McGraw carved out his own identity.

In 1994, Tim McGraw broke into the Top 10 with *Indian Outlaw* and later that year followed up with his first number one country hit, the ballad *Don't Take The Girl*. Soon after, country radio began playing the album cut *Down On The Farm*, a fan favorite in his shows that eventually went all the way to number 2.

> *Every Friday night there's a cloud of dust*
> *That leads back to a field full of pickup trucks*
> *Got ol' Hank crankin' way up loud*
> *Coolers in the back, tailgates down*
> *There's a big fire burnin' but don't be alarmed*
> *It's just country boys and girls gettin' down on the farm . . .*

— *Down On The Farm* (Kerry Kurt Phillips, Jerry Laseter)

New country fans finally had a male star, albeit with a black hat, who *was* different. Someone who could get them up with his uptempo country rockers and set them back down with his soulful country ballads. A country artist who just wanted to have a great time wherever he took to the stage. When the good-times song *I Like It, I Love It* from Tim's third album shot up the country charts and held at number one for five weeks, he was over the top. People were saying, "Move over Garth Brooks and make way for the new outlaw."

Tim McGraw has been able to appeal to working people because he works hard on stage and speaks to everyman and woman when he performs songs like the catchy *All I Want Is A Life*. And when he linked up with Faith Hill, who had broken onto the national charts in 1993 and sold more than two million copies of her debut album, the spotlight became brighter,

MR & MRS COUNTRY MUSIC

their romance and marriage reported as if Tim and Faith were reincarnations of George Jones and Tammy Wynette.

Along with the hats and hunks came a new generation of women. Mary Chapin Carpenter, Lorrie Morgan, and Patty Loveless, then Pam Tillis, Shelby Lynne, Michelle Wright, and Martina McBride immediately scored Top 40 hits. Trisha Yearwood debuted in '91 with *I'm In Love With The Boy*, a number one debut smash. Songs that were written from a woman's point of view like Mary Chapin Carpenters' *He Thinks He'll Keep Her* became anthems for women's rights in country music. Shania Twain's album THE WOMAN IN ME became a rallying point for all country women.

Faith Hill hit the top of the country charts with her first two single releases in the early months of 1994, *Wild One* and *Piece Of My Heart*. Faith and Tim's first collaboration on record, *It's Your Love*, really was the icing on the wedding cake, another number one, this time for a record-setting six weeks, and the most played record of 1997. Faith was with child and in the studio creating FAITH, recording songs that were written from a woman's point of view—including the remarkable *This Kiss*—which introduced a new vocabulary into country music.

It's the way you love me
It's a feeling like this
It's centripetal motion
It's perpetual bliss
It's that pivotal moment
It's 'ahhh' subliminal

This kiss, this kiss
(It's criminal)
This kiss, this kiss

— *This Kiss* (Beth Nielsen Chapman, Robin Lerner, Annie Roboff)

Faith's recording of the song was number one on the country charts for three weeks before it crossed over onto the pop charts. *This Kiss* was featured on the soundtrack of the feature film *Practical Magic* starring Nicole Kidman and Sandra Bullock, and the video for the song was nominated for a Grammy Award. It was a kiss heard around the world. Faith soon found herself performing on the VH1 Divas Specials along with Cher, Mariah Carey, and Diana Ross. This was an exclusive club, but Faith earned her membership card. She had sung at the 1996 Summer

11

Olympic Games to a world-wide television audience of some 3.5 billion people. Faith had sang the national anthem at Superbowl XXXIV to yet another monstrous television audience. In May 2000, she would belt out the *Star Spangled Banner* again—this time on board a nuclear Aircraft Carrier in Hawaii, during the patriotic premiere of the film *Pearl Harbor*—before climbing aboard a jet and flying to Buffalo, NY, to be at her husband's side in a court room in Orchard Park, anxiously awaiting the jury's verdict regarding charges that might send Tim to jail.

Faith had now surpassed Shania Twain as the number one contemporary female country artist in the world. As the first century of country music came to a close, there was no doubt that Faith Hill and Shania Twain were not just country music divas. They were something more—household names, worldwide. Not too shabby an accomplishment for two small-town country girls, one from Timmins, Ontario, the other from Star, Mississippi. Besides astounding the world with their record sales, Shania and Faith shocked traditional country fans with their sensuality and fashion tastes. Shania's navel became a center of seemingly endless fascination, as did Faith's alluring images on the jacket for her BREATHE CD. In Toronto for a show during the Soul 2 Soul 2000 tour with Tim, Faith fielded the inevitable questions about the photos she had posed for during the photo shoot for the album, photos *Toronto Sun* reporter Jane Stevenson suggested "wouldn't be out of place in a Victoria's Secret catalogue." In language reminiscent of Shania's defense of her integrity, Faith explained, "I'm a woman, and I celebrate my womanhood, and it's okay to try and look your best, and if people have a problem with that, then that's when I believe it comes from jealousy. And that's fine. We all have a little of that in us." She added, "I have a husband who I still like to impress. I'm not going to pose nude for Playboy or anything like that. But I wouldn't have done that to begin with. I think having children changes your perspective on everything. But I don't think that I would ever do anything to compromise what I believe in as an individual." For this freedom to express her individuality, Faith was quick to acknowledge Shania's bold spirit. "People compare us all the time. I guess I can see why the comparison would be, because we both came out of country music. We're both women. And people talk about the sex appeal and that sort of thing. But our music is radically different. Our look is not even close to the same. But I certainly credit her with opening a lot of doors. Her music just kind of transcended every boundary that existed."

Shania Twain and Garth Brooks had changed country music forever during the 1990s. By the time the annual Country Music Association awards show rolled around in September 2000, the Garth-Shania era had come to an end. Garth Brooks had accomplished his stated goal of selling 100 million albums in a single decade. He had, his publicists claimed, outsold both Elvis *and* the Beatles, and had announced his retirement, several times. Shania had eclipsed record sales of a single album for women in all genres, toured the world in spectacular fashion, and gone off to her new home in Switzerland for some well deserved rest and relaxation to make babies with her Prince Charming producer husband, Mutt Lange.

Their successors, Faith Hill and Tim McGraw, were not about to rest on their laurels. At the Opryland Theater during the nationally televised CMA Awards Show in September 2000, Faith and Tim McGraw emerged as the new leaders of country music. Faith was named Best Female Artist; Tim was Best Male Artist.

Faith Hill led off the evening's entertainment with a flawless delivery of her power-gospel number *There Will Come A Day*. It was an impressive performance, but many cited Tim's *Times Change* as their performance highlight, a song that was written in response to the ongoing debate between traditional and new country music camps. Despite the decision to vote Alan Jackson and George Strait winners of the Vocal Collaboration Award for their novelty tune, *Murder On Music Row*, written by Lary Cordle and Larry Shell, which traditionalists regarded as a political statement, the winds of change continued to blow through the awards show ceremonies.

The way Tim delivered the lyrics of *Things Change*, which had been written for him by Aimee Mayo, Bill Luther, Chris Lindsey, and Marv Green, they sounded like a direct challenge to *Murder On Music Row*. The song listed those singers who once challenged the tradition with their new voices—Hank Williams, Elvis Presley, Waylon Jennings, Willie Nelson.

*Now some say it's too country*
*Some say it's too rock 'n' roll*
*But it's just good music*
*If you can feel it in your soul*
*And it doesn't really matter*
*It's always been the same*
*Life goes on, things change . . .*

— *Things Change* (Aimee Mayo, Bill Luther, Chris Lindsey, Marv Green)

When Curb Records delayed the release of Tim's long awaited sixth album and issued a "Greatest Hits" package during the Christmas 2000 season, this live version of *Things Change* received sufficient air play that it would chart.

But the biggest story coming out of this watershed edition of the Country Music Awards was the choice of Faith and Tim as their two top vocalists. "For the first time, ever," Mary Arnold wrote in the U.K. magazine *Country Music & More*, "there was a husband and wife with separate careers being voted Female and Male Artist in the same year! It has never happened before. Much has been made by us older fans about the Tammy Wynette-George Jones relationship, and them being the King & Queen of Country. Tim sang *Things Change*, and they certainly have. So, now it is a case of 'Long live the new King and Queen of Country!'"

# LIFE IS A TEAM SPORT

The true story of how 11-year-old Timmy Smith of Start, Louisiana, discovered that his biological father was non other than major league baseball pitcher Tug McGraw, whose baseball card was one of six Topps baseball cards taped to his bedroom wall, and became at least as famous as his famous dad singing country music to packed baseball stadium crowds and national television audiences, reads like a script for a Disney film or the pages from a novel by Horatio Alger Jr. "Timmy's Luck"—the fortunes of a young boy from rural Louisiana who made it big in Nashville, making records about life down on the farm and singing about the green grass of home—would also need to include references to Mark Twain's *Tom Sawyer* because Tim McGraw's talent for delegating tasks and making more than hay while the sun shines steered him toward a vocation where just plain having fun was something he could do very well. So well, in fact, that people would come from miles around to dance and sing along. His easygoing manner and strong inner convictions, which he would later attribute to his father's genes and his mother's influence, coupled with an enterprising spirit and a genuine talent for entertaining, would lead inevitably to his being able to work effectively with the ever-expanding team of musicians, roadies, agents, record executives, producers and publicists that a country star needed in order to make a living playing music in the 21$^{st}$ century. He would also strive to become the father he never had to his children when they came along, and would value his family—his relationship with his wife and commitment to raising his children—as his number one priority.

In the summer of 1966 Betty Ann Dagostino and Frank Erwin "Tug"

McGraw were thrown together through circumstance when Tug was assigned to minor league duty with the New York Met's Triple "A" baseball franchise, the Jacksonville Suns. Three years earlier, McGraw had pitched a no-hitter in his first start as a professional pitcher in the Florida rookie league. By 1965, he was starting games for the Mets in New York City, appearing in 37 games and posting a record of two wins, seven losses and an earned run average of 3:31. During basic training in order to become a reserve in the Marines during the off-season, he acquired a sore arm, an injury that Dave McKenna notes in *The Washington Post* "the southpaw blamed on all the chin-ups and push-ups that the Parris Island drill sergeants put him through."

With this injury plaguing Tug in 1966, he was sent down to Florida for rehabilitation. During this time spent pitching for the Jacksonville Suns he became a relief specialist and developed his unique speciality pitch, a 'screwball'. With Mets' rookie prospects Nolan Ryan and Jerry Koosman already excelling in New York, breaking back into the starting rotation again might have proven difficult for the left-hander, but Tug would make it back onto the roster of the National League club in the Big Apple as a relief pitcher and become a mainstay in the New York Mets bullpen. He rapidly developed into one of the game's best relief specialists—invincible in crucial late-inning assignments—and became one of the first young pitchers to become known as a 'closer'.

Tug McGraw had been seriously into baseball since he starred as a member of the Vallejo Police Junior Peanuts All Star Team during his Little League years in California. In high school Tug continued to shine, playing for the St. Vincent's High School team. During the off-season he was a member of the school's Lettermen Society and was featured as a lead in the production of Gilbert and Sullivan's operetta *The Gondoliers*. Following his graduation, he attended Vallejo Junior College, where as a college baseball star he attracted attention of a New York Mets scout and was signed to a major league contract. In 1968 he would again fail to stick with the Mets, but in 1969 he would pitch in 42 games, along with Koosman and Ryan, during the pennant drive of the "Miracle Mets," winners of the World Series in October 1969.

Betty lived in the same apartment complex where Tug lived with two teammates that summer of 1966. She was 18 and employed in a summer job at a radio station, though she aspired to be a professional dancer. Betty's parents were estranged at the time and she lived there with her mother and an aunt. She was an attractive teenager, but her home life was plagued with unsettling visits from her father. As an escape from this domestic strife she sought companionship with the other young people who lived in the complex and gathered around the swimming pool and at community barbecues during the warm southern nights. A summer romance between Tug, 22, and Betty sparked, then fizzled. When Tug got called up to the parent team in September, he soon forgot all about those steamy nights with Betty. Betty, however, would not forget, if only because she soon found herself living out the consequences of casual sex. She was pregnant.

When Betty's relationship with the minor leaguer led to an 'intimate' liaison, Betty began to avoid Tug. She hadn't exactly felt comfortable about that consummation, and when her mother and aunt relocated in a single-family dwelling a few miles from the apartment complex, Betty felt relieved. However, she soon discovered that she was pregnant and didn't tell anyone until it was too late to do anything but go forward with the birth. "Mom was embarrassed," Tim later explained to an interviewer, "and didn't want anybody to know, and nobody did until it was so obvious she couldn't hide it." Her parents were angry; her father wanted the culprit to marry his daughter. Her mother, Catherine Dagostino, called Tug's parents in California and eventually their son. "When I found out that I was pregnant that winter," Betty recently told a journalist during a phone interview from her home in Jacksonville, Florida, "mama spoke to Tug and told him what the situation was. Daddy was so upset, he wanted Tug and me to get married, but Tug told mama it would interfere with his career." Rejected, Betty decided to go it on her own. "When a situation like that happens when you're young," Tug recently told the same interviewer, "it's confusing. You try to do what's right, but it's hard to know."

In retrospect, the unsettling call to the McGraws out west had alerted Tug's father and mother to the fact that Betty and Tug were not exactly head over heels in love. They were not in touch at all. No doubt, their advice to their son was colored by this perception. While commentators have questioned McGraw's choice of a major league baseball career over a life with Betty and their son, he believed the "right thing" was to concentrate on his career. Tug was in the Big Apple and on his way to becoming a major league baseball star. For Betty, doing what was right meant having her baby. What is surprising to people who are hearing about this story for the first time is that no support payment arrangements were made. Betty was too proud and stubborn to go that route, which in those days would have involved a lot of red tape. She simply dropped out of high school and moved to Louisiana with her parents. Tug never volunteered to offer her any financial support and Betty never asked. In fact, he didn't hear a peep from the distraught Betty.

In order to have her baby, Betty gave up her own blossoming career as a dancer, which must have been tough because she often won dance contests and was unable to attend an audition with the Dick Clark Action Dancers because she had begun to 'show'. She moved back into her parents' home, who had reunited and were now living in Louisiana. No doubt, Betty's parents' off again, on again marriage, which has been said to be filled with frequent turmoil, was not a steadying influence. Betty Dagostino gave birth to Samuel Timothy McGraw on the first day of May 1967 in a medical facility in Delhi, Louisiana.

Betty had become a single mom, a statistic in the archives, but her battle to pursue a happy life and raise her son had just begun. She was still a teenager living with her parents, and when her parents separated again she found herself living in Rayville, a small town not far from Monroe, Louisiana, and laboring as a waitress in a roadside cafe. Times were tough for single moms in the '60s, and when Betty was befriended by Horace Smith, she didn't discourage him from courting her. Smith, several years older than Betty, wanted to marry her. It was a solution to her problems. They married and moved into a small house in Start, Louisiana, an even smaller town than Rayville with merely a gin mill, two churches, and one flashing yellow light on the road passing through to mark its existence.

In New York, Tug was now engaged to be married. Memories of his one-night stands in minor league cities were fading away. He had realized the American Sports Dream and made it in the 'bigs'. He was a member of the New York Mets, World Series Champions in 1969. Still in the back of his mind was his son Tim. In a recent interview Tug said, "Without getting unnecessarily personal, just say that I was aware of Tim and knew that at some point the situation would have to be dealt with." When called to account for himself, he would respond in far better ways than millions of fathers of so-called illegitimate children. He would show up and when it counted he would pay up. In fact, if a lawsuit had ever been brought against him for child support payments, he would most probably have paid up far sooner than he eventually did.

Almost immediately following her marriage to Horace Smith, Betty was pregnant again, and in the fall of 1968 gave birth to a daughter, Tim's sister Tracey Smith. Three years later, Betty gave birth to a third child, Tim's little sister, Sandy Smith. Although Betty was mistreated by Horace,

Tim was treated well by his step-father, who at this time he believed to be his only father. A truck-driving man, Horace also taught Tim to ride horses, which would become an early passion. During long, interstate hauls in the cab of Horace's 18-wheeler, Tim would come to love the country music Horace listened to. "We'd be hauling cottonseed from Louisiana to Texas and listening to the Merle Haggard eight-track tape over and and over and over," Tim recalls. "By the time I was six," he told *Time* magazine, "I felt as if I knew the words to every album Merle Haggard ever recorded."

Tim and Horace sang along with George Jones and Charlie Pride, too, warbling away as they rolled on down the Interstate highways toward their destinations. There was a freedom to be felt out there rambling along. Trucking was more romantic and carefree than reporting to a nine-to-five job at one of the paper mills near Start, or finding employment at the General Motors headlight plant in Monroe. Country music filled the long hours spent away from home with cheerfulness and camaraderie. Tim also remembers listening to the *Grand Ole Opry* with Betty and Horace. At an early age Tim was becoming a country fan through and through, even though, like most kids his age, he was also attracted to the '70s rock bands who were popular throughout the South. Singing along with Horace also encouraged Tim to stick with singing gospel music at the Start Baptist Church and to perform show tunes in school productions and pageants. His first public performance came in 1976 in an elementary school production of *The Wizard of Oz*.

From the first time he saddled up a horse and rode alongside Horace, Tim has been a cowboy in his heart. Years later, when asked what his favorite childhood memory might be, Tim would say "riding horses." His favorite actor has always been Clint Eastwood. And one of the first luxuries he would buy as a country superstar with money to burn was a farm south of Nashville in Williamson County, Tennessee. Working the land and the livestock, whenever he had some time to spend away from his hectic touring schedule, would keep him grounded. He also discovered a fondness for trail riding and camping in the mountains in Montana, savoring the time spent in wilderness settings where a person could get back to basics and away from the consuming occupation of touring and recording.

For his seventh album, Tim recorded Craig Wiseman's *The Cowboy In Me*, which reminded people who had heard him sing the mildly controversial outlaw lyrics of *Things Change* during the CMA 2000 Awards show, that he came by both his country music and his country image honestly.

*I don't know why I act the way I do*
*Like I ain't got a single thing to lose*
*Sometimes I'm my own worst enemy*
*I guess that's just the cowboy in me . . .*

— *The Cowboy In Me* (Craig Wiseman, Jeffery Steele, Al Anderson)

As a boy Tim enjoyed living the country life and remembers the many jobs he performed while growing up in and around the Start-Rayville area fondly. "I grew up driving the cotton picker, the tractor, the bean trucks, the rice trucks," he recalls. "You name it, I did it." At the time, there was seldom enough money to go around, and Tim's efforts were appreciated by Betty, who was determined to make a go of things with Horace, despite his occasional abusive moods. Betty often worked as a waitress during those years. She listened to singers like Rita Coolidge on both radio and records, providing Tim with a grounding in pop. She adored the Beach Boys.

In 1976, Betty separated from Horace and filed for divorce, asserting her right to discontinue the increasingly abusive relationship, but her biggest challenge was yet to come. The following year a medical diagnosis revealed that she had cancer. Surviving cancer in the 1970s was not nearly as common as it is today. Mostly the news that you had cancer meant that you could count the years you had left to live on the fingers on one hand. Betty, however, survived both the life-threatening disease *and* the treatments, which in those days were often as devastating as cancer itself. As a consequence of this harrowing experience, Betty found a new hopefulness and came to believe in her inner strength. With her three children in their formative years, Betty would prevail, establishing a less chaotic home life, remarrying, and eventually becoming known as Betty "McMom" Trimble.

Timmy Smith showed an early love of music, singing at church functions and school concerts. He would sometimes pick up a hairbrush and, pretending that it was a microphone, imitate the singers he heard on the radio, but his passion soon became playing sports, especially Little League Baseball. Tug McGraw was one of his heroes, a member of the 1969 and 1973 Mets teams that had become World Series Champions, and when Tug was traded to the Phillies in 1974, he became the highest paid relief pitcher in professional baseball. Ironically, 11-year-old Tim had taped Tug's baseball card onto the wall of his bedroom along with cards for Cesar

Cedeno, Nolan Ryan, Ozzie Smith, and Greg Luzinski. "My friends and I were fans of Tug basically because he was such a nut," Tim recalls. By now, Tim had sprouted into a sizeable youth, no longer "little Timmy," but still thought that Horace Smith was his father. After the divorce and several relocations in and around Richland Parish, he would hear things, now and then, at family functions, overhearing relatives who would shush up once they noticed his presence. Then one fateful afternoon in 1979, while his mother was at work, Tim, home alone, opened Pandora's box, so to speak, and his tears began to flow. Tears of grief because his "real father" had left him and his mom and gone off to the big city. He was merely rummaging around in a closet trying to discover what he and his sisters were receiving as Christmas presents that year when he came upon that box and discovered his birth certificate.

Tim had already had his suspicions. "I might have heard a comment or two from relatives or something," he later told one interviewer, "and I started asking around. I found a birth certificate and the names were a little different. One was scratched out, I think. Something that set my antenna up." Dave McKenna, writing in *The Washington Post*, reported that "Tim came across his birth certificate in an unopened box. The space designated for the baby's father contained only a scribbled out name. But beside the scribbling, under 'occupation', Tim could make out 'baseball player'." He called his mother at work and said, "Mom, can you come home? We have to talk."

"I was planning to tell him when he got a little older," Betty has said in interviews, "when I thought he could handle it better." When she received the troubled phone call from her son, she left work and was soon at her son's side. Yes, she told him, Tug McGraw, the man whose baseball card was taped to the wall of his bedroom, was his real dad, his biological father. At the time, it was impossible for Betty to explain to her son why his "biological father" had chosen not to be his "dad." In the opening chapter to her book, *Tim McGraw: A Mother's Story*, Betty explains this situation from a mother's point of view. "Tug's treatment of Tim," she wrote, "broke my heart. But Tim has always been a survivor. Instead of becoming angry, the experience made him stronger and more compassionate." She could have been speaking of herself.

"We had a good talk," Tim has recalled, "and then a good cry." Now that the truth was out in the open, Tim wanted to meet his father. Betty sent messages to Tug, but her requests for a meeting were not answered. Betty had not spoken with Tug since their night of intimacy in 1967, but she was no longer a shy, embarrassed teenager. She was not prepared to merely let this slide this time. Armed with a new determination, she persisted until she spoke with Tug himself, laying it out that he owed it to his son to at least meet with him. Tug agreed to meet with Betty and Tim in Houston before a Phillies-Astros game. Betty and Tim made the trip to east Texas in the family car. They had lunch with Tug in a private dining room at the hotel.

"Tug handled it real well," Betty recently told *People* magazine. He said, " 'Hey, son, I'm your father. I haven't been much of a father, but I am a friend. Do you want to go to a ball game?'"

With the ice broken and the three on their way to the ballpark, Tug told Betty, "If anyone asks, just tell people you are an old friend and Tim is your son." Which Betty now finds to be a chuckle whenever she relates this story to an interviewer. "And that is what I told people," she continues, "but they figured it out." She was asked, "How long have you known Tug?" She said, "Eleven years." Then she was asked, "How old is your son?" The cat was out of the bag when she answered, "Eleven years."

Tim's most vivid impression of Tug was that he was big. "I was so shy that I just sat at lunch looking down at my plate," he recalls. "I remember Tug asked me, 'Do you have any favorite Phillies?' And when I started naming some—Bake McBride, Mike Schmidt and some others—Tug laughed and said, 'Name me!'" Tim has also said that things didn't exactly get off to a smooth start that afternoon. "He gave up a grand slam," Tim told Dave McKenna. "That didn't bother me, but I could tell it bothered him. He told me he was trying out a new pitch, and that's what got hit. I'd never even been to a (Major League) baseball game before that, but I knew enough about pitching to believe him."

Another report has the six-foot, 185-pound Tug saying, "I can't be a father to you, but I can be a friend." It would be several years before this friendship would take hold. In fact, Tim and Tug would not meet face to face again until Tim was in his final year at Monroe Christian High School. As he told Dave McKenna: "I still thought of him more as the baseball player than as my father, until I was 18, and changed my name to McGraw, most people didn't know." Tim had confided in a few close friends, however. One of these friends, Lance Butler, a Little League teammate of Tim's at the time, later told McKenna, "Knowing that his dad was this guy on television who won a World Series was impressive to me and the rest of the kids in the neighborhood. But Tim never acted like it was a big deal growing up. I don't think it changed him at all."

Betty would slug it out for years, working two jobs and studying to further her education, before she saw a more successful father and son reunion. Tim had taken to his father even before he knew him as a father. Tug had showed tenacity in the difficult role of relief pitcher, and his "You Gotta Believe" motto had become the spirited slogan of the '73 Mets team in their pennant run and post-season victories. By the time they met in '79, Tug was pitching for the Phillies and Tim was a big fan. Now that he knew his genetic background, Tim would no longer be surprised that he had a talent for sports, which Horace had not had, and, as he learned more about Tug, no longer surprised that he had a talent for singing, which Tug had also shown during his high school years.

*Screwball*, Tug's autobiography, co-written with *New York Times* sportswriter, Joseph Durso, had been published in 1974 and then issued as a paperback, so there was a wealth of information available concerning his millionaire biological father, who had not possessed the same overpowering fast-ball that had powered Nolan Ryan's career, but had nevertheless prevailed due to a pesky screwball that baffled batters. Tug's outgoing personality had also led to the creation of a comic strip called *Scroogie* based on a cartoon character modeled on Tug that was drawn by Mike Witte. Scroogie was a left-handed screwball pitcher who played for the "Pets," a combination of Mets and Phillies that delighted sports fans from coast to coast. Tug had married and was father to two children; Tim's half-brother Mark, and half-sister Cari. Then in 1981 when Tim was 14, Tug authored a book titled *Lumpy*, the story of a baseball who realized his lifelong dream of appearing in the Fall Classic. This was a creative children's publication, which also included a 45 rpm record, and has become a collector's item along with baseball cards of Tug McGraw and other signed and unsigned memorabilia such as baseballs and game jerseys. Although neither father nor son knew this during the '80s, it would not be long before memorabilia signed by Tim McGraw would be as sought after as the sports memorabilia signed by his famous father.

Tim soon developed a more outgoing personality and interests not merely confined to excelling at sports. He is remembered by high-school classmates for a classy duet performance of *Silhouettes*, the finger-popping ballad first made popular by the Rays in the 1950s and covered during the British Invasion in the '60s by Herman's Hermits. Tim also kept up his attendance at Choir practices at the Monroe Christian High School, where he gained valuable experience in harmony singing. Like many teenagers, he was inspired by Elvis to yearn for a career as a rock star, although an illness kept him from his one chance to see the King live. Elvis's influence in those days was huge, especially on teenagers who did any singing at all. In recent interviews, Tim has said, "Doesn't everybody think they're Elvis when they're by themselves?" And although he continued to collect baseball cards and listen to country music, his widening interests included the brash stadium rock music of Rush, Journey, and Styx. Betty encouraged Tim's musical interest by purchasing a set of drums, but the teenager drove the whole family bananas when he played along with his favorite rock records. Pounding drum skins and whacking cymbals, however, would not become an overriding passion. For Tim McGraw, like most teens who envision the experience from afar, a career as a rock star meant fronting a band. "When you're 14 or 15," he says, "and you think about being a rock star or a country singer, the thing you think about is being out on stage in front of screaming fans."

In 1980, with the Phillies making it into post-season playoffs, Tim's father, Tug, *was* in front of tens of thousands of screaming fans in major league stadiums—millions of television viewers, too—as he strode fiercely in from the bullpen to put out late-inning fires night after night. Once again, Tug had himself a World Series ring, this time for defeating the Kansas City Royals as a member of the Philadelphia Phillies. Tim was 13, and even though he had experienced mixed feelings about their relationship, he was still a loyal Tug McGraw fan. In a few short years roles would reverse themselves, but not before Tug made a commitment to help Tim with his education. As it was at the time, Betty had kept on keeping on with no help at all from Tug and had become a bookkeeper, eventually purchasing a family home for herself and her three children. She survived yet another marital and personal crisis when she discovered that her second husband had sexually abused one of her daughters, a crime that might have gone unpunished in the past, perhaps even been tolerated in some circumstances. Fortunately, society had come to view this behavior as reprehensible, and she had plenty of support in dealing with the situation. Her catharsis would come when she wrote her book *Tim McGraw: A Mother's Story*. She would also be rewarded when Dick Clark, not one to be put off at all by aging, learned of her story and 'made her day' by presenting her with a dance 'contract' during an appearance on the *Leeza Show*, 30 years after she had put family before career and chosen to bear and raise her son.

By the time Tim was 16, he had given up on playing baseball and became a coach, helping out the younger kids whenever he could. He had also played a whole lot of football and became an avid NFL fan. His favorite NFL team was the Green Bay Packers. "I played everything in high school. That was what I felt my calling in life was going to be, to be an athlete," he has recalled. "Once I got out of high school, I realized I wasn't dedicated enough to be an athlete." Growing up in a small town in rural Louisiana meant that many of his influences would come to him through the media, through television and Hollywood films. Television was the primary medium through which he had learned about his baseball heroes, but it was a movie starring Al Pacino that piqued his interest in getting a college education. "I wanted to be a lawyer, ever since I saw Al Pacino in *And Justice for All*," he has recalled, "but money was a problem." Tug had not answered Tim's letters after their initial meeting and nearly seven full years had passed by. Seven years in which Tug had seriously wondered if Tim were really his son. Seven years colored by consultations with attorneys. By the time Tim was in his final year of high school, Tim had formed his own opinions of the man who would not be his father. Especially when it came to how poor their family was and the fact that he didn't have the money to attend college.

For the first time since he had learned of his birth father's identity, Tim spoke out boldly to his mother, saying, "Mama, this is just not fair. You never asked Tug for a dime. The least he could do is help me out with college." At this point Betty acted firmly, enlisting the help of an attorney before she wrote Tug a "stern" letter. "It went back and forth with the lawyers, who, I guess, were concerned that I wanted to cause Tug trouble," she recently recalled. "Heck, if I had wanted to do that, I would have walked out on the field when I was pregnant." The agreement reached by the lawyers stated that Tug would pay for Tim's education, but also laid it out that Tim not contact Tug again. Tim was not satisfied with this stipulation and asked for one final meeting with Tug. Nervous in the days leading up to this meeting, Tug requested that an attorney accompany him to their meeting in a hotel lobby in Houston. When Tim ambled into view that lawyer said to Tug, "You had no need to bring an attorney with you. Here comes your son. Heck, he even walks like you." As Tug would later say, "Genetics is a scary thing."

Tug, now retired from professional baseball, relented. He introduced Tim to his wife, Phyllis, and his half-brother and half-sister. Tug realized what he was missing by not seeing more of Tim. Tim really had turned out to be a nice guy and had an intelligence about him and a conviction that he wanted to make something of himself in this life. The father sensed the same determination in this young man that he himself had possessed when it came to focusing on a career in his teenage years. Eventually, the relationship would warm right up with Tim and Tug becoming pals. They have had their heart-to-hearts and they have done their share of drinking together, as well, including, as Tim puts it, "nights we got drunk and came close to getting thrown in jail."

Country singers who go to college don't always stick all that long. Willie Nelson has said that he "majored in dominoes" during his brief stint at Baylor University in Waco. Tim began to create a legend of his own by majoring in 'happy hour'. "I did get into the party scene just a little bit too much, and that's probably what turned me toward music," he confided to one journalist. "I knew I had to do something that didn't require much education." This was the same sort of sensible decision he had made when he had decided not to become a professional athlete.

In high school Tim had been a popular and talented football and basketball player, but he realized he didn't have the focus it would take to become a 'pro ballplayer', and he didn't go to college on a sports scholarship, although, apparently, several were offered to him. He had decided he wanted to be a lawyer; that was his focus at the time. At first Tim was resolved to be more serious than Willie Nelson had been about his university classes in Texas. But Tim had not developed good study habits in high school, coasting along on his natural abilities and seldom preparing himself for exams. He knew he would have to bear down and get serious in order to make it in post-secondary studies. Tim enrolled in courses at Northeast Louisiana State in Monroe and attended classes for three years. It wasn't long, however, before he began to realize that he was not cut out to be an attorney. "I realized that after my first semester, when I got my grades," he has said. A "C" average was not going to get him into law school. Then as he was adjusting to this reality, a random trip to a pawn shop during summer break resulted in a change of direction that would become his focus from that point onward.

"I bought a guitar and taught myself to play," he says. "I bought it at a pawnshop for $25. I was bored and I thought, 'How hard can it be? It's got six strings'. . . but it was a slow process. I lived in a house with five or six guys and they hid my guitar when I first started. Of course, after I got better, they used to make me bring it out when girls came around." It wasn't long before Tim was sitting in with local bands. The next step was to form his own band, the Electones. Their first paying gig was the "Pig BBQ in Jacksonville."

Tim had come full-circle by this time, back to the honky tonk music that he had first listened to with Horace, that he had heard everywhere in the South played and sung by Lefty Frizzell, George Jones, and Merle Haggard. "I grew up in rural Louisiana," he has reminisced, "and I think my music reflects that." Horace would remain the "daddy" in his life, coming to his shows, once he got a band. "That's who I called 'daddy' until I was 10 or 11," he says, "and I still call him daddy. When we play down in Louisiana, he comes to the shows and hangs out."

For Tim, "honky tonk" would be a hard-driving style that early Tim & Faith biographer Scott Gray, author of *Perfect Harmony*, refers to as "turbo-tonk," a sort of Haggard meets Lynyrd Skynyrd hybrid. Southern rock, as played by Lynyrd Skynyrd, the Jacksonville-based band that released the rock anthem *Sweet Home Alabama* in 1974, the Allman Brothers (with Dicky Betts), and the Charlie Daniels' Band, has always had country roots. Tim McGraw can rock with the best Southern rockers, but like fiddle-playing vocalist Daniels' best tracks, including the classic *The Devil Went Down To Georgia*, Tim's rocking cuts have undeniably country underpinnings. His own country roots, which betray a full knowledge of the Possum's seminal east-Texas honky tonk style, and Tim's oft-acknowledged worship of the Bakersfield based Haggard, have infused his vocals with essence of honky tonk, especially his ballads. As a teenager he came to love the Eagles and respect everything George Strait ever did. But it was the Little River Band, a country pop act that broke out of Australia and became known internationally, that seemed to bring it all home for Tim. Their vocal harmonies showcase a vibrant country pop style that also influenced Tim McGraw during the years when he was learning to play the guitar and working out with his first band, the Electones.

Tim hung around the college scene, now merely enrolled in a partial program. He wanted to switch careers, and, in effect, already had, but he had not made the inevitable move to Nashville to seek his fame and fortune as a country singer. "The only thing I learned in college was how to float a keg," Tim confided to Dave McKenna, "and I didn't figure that was going to get me far. So, even though it was scary, I wasn't giving up much. I thought I could make it."

A chance encounter with Randy Travis and manager Lib Hatcher in a cafe, during a visit with mother Betty in Florida, helped Tim decide on his course of action. Right away Randy said sure, go to Nashville. Hatcher, who would soon wed Randy, had steered Randy Traywick's rapid rise to fame as "Randy Travis," country's leading new traditionalist star. She told Tim, "If you sing as good as you look, you'll make it in country music." No doubt, Tim figured she knew what she was talking about. The owner-operator of the Nashville Palace, where Traywick had worked as a singer and cook before getting his break with Warner Brothers Records, was not the only person advising Tim to head to Music City. Betty was saying, "Go for it!" But still Tim hesitated. There was one more person he knew he must speak with before making the move, his birth father and current benefactor, Tug McGraw. But he would not make his phone call to Tug until he was already in Nashville.

"I sold my car and my shotguns and water-skis and everything I had," Tim later explained to a reporter from *Music City News*. "So, I had saved a little money when I got there. I stayed in a hotel for a couple of weeks and that took care of most of the money. I stayed with friends for about a month and then actually found an apartment. I got lucky in a lot of ways. I had friends that helped me out. And then I worked in clubs and sang around town."

Tug was not thrilled at the idea of Tim quitting college. Tim, however, resorted to his considerable knowledge of how Tug had gone and done it during his own rise to fame, reminding Tug that he had quit his classes at Vallejo Junior College to pursue a career as a major league pitcher. "He *had* me there," Tug admits. "Okay, end of story." Convinced and impressed at his son's resourcefulness, Tug agreed to continue his basic support payments a while longer. "Good," Tim said over the phone line, "'cause guess where I am?"

Stories are everything in country music. Legend has it that Willie Nelson drove a battered Buick into Nashville which gave up the ghost out front of Tootsie's Orchid Lounge. There Willie met the songwriters who helped him get his songs recorded by Faron Young and Patsy Cline. Tim's story has him arriving on a Greyhound bus on May 9, 1989, the fateful day that one of his personal heroes, the immensely popular Keith Whitely, who had brought a high lonesome bluegrass flavor back into popularity on his country records, died from alcohol poisoning. Tim learned of Whitely's death while hoisting a few cold ones with some songwriters he met at a bar in the Hall of Fame Inn. Country fans were saddened by the passing of Whitely, who had recently married local singer Lorrie Morgan. Keith and Lorrie had been viewed as successors to the George Jones and Tammy Wynette legend, but the bottle had let Keith down, and his tragic death reminded fans and artists throughout the country community of the days when the Possum nearly lost his battle with booze and his marriage with Tammy came to a sorry end.

As fate would have it, one of those songwriters in the Hall of Fame Motor Inn bar—which at one time had been a favorite refuge for George Jones during his binges and was now part of the Quality Inn chain of hotels—was Tommy Barnes. Once the two men got to know each other, Barnes played Tim some of the songs he had written, including a song he called *Indian Outlaw*. "I knew it was a hit the first time I heard it," Tim has recalled. There was little he could do with the song at the time, but he stuck it in his back pocket and began knocking on doors on Music Row. The odds of a country singer making it in Nashville are not good. Thousands try their luck each year and less than a dozen are signed to contracts. One or two of these new artists is successful at selling records, the bottom-line for a country singer in Nashville. Each new crop of hopefuls faces a Music Row elite who have their own ideas about finding the "next Randy" or the "next Ricky." Of course, after Garth Brooks' breakthrough string of number one hits—beginning with *If Tomorrow Never Comes*, *The Dance*, *Friends In Low Places*, *Unanswered Prayers*, and *The Thunder Rolls*—plus his unprecedented multi-platinum album sales and sensational stadium shows, all the Nashville label executives wanted to find and sign the "next Garth." Fortunately for Tim McGraw, the current elite had decided that youth was "in" and the older artists, who sometimes appeared "hokey" in the new music video medium, should be put out to pasture. That meant that George Jones and Merle Haggard were not heard on country radio very much any more in the '90s, but it did make way for a generation of "hat acts," including Tim McGraw. So, Tim came to town at the best possible moment. Tim soon signed to a management deal with RPM Management; Mark Hurt at RPM believed he could get Tim a record deal. "All the labels," Hurt recalled during an interview with *TV Guide*, "started signing everybody that could hold a guitar."

During his earliest days in Nashville, Tim's background in sports provided him with an unsuspected resource. Visualization and focus, which are important to athletic success, were two mental disciplines that he was able to adapt to the task of making the rounds to the Music Row offices and showcasing his talents. "The way sports helps is the discipline," Tim explains. "You have to have visualization. You visualize yourself catching the touchdown pass while you're lying in bed at night and if you visualize it enough times, when it happens, it becomes natural. That's what helped me in this business, visualizing what I wanted to do and become." Tim's father Tug had been able to visualize dealing with the tough hitters he faced during critical late inning relief appearances. But Tug had merely been a team player on clubs comprised of many such motivated and dedicated baseball players. He hadn't won those three World Series rings on his own. Tim was called on to combine the best of team sport values with an intense individual drive to succeed on his own if he was going to secure a deal with a Nashville label.

Like Tug, Tim had always been a team player, willing to lend Horace a hand whenever he could, always helping Betty mind his younger two sisters, and doing well with his baseball, basketball, and football teams. Now he found it necessary to deal with musicians in order to form a band; songwriters in order to find hit songs to record; and the various agents, managers, tour managers, and record label executives who conducted business on Music Row. For an artist to 'make it' in country, it was necessary to put together an entire team of people. Tim was learning all over again that life just seemed to be a team sport. Once he put together his band the Dancehall Doctors, they would spend their afternoons playing flag football until they wore themselves out and headed back to their hotel or motel rooms for a brief nap before their evening show.

# A ZEST FOR LIFE

The artist currently known as Faith Hill was first named Audrey Faith Perry by Edna and Ted Perry, the couple who adopted her one week after she was born in Jackson, Mississippi on September 21, 1967. While "Faith" wasn't exactly in vogue as a name for a youngster in the 1960s, the designation has turned out to be fortuitous, especially in light of her story book marriage and family life with Tim McGraw in the 1990s. During her formative years she accepted being named "Audrey Faith" as Edna and Ted's way of saying they regarded her as a God-given addition to their small family. They had *faith* in her—how could she quibble with that?

The Perry home was in Star, Mississippi, not far from the metropolitan center of Jackson, but tiny in comparison. At the time they adopted and named Audrey Faith, Edna and Ted had two sons, eight-year-old Wesley and five-year-old Steve. Edna, however, desperately wanted a daughter. Ted wasn't so hot on the idea, especially when his wife told him she wanted to *adopt* a baby girl. "She finally talked him into adopting me," Faith says. "Once I was theirs, he was putty in my hands." The issue of being adopted was never hidden from Audrey Faith, which is something she has said she appreciates; eventually, when she was in her 20s, she would become curious about her biological parents.

During her childhood years Faith received unconditional love from both Edna and Ted. "My mother and father," she says, "have given me everything. They gave me a backbone, first of all, that has allowed me to be independent and a career woman and a wife and a mother, and I give them full credit for that." Key to this development of shared love among the Perry family was the way that Faith's parents encouraged their off-spring to express their feelings, especially their feelings of affection, although they were not discouraged from expressing their feelings of concern, either.

Edna and Ted loved all three of their children equally, and Edna regularly read to them before bedtime—books like *The Grinch Who Stole Christmas*, which became one of Faith's favorites, a story she would read to her children when she began her own family. When Edna felt that Faith was old enough to understand the concept and able to handle the emotional turmoil involved, she told Faith that she had been adopted. So far, Edna was handling this dicey issue as well as any mother of an adopted child could hope to do. This forthright approach would ensure that Faith and her brothers would continue to feel that they were family, no matter what happened in later years. Faith had bonded with Edna and would always regard her as her mom, but she did wonder, now and then, just what her birth mother was like.

Curiosity about her heritage was merely curiosity, not a deep sense of loss and longing. As an adult Faith remembered during a revealing interview published in *Redbook* magazine that "I would be lying to you if I said that I didn't have some kind of feeling, not of emptiness, but of curiosity about my biological mother. I was so ambitious as a child. I was a dreamer, the kind of dreams that made me know things were going to happen to me. So, I always wondered where that quality came from. And there are all those other questions. Who do I look like? Do I have a brother? Do I have a sister? So I went on a search, but I didn't do it without the support of my family."

Remarkably, Faith also felt considerable insight into Edna's dilemma as an adoptive mother and the pathos she must have been going through. "She's encouraged me," Faith told *Redbook*, "to do what I needed to, but I know there's been pain for her. Once the ball started rolling, I'm sure she was thinking, 'I don't want her to find her birth mother because I'm her mother.' And that just truly broke my heart. We never talked about it. But, as a woman, I knew what she must have been feeling. The search took me three years. I wouldn't settle for 'no.' I prayed so hard and my family prayed, too, but I think everyone felt that there was so little information to go on that it would basically be a miracle if this woman was ever found."

Finally, Faith went to a judge in Jackson, in the court where she was "given over for adoption." She arranged for an intermediary to be appointed "in case my biological family didn't want to see me." The judge, who happened to be a woman, agreed to this plan of action. Soon after that Faith met with her birth mother for the first time, a woman who has sometimes been referred to by journalists as a "Faith Hill look-a-like," which may be ass-backwards when you first encounter it, but is a biological clue, nevertheless. Because Faith has chosen not to reveal the identity of her birth parents, who are not celebrities like Tug McGraw, for example, and who prefer to live out their private lives without being invaded by members of the media and photo-hungry paparazzi, this remarkable physical similarity is all we have to go on when it comes to describing Faith's birth mother.

Faith has painted one exceedingly glowing portrait of her mother as an artist. "I found out that she was a painter, an artist," Faith told *Redbook*, "and she has an incredible sense of style. She's very tall. She's a sweet, sweet woman. I have a lot of respect for her, and I had no feelings of anger or any of that. I'm a mother now, and I know she must have had a lot of love for me to want to give me what she felt was a better chance. Thank God she let me live!"

For Faith's biological mother becoming pregnant before becoming married to Faith's biological father and bearing a child out of wedlock in the 1960s was something she could not face. "She said she was very young," Faith confides, "and did not feel she could go to her family and tell them that she was pregnant before the wedding. I had always been told a different story—and I don't know where this came from—that she'd had an affair with a married man who didn't want to leave his wife to marry her, so she gave me up for adoption. But it was completely untrue." Faith does speak with her biological parents, occasionally, but for her Edna and Ted Perry will always be Mom and Dad.

Faith Perry's love of singing was first noticed during youth choir rehearsals at the local Baptist church, even before her 'talent' for doing it became apparent. She was the loudest voice in the choir. Beginning at age three, she belted out her lyrics with confidence. "I can't remember a time when I wasn't singing," Faith told Larry Delaney for an article printed in the February 1994 edition of *Country Music News*. "My momma tells the story that I used to hold the hymnal upside down, pretending I could read the words as I sang along with the congregation."

She was inspired by the fervor of fundamentalist church services and gospel singing. It wasn't long before she was singing at 4-H Club events and family reunions. "My mom," Faith told Delaney, "used to pay me to sing at the family get-togethers. Yup, she used to pay me 50 cents when the really big family reunions happened. If it was just a close family thing, I'd only get 25 cents. Those were my first paying gigs!"

As a teenager, Faith would continue to sing gospel music, sometimes at black Baptist church services where she was a physically demonstrative participant, and often felt "filled with passion." "People were on their feet the entire time at those churches," Faith told an internet interviewer at *Country Music World.com*. "Even my black friends would joke me and say, 'Girl, you've got a black soul. You should've been born black!'"

With mother Edna working as a bank teller and father Ted employed as a factory worker at the Presto Manufacturing Company plant in Jackson, there wasn't a surplus of money during Faith's childhood. Still, the Perry family was not poverty-stricken as so many families of country stars have been. Nor was she forced to quit school at a young age and work on the family farm as her father had been forced to do in order to help feed the 13 other children in his large family. Faith would become inspired by her father's dedicated work ethic and her mother's equally loving devotion to her children. "They were strong," she says, "the hardest working people I have ever known. Mom financially stretched a dollar into $10. That's impressive!" The fact that Ted Perry was illiterate, that his lack of schooling meant that he had not learned how to read, was not a negative factor in their happy and stable home life. It was known, but it was never an issue while Faith was growing up. The Perrys were too busy having fun and making do with what they had to worry about what they didn't have. This warm family environment, despite the lack of luxuries, would become a huge asset when Faith chose singing country music as a vocation. "God was watching over me and put me in this incredible home where I had a great family life," Faith told *McCalls*. "If you show love to someone, it's amazing what possibilities it gives that person in life. I know how lucky I am."

Like many parents in the '60s, before television viewing changed American family activities from active participation to passive couch-potato addiction, Ted and Edna cultivated a vegetable garden. Edna was somewhat of a green thumb, and Faith remembers the vegetables that grew and the flowers that blossomed in their yard each year. "My parents and I grew up eating out of the garden," she recalls, "fresh vegetables, and they still do that, and they bring them to the kids, to both my brothers and myself. It's wonderful." When asked what she most wanted in the future, she mentioned gardening. "I don't garden because I don't have time. My mother is such a talent, she has a gift for that. I just want to be able to go outside and pick my flowers and bring them back inside and smell them and set them up inside the house." No doubt, her nostalgia for the times when Edna Perry did just that are comforting memories for Faith today.

With Faith's rise to superstar status in the late 1990s people 'round the world have come to view her as one of the 50 most beautiful women in the world. People who read *People* magazine, that is. During her junior high school years, however, Faith Perry hated how she looked. She might be able to emulate Aretha Franklin during gospel concerts, but her braces and her tall, skinny body did not provide her with a whole lot of self-confidence. "I had long skinny arms, long skinny legs, long skinny hair," she recalls, "and braces." At the time she wanted to be 'five-foot-five' but was well on her way to becoming five-feet-nine-inches in height. These awkward growing pains were not to last forever, but for a few years they were a major challenge for Faith. Childhood friend Gaye Knight would later tell an interviewer that Faith was "brutally hard on herself," even though "when she sang a cappella she could bring the roof down."

In high school, armed with advice from mother Edna that winning was not as important as the family love they shared, coupled with a solid Christian upbringing during which her mom had stressed the Golden Rule and putting herself in "other people's shoes," Faith persevered and eventually distinguished herself in cheerleading and basketball and became her junior class president. "Faith never did anything halfway," another high school friend, Kathy Jones, remembers. "In cheerleading she didn't just chant, she screamed."

Faith Perry was already blossoming into a willowy teenager who showed early promise of adult beauty, and would eventually be cited as "most beautiful" by her classmates. For another high school yearbook, Faith was named "most popular." Her down-home charm would win over many people along the way as she took to entertaining and eventually made the trek to Nashville. Still, as the familiar lyrics of Bobby Rydell's 1960s hit suggested, she *was* a bit of a *Wild One*. By the time that Faith was in her teens, the troubled and tragic roles of rebellious teenagers played by Sal Mineo and James Dean in the popular Hollywood movie *Rebel Without A Cause* had achieved cult status. Being a "rebel without a cause" had also become a slang expression, but Rydell's song lyrics could more appropriately be applied to Faith Perry's teenage years. She was a "wild one," not a "bad seed." No doubt, there were times when her pranks got her in deep doo doo, and surely this same "down-home charm" helped keep her out of serious trouble. Her pal Gaye Knight remembers that "I was afraid to get in trouble, but Faith would say, 'you've got to live a little.' "

"I was fearless," Faith says, "I enjoyed doing crazy, daredevil things." But her exploits, such as the time she kissed Bo Tanner, a grade-two class-mate, during a classroom session, were never the activities of a juvenile delinquent. "It was second grade," she remembers. "We were sitting across the aisle from each other, and the two kids in front of us held up note-books, and we leaned across the aisle and kissed in front of the teacher. She was reading or something. It was a conspiracy." That 'first kiss' was a good-natured prank, the sort that made the protagonist in *Anne Of Green Gables* endearing to readers of all ages. Like the mischievous Anne who once dyed her hair green in Lucy Maud Montgomery's novel, Faith—who is a natural brunette—would also screw up when dying her hair blonde and be forced to go on stage with pink hair.

All in all, while she was no goody-two-shoes, she was scarcely a bad apple, and her pranks, which included messing up neighbors' yards with toilet tissue and racing across level crossings just in the nick of time before trains arrived, would scarcely have been noted if they had been performed by teenage boys. Journalists would later latch onto the image of her as a "wild one," but to gain a perspective on what her teenage years were really like it is helpful to note that her favorite television show was *Little House on the Prairie*. When questioned on these seeming opposites during the promotion of her first Nashville hit, *Wild One*, Faith would say, "I wasn't a hoodlum or anything like that, but I liked to get in trouble a little bit, to see how far I could go." While similar behavior had gotten other girls in even more trouble and conflict with their parents, Edna and Faith's strong bond of love and loyalty proved to be stronger than most. Perhaps this explains Faith's devotion to her favorite television show. "I cry every time I see one of those shows," she told interviewers in 1994. "When I have kids, I want them to see 'em. They teach you so much about morals."

Daring to be different would eventually distinguish Faith from the rest of the hopefuls vying to be a country music star in the early '90s. And the need to escape the hum-drum day-to-day existence in a small town would eventually provide enough daredevil energy that she packed her bags and headed to Tennessee to pursue her dream. Just like Elvis Presley, who had been born in Tupelo, Mississippi on January 8th, 1935, had done before her. "Like everyone else," she recalls, "I really liked Elvis a lot. I think the first record I ever had was his LEGENDARY PERFORMER VOL. 2 album. I used to sing all the songs on that album." While in England to promote the release of her album BREATHE, she would explain to interviewers that recording the song *Bringing Out The Elvis* was not only appropriate, it had also brought her full circle, back to her earliest roots. "The first music I ever heard," she recalled, "apart from in church, was Elvis Presley. I heard Elvis on the radio and bought some of his albums, then in 1975 when I was eight my mother took me to see him in concert."

For Faith, Elvis was something else, as was Tanya Tucker, who also idolized Elvis, dressing up as a teenager to imitate the King. Faith learned the radio hits that teenage phenomenon Tanya Tucker put out during the '70s, including *Delta Dawn*, which became a staple in her early repertoire along with *Jesus Loves Me*. For a while during her pre-teen years, Charlie Pride's *Kiss An Angel Good Morning* was Faith's favorite country song. Patsy Cline, Tammy Wynette and Emmylou Harris were also influences before she became a teenager. Faith loved the way Aretha Franklin sang. "In high school," she told Larry Delaney, "I grew up listening to Reba." Reba McEntire would become her favorite. In 1994 when Faith toured with Reba McEntire and John Michael Montgomery, she would tell *Country Music People*, "Reba has to be the top of the cake of all that has happened to me so far . . . Someone whom I was truly influenced by, really deeply, in more ways than just music. I thought she was a cool lady, a smart business woman. I wanted to be that person."

Faith finagled her way backstage to meet her idol at a Reba concert. When the long-anticipated moment finally came, Faith was unable to speak. She received her autograph . . . time to move on . . . before she had a chance to say a word. But Faith was not done, yet. "I love you, Reba McEntire," she called out as she left the little knot of autograph seekers who were lined up to meet the Nashville star. "I love you, too, honey," McEntire called back.

While Reba did not remember this occasional meeting with an autograph seeker, she would smile wryly when she recalled meeting Faith Hill for the first time in Nashville, commenting, "Faith was a bright, spunky, feisty girl—real sweet and open, but a little mischievous. She reminded me a lot of myself. When she got nervous or a little flustered, her neck would break out in a rash."

For a teenager growing up in a small town, realizing a goal as ambitious as becoming the next Reba was indeed a huge dream. But with devoted parents who instilled strong family values in all three of their children, as well as her churchgoing and choir singing, Faith had both the support she needed to pursue her goal and the upbringing that prepared her for the inevitable trials and tribulations pursuing that "dream" would entail.

From an early age, she wanted to sing more than anything else. "Music was what I always wanted to do," she recalls, "and I'd had my sights set on it after leaving high school. At college, I just couldn't focus. What was on my mind was music and how to get to Nashville, Tennessee." There was no doubt in her mind that she could accomplish anything she put her mind to. "I really believed I'd just get on the *Grand Ole Opry* stage, start singin', and be on the bus the next day," she has stated. To help realize this dream, Faith taught herself to play guitar.

On the road to becoming a professional singer, Faith played a goodly number of family reunions, as well as women's social luncheons, school lunches, and—when she joined a country band—fairs and rodeos, but the paying gigs were not always normal. At age 16, she found herself in Raleigh, Mississippi singing at a 'Tobacco Spit'. "They would have the competition before the entertainment," she later explained to *People*, "so they would set these spittoons at the end of the stage and the men and women, some with teeth, some without, would stand way back to see would could spit the furthest into the spittoons. It was *so* gross. They had to clean the stage off with a towel before we played, but I was used to it— my grandmother used to sip snuff, so it didn't bother me too much then. But to think about it now, makes me laugh."

While she was in high school, Faith added George Strait to her list of heroes after attending a concert by the Texas singer, his twin fiddlers, and seven-piece band in east Texas, the closest the George Strait Show got to tiny Star, Mississippi. At age 17, Faith had a crush on George Strait and thought Tom Cruise was "real cute." Her favorite movie was *Top Gun*. Her favorite place to shop was Wal-Mart. She had taken a part-time job working after school at a MacDonalds franchise to provide herself with some pocket money. She was proud that she "had passed my driver's test on the first try," but singing was her overriding passion. "You could find me in my bedroom watching nothing on television," she told *Seventeen* magazine. "I didn't have a tv in my bedroom. I was lip-syncing to Reba McEntire, Rod Stewart and Elton John on my stereo."

Faith Perry's first band gigs would come about as a result of entering a singing contest in Meridian, 100 miles east of Jackson on I-20, and impressing the members of a country band who heard her sing that afternoon. Invited to join this group, the 17-year-old leapt into the fray. She would come to enjoy fronting a band more than anything she had known before this. "I just loved the way singing made me feel," she later *Glamour* magazine. "The excitement and energy that happens on stage is unbelievable.

The only thing better than that is sex, I swear!" Performing with a country band that played rodeos, fairs and dances, she sang harmonies on covers of George Strait records and lead vocals on covers of Reba McEntire hits. At that time in the mid-'80s, George Strait and Reba McEntire were becoming the reigning king and queen of country, riding the new traditionalist revival right into the "new country" era. The group had also performed gospel numbers before she joined them. Faith knew gospel really well. So, without auditioning, she had found a band that was the perfect fit.

That Faith Perry was attracted to the music of Patsy Cline, Tanya Tucker, Tammy Wynette, Emmylou Harris and now, during her later teen years, to Reba McEntire was not coincidental. These women represent a tradition of strong-willed, assertive female artists who resisted the "girl singer" mentality that existed in country music. During their most popular and influential years, these women helped change that perception—and they did not do so by toeing the line. Patsy Cline was well-known for her penchant for swearing and speaking her mind, especially when she encountered entrenched male chauvinist situations. Yet she sang like an angel, and once she escaped from an exploitive contract she had signed with "4 Star" Bill McCall and signed with Decca Records, she crossed over big time. If she had not died before her time, there is no telling where she would have taken country music.

Before tragedy struck and took Patsy's life, Loretta Lynn had become a close friend. Loretta inherited a legacy, but she never became the 'next Patsy'. Loretta simply could not sing with the same power, assurance, and vocal technique. Even though Loretta recorded several women's issues country songs, working with Patsy's producer Owen Bradley, she was unable to cross over onto the pop charts as Patsy had done. Loretta had heart and charm and she was fiercely loved by country fans, but it was Tammy Wynette who possessed the vocal ability to became the next Patsy. Like all country fans in the early 1970s, Faith Perry heard Wynette's records on the radio and sang along with them. "You can probably hear a bit of Tammy in my voice," Faith admitted in a recent interview published in a British magazine. Some of Wynette's technical polish and country soul did rub off on the aspiring teenager.

Tammy Wynette could sing like an angel, even though her first hit announced that *Your Good Girl Is Gonna Go Bad*. She crossed over onto the pop charts with *Stand By Me*, then married George Jones, the most popular singer in the South. But when things went sour, Tammy divorced Jones and struck out on her own. She was just as independent-minded as

Patsy Cline. In 1976, when Faith Perry was nine years old, Tammy released four number one records: 'Til I Can Make It On My Own and You And Me, as a solo artist, Golden Ring and Near You, number one duets with ex-hubbie Jones. In 1978 Tammy released Womanhood, one of the first pro-women's rights country songs, a rhythm and blues flavored record that became controversial when critics compared its lyrics to those of her signature tune, Stand By Your Man, which Tammy had co-written with her producer, Billy Sherrill. Tammy answered her critics with her autobiography, Stand By Your Man, which, along with Loretta Lynn's autobiography, Coal Miner's Daughter, represented the first time in print that country singers had become best-selling authors—and the first time women authors had described not only the plight of a "girl singer" in the male dominated world of country music but also the plight of women in the South.

Contemporary journalists often refer to Faith Hill as the 'next Shania'. More to the point, Faith is the 'next Tammy', the next heir to Patsy Cline's legendary ability to sing country and hit on the pop charts. Shania Twain did the same, but she belongs to a pop country 'snowbird' tradition begun by Anne Murray and continued by kd lang. Faith would acknowledge Twain's role in her own career, especially when Shania was being knocked by male journalists. "I've always defended Shania," Faith said during one interview. "She's not only opened doors, she knocked several down!"

Shania was not the first to knock down doors. Emmylou Harris had broken new ground, recording country rock with Gram Parsons in southern California, then teaming up with Linda Ronstadt and Dolly Parton to create the high harmonies of Trio, before becoming the queen of alternative country. Dolly Parton pried control of her career away from her singing partner and employer, Porter Wagoner, got herself an LA manager, and became the first bona-fide country singer-actress, starring in 9 to 5, her first Hollywood film with Jane Fonda and Lily Tomlin. Once a child country star, Tanya Tucker broke out of the Nashville mold and away from the overbearing control of her father to rock her country in Los Angeles. When she revived her career in the late 1980s, she took full advantage of the country video medium to strut her stuff on songs like Strong Enough To Bend. She knew full well the Highway Robbery that had been pulled on her sister country singers. She put on her Walking Shoes and let everybody know that if there were going to be further victims of the Nashville 'system', It Won't Be Me.

Like Dolly, Reba McEntire wrested control of her recording sessions from her male exploiters, divorced her good ole boy husband, and took control of both her record production *and* her business affairs. The first female country artist capable of headlining her own major tours and filling arena-size stadiums, Reba became an example that all of the young "new country" women artists of the '90s would admire. Like Faith Hill, they loved the way Reba sang; they liked the way she stood up to the male establishment even more.

Faith Perry had never exactly behaved herself, either. Not even in grade two. So, it is understandable that she didn't last very long in college. She enrolled in Hinds Junior College in nearby Raymond, but she did not graduate—she had other things on her mind. On stage, singing with her band, she felt exhilarated. At rodeo events, singing Reba's hits, she felt empowered, enough so that she could put any possible stigma of not completing college behind her. "People assume southern girls are unintelligent," she once observed, and amid the international glamor of being dubbed a 'country diva', she made much mileage out of playing up the hick-from-the-sticks shtick, telling journalists, "I've never seen real snow, I'm from Tennessee. I'm just a country girl." This 'unintelligent' Southern girl from Star, Mississippi was more than capable of 'snowing' those city-slickers from time to time when she was pressed to reveal the most intimate details of her famous marriage to Tim McGraw. For Faith what distinguished country girls and the country girl singers she idolized was what she once described as "a zest for life."

Faith Perry left Hinds Junior College after one semester with a zest for life and a desire to be a country singer. Her dad drove her in his pickup to Nashville, Tennessee. "That is where the wild child in me kicked in," she says. "I didn't worry about being safe or where I was going to get money. I just had faith that it was going to work." Edna and Ted continued to support her when she began knocking on doors on Music Row in search of someone who would let her sing. "It was very scary and intimidating," she has confessed, "but at the same time I had to be confident. I was being given a great opportunity and I didn't want to blow it."

# WELCOME TO THE CLUB

W hen Tim McGraw first arrived in Nashville, he was still a green-horn in the music business, but he proved to be a fast learner. Before long he had found a roommate, secured lodgings, and put together a band to showcase his talents. He was acting purely on instinct with a strong belief that he could become a country star. Like his father, Tim had grown to six feet in height. He had rugged good looks, brown hair, brown eyes, and a winning combination of his father's youthful com-petitive spirit and his mother's good-natured beliefs. When asked about his father's character during a 1994 interview, Tim smiled and com-mented, "He was 22 and immature when it happened. Hell, he's still immature." About his mother he said, "My mother's always taught me to treat people the way I want to be treated." When Tim finally hit on the radio, he was ready and willing to credit his biological father, Tug, telling interviewers, "What I got from Tug is athletic ability and a big heart. He never gives up on anything." But Tim has always credited his mother, Betty, as his most important influence. "I got my drive and determination from my mom," he says. "Nobody knows her, they only know Tug, but she is an unbelievable person. She is the most tenacious person you'll ever meet in your life, yet, at the same time, the most laid-back. She was my biggest influence. I know that 90 percent of what got me to where I am, I got from her."

Even though many people will tell you that getting into the music business can be a lot like taking a dive headfirst into a shark tank, Betty's application of the Christian "Golden Rule" would turn out to be good advice in Nashville, where Tim became known as a genuinely nice guy.

While this sometimes worked against him, as it did when he first began pulling in enough money from his band gigs that people would hit on him for loans, his fair-minded good nature was respected by the people who counted the most in his career. Although at first he was easy mark, Tim's education in the ways of the music business would not jade him. "I would loan money to songwriters whose royalty checks were comin' next week or next month or whenever," he recalls. "I never saw a lot of that money again, although some would pay it back."

One of the local bars in Nashville that Tim first discovered to be a hang out favored by songwriters and guitar pickers was Skull's Rainbow Room. Tim got to know some of the regulars and was sometimes invited up to perform a song or two. At Skulls he met guitarist Darran Smith and drummer Billy Mason. Smith was a veteran of the road wars. He'd spent several years with Dave & Sugar and several more touring with acts like David Frizzell and Shelly West. His guitar heroes were Eric Clapton and Stevie Ray Vaughn. Tim and Darran hit it off well, especially during the time Tim was putting together his first Nashville band. Darran's motto was, and still is, "Just have a great time." Which was what Tim had on his mind for his stage shows. Darran would become Tim's bandleader and show up for every music video Tim made, beginning with *Welcome To The Country Club* in 1992. Billy Mason would also stick with Tim for the duration. Right from the get go, Tim and the guys in his band would be just that, a "band of guys" who stuck up for each other. They banded together, so to speak, exploring the local sights together while on tour, playing flag football to while away their afternoons after sound check, sticking up for each other when the going got tough.

There were tough times when Tim and his friends had no money at all. Sometimes it becomes necessary to invent your own employment. Several aspiring songwriters have created employment by operating their own home cleaning services in Nashville, doing housework for people who have better things to do. For Tim, cleaning and repairing shopping carts for local supermarkets turned out to be a job that kept the wolf from the door. "Me and my buddy," he confessed to *Music City News*, "used to go out and clean shopping carts from grocery stores. We would go out and clean them up and fix the wheels and all of that stuff." This was the Tom Sawyer side of Tim, a hustle that no one else was working at the time. And when interviewers would prod him for more information, asking if that sort of manual labor provided incentive to make it as a recording artist, he would quip, "Absolutely. You ever washed a shopping cart in 30 degrees?"

Tim called his band the Dancehall Doctors, which suggested to fans even before they arrived at band gigs that they would be treated to feel-good music. They pulled their equipment in a trailer behind a van that Tim had acquired. Their gigs ranged from showcases in the tiny clubs in Printer's Alley in Nashville itself to strings of one-nighters in country clubs throughout the South. Tim continued to hang out at Skull's Rainbow Room and other local night spots where he got to know many other aspiring songwriters and artists. The goal was to get into a recording studio and make a record, a demo tape, and shop that tape until you secured a record contract. It took two years before Tim made his first demo. Tim had a small but loyal fan base back in Louisiana, and one of these fans, a farmer who believed in Tim, put up several thousand dollars to make a demo. Joe Diffie, who was just beginning to hit on the radio with cuts like *Home* and *If You Want Me To*, sang harmony vocals on the session.

One of the producers who heard that demo told Tim to "pack it up and go home." Tim remembers with a smile, "He said I was never going to make it." Getting known in the capital city of country music was a struggle, but he persisted. This recording session led to more work as a 'demo singer', recording for some of the many songwriters who make their home in Nashville. Making demos is a thriving business in Nashville, and many of the singers who eventually make it as country stars hone their skills singing on these demo sessions. Singing demos is one of the few ways a singer can make money in Nashville. Garth Brooks met Trisha Yearwood during a demo session; he didn't forget her when he made it big time. In addition to meeting and working with Joe Diffie, Tim met people like Lefty Frizzell's nephew, Jimmy, and a young woman by the name of Jo Dee Messina. Messina was a classy redhead with a huge talent for singing and a possible deal cooking with RCA. The two became friends and vowed that if either made it like Garth, they would help the other out. "I've known her since the beginning of my career," he told the *Boston Herald* in 1999. "I just knew she was going to get a record deal back in 1990, so I kept telling her, 'When you get a record deal, tell them about me. Get me a deal.'" Tim also befriended Kenny Chesney and Tracy Lawrence and the three aspiring singers often hung out together. Jo Dee Messina's deal with RCA derailed, but once Tim was in a position to help out, he gave her a call and offered her a backstage pass that would put her career back on track.

When Tim's demo was eventually pitched to Curb Records, he was offered a recording contract. Tim now concentrated on finding the songs he would soon need for his debut album. Song selection is key to the success of a country album. While some artists find themselves reigned in by their label executives and an unsympathetic producer appointed by the label to run their sessions, Tim, once again, lucked out. The people at Curb, it turned out, were not the only Nashville entrepreneurs who had noticed him during his showcase performances. One of the people who attended Tim's showcase at the Diamond in the Rough club was producer Byron Gallimore. A songwriter and guitarist, Byron was a native Tennessean who hailed from Puryear, TN, and had a background in rock & roll before winning the Music City Song Festival competition. Encouraged by this songwriting success, Gallimore had given up on farming for a living and moved to Nashville where he set about becoming a session musician and producer.

Establishing yourself as a record producer demands that you have some aptitude for recognizing new talent. Byron thought that Tim was, indeed, a 'diamond in the rough'. "I watched him do six songs," the producer told *Mix* magazine, "and he was phenomenal. I wanted to produce him but Curb Records wouldn't let me."

Not one to be put off by this, Gallimore turned to his friend and golfing buddy, James Stroud. Stroud was already a legendary musician and producer, having drummed on sessions for superstars like Paul Simon, Bob Seger, and Dionne Warwick in Muscle Shoals and Los Angeles, before making the move to Nashville. During the late '80s and early '90s, he had crafted radio hits and best-selling albums for country acts like John Anderson, Clint Black, Little Texas, and Tracy Lawrence. He had been Jimmy Bowen's right-hand man at Capitol Records in Nashville before accepting an offer from David Geffen to run Geffen's Nashville-based Giant Records. James Stroud had the 'clout' that Gallimore did not yet possess. Perhaps, Gallimore speculated, Curb would listen to his friend.

"I went to Tim's showcase," Stroud told *Mix*, "and what hit me hard was his passion for what he wanted to do. We went to Mike Curb and the deal was done. We were able to make a record, and it was the first time Byron and I, who have been friends for quite a while, had the chance to work together." The two have gone on to become one of the most successful Nasvhille production teams of all time.

"You could call Gallimore and Stroud the most influential production team in Nashville," music journalist Elianne Halbersberg wrote in a recent article published in *Mix*, "but they're too modest to accept such accolades. You could describe them as workaholics, but they make what they do— producing, engineering, recording and, for one of them, running a record label—sound like so much fun that it's almost a mistake to call it work. You could say that they're responsible for a large percentage of the hit records currently on the charts, but they'll reply that it's all because of the artists. You could even tell them that they have remarkable intuition and musical instincts, or use trendy words like 'synergy', but they'd contradict that by telling you that they're a 'hillbilly and a redneck, just some old farmer and a half-assed drummer who don't know shit.'"

Byron's wife, Missi, listens to literally thousands of song demos, isolating the most promising ones for her husband to hear. Right from the beginning there was teamwork. There was chemistry, too. "Early on," Stroud told Halbersberg, "Byron and I saw that there was something special we could bring to the table as producers. We're a good combination. He has great ears and is a great player. He knows, tonally, how to make things great. My side of the expertise is in rhythm and structure on the tracks, so, it's the best of both worlds, and we never step on each other's toes."

Tim had played a role in bringing Gallimore and Stroud together in the studio, so he became a favored son. Tim still had a whole lot to learn about recording. His live performance is what attracted the initial attention from Stroud and Gallimore, but recording killer vocals in a studio atmosphere where there is no audience rapport at all would prove to be a challenge. While singing effectively into a Neumann 47 tube microphone in an isolation booth was a skill he had not yet refined into an art, the bottom-line was that Tim now had some heavy-hitting people on his team.

While they may have all had fun during those recording sessions for Tim's first album, it did not do all that well in record stores. The package was put out as a self-titled album, and while the lead single, Welcome To The Club, showed promise, it did not do the same for Tim as Travis Tritt's 1989 debut Country Club, which had hit into the Top 10 and paved the way for his next singles, Help Me Hold On and I'm Gonna Be Me Someday, to go all the way to number one. Welcome To The Club got regional airplay but did not crack the Billboard Top 40. Like Shania Twain, another member of the Class of '93, Tim's first album did not really capture his best side. Shania would soon shine when she met rock producer Robert John "Mutt" Lange who did hear her potential and produced her second album. But both Tim and Shania's debuts had stiffed at radio, whereas rookie singers Toby Keith, Doug Supernaw, Clay Walker, Martina McBride, Faith Hill, and Tracy Byrd had all hit into the Top 10 with their singles in 1993 and early 1994, some of them making it all the way to the number one spot.

Still, Tim had a record on the radio, and audiences at his shows began to pick up. Tim and the Dancehall Doctors no longer had to sell cheap, silk, department store roses before their gigs and recycle them to sell again at the next stop down the road, a Tom Sawyer-like tale which has become part and parcel of the McGraw family legend. "The guys would buy them for their girlfriends," Tug told one reporter, speaking fondly of his son's enterprise. "Tim would perform, and the girls would throw them on stage. Then, the band would collect them and sell them at the next bar."

The motto for the Dancehall Doctors has remained the same over the years, as Darran Smith reminds visitors to Tim's website: "Just have a great time!" These road hogs may tell you, as percussionist and background vocalist Dave Dunkley does at this same website, that the "threat of having to work a real job" is the reason he became a drum tech and musician, just as Tim has said that he turned to music because he knew he wasn't going to cut it as a law student. Today they wouldn't have it any other way. Dunkley first signed on with Tim's production crew in 1995 as a drum tech. Once Tim heard Dave smacking the skins during sound check, Dunkley's talents were incorporated into the show playing congas or additional percussion. "I'd be the drum tech," he recalls, "then I'd throw on a shirt and play a few songs, too. I would go out and play two songs. And I sang a lot, too, because they needed extra harmonies." By 1996, Dave was asked to join the Dancehall Doctors on a full-time basis, but he will never forget the first night he joined Tim McGraw's band on stage. "The first night, I came out to play on one song," he recalls. "Later in the show, the guitar player dropped a chair off the stage in the dark and it hit me. I got 17 stitches in the head." A unique initiation, to be sure, but Dave had what it takes to survive in the helter skelter busworld. Keyboard player and background vocalist Jeff McMahon confides that the road has taught him that "small acts of kindness can mean so much to people."

Tim McGraw and the Dancehall Doctors weren't exactly setting the world on fire, but their shows were heating up. Tommy Barnes' song *Indian Outlaw* had become their signature tune, even though Tim had not yet recorded it. Despite the poor record sales numbers, as Dave McKenna points out, "the label didn't put McGraw back on the bus for Louisiana. Instead, it put him on the road with his band, the Dancehall Doctors, and allowed him to build an audience with a live show heavy on twangy party anthems, melodramatic power ballads, and '70s covers. Steve Miller's *The Joker* became a concert staple." In retrospect, this seems like a smart move for everybody concerned; after all, it *was* Tim's live performance that had attracted his producers to his project. His label had been more impressed with his rugged good looks. Which was understandable. By 1990 country videos had become key to promoting new artists, and hunks with hats were what the labels wanted. Garth Brooks was not exactly a hunk, but what Garth lacked in looks he more than made up for with his intense performances, which is also where Tim shone the brightest. When Billy Ray Cyrus' 1992 debut, Achy Breaky Heart, rocketed to number one, stayed there for five weeks, and propelled sales of his Mercury Records debut album SOME GAVE ALL toward the eight million mark, 'looks' rather than vocal talent would become the most sought after commodity label scouts were looking for. Tim had no problem in that department, nor did he have any problem putting on shows that had the same voltage levels of electricity as Garth's stadium performances.

With a single kissing the bottom of the national charts, Tim managed to get himself onto some bigger shows as an opening act for country veteran Gene Watson. One night, he came full circle when he opened for the traditional honky tonk singer and his Farewell Party Band during the Jacksonville State Fair, singing in the same arena where his mother Betty had danced in those long forgotten contests in the 1960s. As Tim's second single, Memory Lane, and the third, Two-Steppin' Mind, failed to click at radio, Tim's team began putting together a song list in preparation for the recording of his second Curb album. Producers Stroud and Gallimore, always networking with musicians and songwriters, were also putting together a tougher studio band to back Tim. One of the additions, Lonnie Wilson, would become Tim's regular studio drummer. Lonnie had an ability to lay down drum tracks that were closer to the sort of live feel that Tim's road drummer Billy Mason put into Tim's shows. That 'live' feel was the ingredient the team felt they needed to capture on this second album.

Coincidentally, Lonnie Wilson had co-written Memory Lane with Joe Diffie. Diffie had, of course, helped Tim out with his demo sessions. Country music, as they say, is just one big, happy family, which is just as evident in Nashville as it is down on the farm. According to one reporter, the people in California who had introduced Tim to the label executives who had signed him to a recording contract had been "friends of Tug." What goes around comes around, as they say. It was not different for producers James Stroud and Byron Gallimore. "Being here does make a difference," Stroud told Mix. "It's a totally unique situation. We're like family. If I didn't see Byron and we didn't golf together, I'd have withdrawals."

Tim's situation was, truly, unique. One of his producers headed up a rival label, Giant Records. The other was an independent. Both were accepted on the Curb Records project by Mike Curb. "Nashville's record-making process is markedly different from that of other music cities," Elianne Halbersberg remarks. "Music Row—the area that houses the business side of country music—makes it possible to walk from office to office, label to label. Gallimore and Stroud agree that the intimacy offered by this closely knit sector would be unimaginable in New York or Los Angeles." Tim's strong family values were well-suited for the sense of camaraderie and loyalty that came with this team, qualities that enabled him to survive the vicious competition between vested interest groups.

This 'team' was given a rare second chance. As the scheduled recording sessions for Tim's second album neared, the team prepared to meet the challenge. Second albums are notoriously more difficult to make than first albums, especially if the debut has been any kind of success at all. In Tim's career, however, things were different because the people on his team were willing to let him develop without rushing things. "Tim had never been in the studio when he made his first album," Byron Gallimore points out. "So, he was getting acquainted with microphones, how to sing. He'd listen back and hate the way he sounded, so he'd try something different. It was almost a learning experience for all of us to figure out what to do."

James Stroud's approach to producing in Nashville heralded in the brash "new country" sound of the '90s. Because he had worked for so long in Los Angeles on projects for artists who sold millions rather than thousands of albums in a competitive world-wide market, the wily producer devised a new game plan that other Nashville producers would also come to embrace. "When I started making successful records," he told the *Nashville Banner*, "there was an edge to it; there was a heft to the sound. I tried to make the record as loud and bold as I could because I thought in order to compete with other markets we had to do what they did and do it better, while maintaining our tradition and our heritage." Stroud's "loud and bold" productions, along with sensitive dynamic passages that provided dramatic ambience, would become Tim McGraw's trademark sound on his records. His vocals were another matter—that was where Tim would come to shine, with critics referring to his "achy breaky tenor." By the time the team went into the studio to begin recording his second album, Tim had his vocal identity down pat and he had opinions to offer as they began to lay down tracks.

"The difference between his first album and all the others," Stroud says, "is that, after the first album, we listened to Tim McGraw. When he

49

was able to say, 'Here's what I'm going to do. The first one didn't work and here's what I want,' in my view, that was the biggest change his music took from the first album to all of these. . . ." One of the songs that Tim brought to the pre-production meetings was Tommy Barnes' song *Indian Outlaw*. It was working well in his stage shows, why not record this one? Novelty songs had done well for George Jones throughout his career and country fans usually ate them up. At first, he met resistance from Curb.

"My first record didn't work," Tim admits, "but some of the songs we were playing live were getting incredible reactions from the fans. My record label didn't want to record one song in particular, until they saw me do it live." Tim and his band mates had fun with Barnes' song on stage and often ended it with a passage from Paul Revere & the Raiders' 1971 novelty number one hit, *Indian Reservation*. This was included on the track as an extro, which conveniently—if they wanted to—deejays could fade and rap over. Nashville singles are notoriously shorter than rock singles and often much shorter than the live version the artist performs in their shows. Brevity would not be a factor at all when the first single from NOT A MOMENT TOO SOON was released to radio in the early weeks of 1994. Controversy from a totally unexpected quarter would be what put Tim McGraw in the national spotlight for the first time in his short career as a recording artist. A cool video that featured Tim as an appropriately scruffy country rebel without a cause riding a Harley provided an early image that also drew in fans.

Success came with the release of *Indian Outlaw*, the novelty tune that Tommy Barnes had handed Tim when he first arrived in Nashville.

*I'm an Indian Outlaw*
*Half Cherokee and Choctaw*
*My baby she's a Chippewa*
*She's one of a kind . . .*

*You can find me in my wigwam*
*I'll be beatin' on my tom-tom*
*Pull out the pipe and smoke ya some*
*Hey, and pass it around . . .*

— *Indian Outlaw* (Tommy Barnes, Gene Simmons, John D. Loudermilk)

More than 600,000 copies of the single would sell while it made its way into the Top 10 on the *Billboard* country chart and then slowly slid back down. Even though the cut did not gone all the way to number one, a storm of controversy flared up over the song that put Tim into newspaper headlines from coast to coast. A letter written by Cherokee Nation chief Wilma Mankiller created the initial controversy. In her letter, Mankiller claimed that the record was "extremely insulting to Indians" and that the lyrics "promoted bigotry." Chief Mankiller's letter was delivered to Oklahoma country stations, urging them not to playlist Tim's *Indian Outlaw*.

Chief Mankiller's criticisms were directed specifically at Tim: "Tim McGraw appears to be one of those who appropriate Indian culture and then corrupts it for his own gain." Tim maintained that "no offence was intended. ... It took me by surprise but just about everything you do people are going to interpret one way or the other. I just never thought anybody could take something like that serious. That song isn't serious."

Even though Mankiller's letter resulted in some stations in Arizona, Minnesota, Nevada, and South Dakota, as well as Oklahoma, not playing *Indian Outlaw*, it didn't seem to matter one iota. No news is bad news, as they say in marketing departments, and the fact that people all over America were debating the issue was publicity that no press agent could have generated for Tim.

One night in February 1994 outside a concert venue in Tulsa, Oklahoma, a group of people picketed Tim's show. Tim met with them, but he did not agree to drop the song from his set-list. Tim knew he was on a roll—everywhere he and the Dancehall Doctors went there were journalists poking their microphones at Tim. "We played it for about four years live before we recorded it," Tim told one interviewer, "and I could tell it would be a really big record because of the crowd response. You have to remember this wasn't meant to be this great piece of work, this great piece of art, or some social statement, but I guess anything you do is up to interpretation. All this is about trying to pick the ten best songs you can to make every album better." Throughout this period of turmoil, Tim maintained that the incident had simply been blown out of proportion. "We only had, like, four or five letters," he noted, "and there were only a few small groups of people who objected. I've talked to some people from the American Indian point of view—they were the main people who were against the song—and we just had different points of view."

Nancy Ragdale, director of Southeastern Michigan Indians Inc., an activist group based in Center Line, said, "I have mixed feelings. The song's catchy, but every time I hear it, I'm mixed up inside about it. I don't feel good. I'm just not sure whether he's portraying us in a positive way or not." Ragdale did admit that she hadn't heard any storm of protest or reaction either way from any of the 40 tribes in her organization. Not all Native groups objected to the song or had misgivings, however. Gerard Barker, vice president of the North Carolina-based Eastern Band of Cherokee Indians and a well-respected spokesperson for Native rights, said, simply, "We hope he sells a million copies." Radio stations on many reservations decided to continue playing the cut, and one station, KNNB-FM on an Apache reservation in White River, Arizona, played the record in heavy rotation. When all was said and done, *Indian Outlaw* was simply a fun-tune aimed at people who like kicking up their heels. One national critic described the song as "a rocking tune with changing tempos and a layered guitar arrangement that recalls the Eagles' *Witchy Woman*."

Several years later, when asked by a reporter from *Music City News* what the "riskiest thing he ever did" might be, Tim would refer to recording *Indian Outlaw*. But he was also not shocked at its success. "I always thought it was going to be a hit," he told this same Nashville reporter. "I was tired of it by the time we recorded it because I had been doing it in bars forever. As a club band, playing the circuit out on the road with our van and our U-Haul trailer, that was our signature song. By the time we actually recorded it, we were tired of it."

Just when the controversy over Tom Barnes' song had led some critics to speculate that Tim would be a one-hit-novelty-tune wonder, his showcase appearance during the Country Radio Seminar in Nashville in March 1994, where he performed *Don't Take The Girl* to an audience comprised of key radio programmers, changed everybody's perception of Tim McGraw.

*Johnny's daddy was taking him fishing*
*when he was eight years old*
*a little girl came through the front gate*
*holding a fishing pole*
*His dad looked down and smiled*
*said we can't leave her behind*
*son I know you don't want her to go*
*but someday you'll change your mind*
*And Johnny said*
*Take Jimmy Johnson*
*Take Tommy Thompson*
*Take my best friend Bo . . .*
*Take anybody you want as*

*long as as she don't go*
*Take anybody in the world*
*daddy please — don't take the girl . . .*

— *Don't Take The Girl* (Larry Johnson, Craig Martin)

Here was another side of Tim, a softer more romantic side that was 100 percent country, yet mysteriously the song hinted at crossover potential. Tim would later refer to his performance of the song on this CSR New Faces Show as the turning point in his career. "It was the second time I ever played the song," he told *Closup* magazine's Angie Crabtree, "and I got a standing ovation for it. Everybody ran back to their radio stations and started playing it. I think it was in the Top 10 before it was officially released as a single." Deejays were readily agreeable to playing the album cut for their audiences. The momentum of this second single, which went all the way to number one, mowing down *Indian Outlaw* on its way to the top of the country charts, also invigorated sales of NOT A MOMENT TOO SOON, which would be named the 1994 Album of the Year at the Academy of Country Music Awards in California and go on to sell more than six million copies. Tim would also be named the ACM's Top New Male Vocalist.

"We were trying to get in the studio and cut a good enough album to sell enough records to keep our contract," Tim told interviewers. "So, everything else is gravy." When a third track, *Down On The Farm*, was heavily requested before it was officially released as a single and shot up to number 2 during the summer of '94, that "gravy" was beginning to look like platinum. Then in November, when the title track, *Not A Moment Too Soon,* was released as a single, Tim would soon have his second number one. This song, written for Tim by Joe Barnhill and Wayne Perry, would become a favorite of Tim's mother, Betty. "I think that song will be special to me for a long time," she said at the time. "The words, taken spiritually, fit my life."

Although panned by numerous critics, NOT A MOMENT TOO SOON hit a sweet spot with country fans, and its triple-platinum sales made it the topselling country album of 1994. When a fifth track, *Refried Dreams*, was released in March 1995, it would again hit into the Top 10. By that time, Tim's "team" was hard at work selecting songs for his third album. A whirlwind promotional tour through several European countries led to Tim meeting one of his guitar heroes, Jimmy Page. The two spoke in London after a Curb Records sponsored showcase featuring Hal Ketchum. "I got to meet him (Page) after the gig," Tim told *Country Weekly*, "which was really cool." Another celebrity, Green Bay Packers quarterback Brett Favre, would also become Tim's friend during this same period. Just as fate had led Tim to meet one of his baseball idols in the '70s, in the '90s fame led him to an inner circle of performers and celebrities, many of whom were already his heroes. What was coolest of all was that Tim's unassuming manner and genuine character allowed him to become friends with some of these rich and famous people. Few of them seemed to resent that he was the new kid on the block. He was so humble, unassuming. "As he strolls into his dressing room several hours before show time at the Westbury Music Fair," one journalist wrote, "Tim McGraw looks like anything but the red-hot country star that he is. For starters, he's got no attitude and no entourage. What's the sense in having a multi-platinum album, NOT A MOMENT TOO SOON, with a couple of gold singles, if you're not going to get yourself an entourage to boss around? Instead of the standard cowboy hat, McGraw is sporting a baseball cap. It's logo: 'Don't Dream It—Be It.' His demeanor is so unassuming he could be mistaken for one of the Long Island cowboys picking up tickets for the evening's show."

With his breakout success on radio and in record marts, Tim had gone from playing honky tonks and clubs and occasionally opening for someone like Gene Watson to becoming a headliner capable of staging his own tours in less than a year. "It was a crazy time," he recalls. "We just wanted to play. I think we played 250 shows that first year." Out on the road head-lining a package tour that included BlackHawk and 4 Runner, Tim was fielding more and more requests for phone interviews. Nick Krewen wanted to know how making the switch to being the closing act was going. "The coolest thing about it," Tim told the *Country Weekly* reporter, "is that you've got a guaranteed sound check every time. Being able to close it gives me a little bit more leeway in what kind of show I want to do. I feel like we're just out there having a good time and I don't think there should be any pressure."

While Tim was becoming known as a wild and crazy guy in his shows, he cautioned journalists, reminding them that once he stepped off stage, he hadn't really changed from the person he had always been. "I think there's a lot of misconceptions," he told CMA *Closeup*, "that I'm some kind of wild man, and I'm not at all. I may be a wild man on stage, but any other time I'm about as boring as you can get. I'm basically pretty shy."

The first single released from Tim's third album ALL I WANT was the infectious, fun-loving *I Like It, I Love It*, another great performance number in his shows. The song spent 19 weeks in the *Billboard* Top 40, five of them at number one. The second single, *All I Want Is A Life*, also climbed into the Top 10, while album sales once again ballooned into multiple-platinum figures. ALL I WANT became one of Tim's personal favorites. "I love that album," he said recently. "It has some of my favorite songs I have ever recorded like *Can't Be Really Gone.*" At the time, his fans loved it, too. Which, Tim maintains, is a barometer he has always monitored. "That's one of my guiding thoughts," he says. "I am a fan myself. I go to shows, I listen to the radio, and I watch other acts. I like to think about what the fans want."

No doubt, in January 1996 Tim was absolutely positive that his fans would like Faith Hill, if she agreed to tour with him. As Tim prepared to launch his Spontaneous Combustion Tour, it appeared that his career had truly caught fire. And when romance with his opening act blossomed during that tour, critics like *Billboard* magazine's Chet Flippo would soon be writing, "He's definitely the guy the industry is grooming as Garth-to-be. He's what country needs now. He's macho and he's vulnerable. He's boisterous and he's sensitive. And he's one of those rare males whose voice you can immediately identify. His voice seems like it could break at any moment, with an achy element and even a little knot of pathos."

# TAKE ME AS I AM

When Ted Perry dropped off his daughter Faith in Nashville, he helped her unpack and then gave her his blessing, but he was concerned, all the same. "I can still see his face to this day, sitting with empty boxes all around him," Faith remembers. "He had tears in his eyes. He just waved goodbye and said, 'Take care, I love you. We are behind you one hundred percent.'" She had come to Nashville acting purely on the belief that she could make it as a country music star but she had no game plan whatsoever. After bruising her knuckles on one too many Music Row doors, she must have thought that the lyrics to Charlie Rich's number one country hit, *Behind Closed Doors,* represented some kind of insider joke to the men on Music Row who controlled the action and raked in the spoils. Before long she also realized that every taxi driver, bus boy, waiter, and bell hop that she met was an aspiring songwriter, guitar picker, or vocalist, still hanging in, hoping that someday they would strike it rich and win the Nashville sweepstakes to become the next Hank, Tammy, or Chet.

Most of the decision making that takes place in Nashville does take place behind closed Music Row doors. Country stars, managers, agents, publicists, musicians, songwriters, publishing company reps, and record label executives—plus an assortment of movers and groovers whose job descriptions are less well defined—are all members of a private club, so to speak, who hob nob with each other at showcases, fish fries, and barbecues. They all have back stage passes to each other's shows and media events. As country music evolved from a hokey, hoops and skirts, hats and rhinestone suits, big-haired, big-ego, rural industry into the big city, corporate, music video era, with paparazzi pursuing the current stars, the stars and their handlers began posting security guards at the candy store door, which made it increasingly difficult for talented newcomers, like Faith Perry, to get inside.

With no insider contacts, times were tough for 19-year-old Faith. For several years, she found herself shut out of much of the good jobs and the good times. "I thought I was so mature and grown up and ready to be away from my family," Faith later told *Billboard* magazine, "but after a couple of weeks I realized I wasn't so mature after all. It was tough. I lived off Kraft macaroni and cheese and Hamburger Helper for a long time."

Not only had Faith come to Nashville not knowing some member of this inner circle, she was also totally naive about what went on in the country music capital. She didn't even know that Fan Fair was the largest single fan event of the year, where 25,000 eager fans snapped up the available tickets long before the event was staged each June. Fan Fair was be an eye opener for Faith, and, as it turned out, she did not have to pay admission to attend. "My first job in Nashville," she often told interviewers during the promotion of her early albums, "was selling t-shirts at Fan Fair. I had no idea what it was. I saw an ad in the paper, for a week's worth of work. I was selling inside one of the exhibit halls, but I was selling for a company that sold 'Music City USA' t-shirts—Nashville t-shirts. There were lots of people there; it was busy all day. I was thankful for that job, because, at that point, I was not really finding much work." As she labored in the exhibit hall day after day at the t-shirt booth, she began to realize just how huge Fan Fair really was, with fan-club meets, autograph sessions, and showcase concerts all staged for the thousands of fans who showed up each year. Her first reaction was to think, "Wow! This is crazy!" After a while she began to appreciate just how loyal country fans were to the stars they idolized. "I didn't understand," she later recalled, "what people had gone through and the money they had saved. I didn't get what the whole thing was. In the course of the week, people would come by and say, 'Yeah, we're here to see so and so.' I was, like, 'Wow, you came all that way?'"

Faith has often said that she is a dreamer, so it wasn't much of stretch for Faith to imagine herself there at Fan Fair in some future year, signing autographs along with Kathy Mattea, the Sweethearts of the Rodeo, the Judds, Steve Wariner, Marty Stuart, Randy Travis, and Reba McEntire. Having an autograph booth at Fan Fair became part of her country music dream, along with opening for Reba McEntire and George Strait. Pursuing that dream, Faith next sought employment at Reba's Starstruck Entertainment complex.

She was offered a job in the merchandise department, packaging up fan-club items and stuffing envelopes. After a few months, Faith had seen enough images of her idol to last her a lifetime. "They had a mail order business," she confided to *Housekeeping* magazine, "and I was in charge of filling orders. I was so sick of Reba . . . I love her so much, but after eight hours a day of Reba shirts and pajamas, clocks and watches, necklaces and key chains and hat pins . . . Oh, my Lord!" The superstar would later remember Faith's time spent there fondly. "She was a very outstanding lady," Reba told *People* magazine in 1995, "because she was so bubbly and full of life. That's the way it was, even in the fan-club days, when she was back there stuffing envelopes."

Stuffing memorabilia into fan-club packages and mailing them out was not a job with a future, but no one at Reba's Starstruck Entertainment company was asking her to cut demos or sing at showcases. Frustrated by the lack of interest in her real talent, she decided that a job somewhere else in Nashville might provide her with an opportunity to meet someone who would give her the break she needed. In an attempt to get a bit closer to the action, Faith began to interview for job openings in the offices on Music Row where song publishing deals were made and artists were signed to recording contracts. Again, she discovered that nobody was interested in hearing her sing; even worse, she learned that telling people she was an aspiring singer meant that the executives doing the interviewing became uninterested in hiring her. They had already employed one too many wannabee singers who merely wanted the job as a stop-off along the way to realizing their eventual dream of becoming a Nashville star. So, she lied during one interview, mentioning a college education, not a career as a singer, as her reason for moving to Nashville, and secured a job working for recording artist Gary Morris in the office of the Gary Morris Music publishing company. She would have to pursue her dream on her own time, haunting clubs and showcase venues after working hours, trying to make some sort of impression on someone who cared.

Although Faith Perry's bid to make it as a country star in Nashville had slowed to a crawl while she worked at Gary Morris Music, answering phones and performing secretarial duties, she caught her first glimpse of the wheeling and dealing that takes place inside the star-making machinery. For a country music fan from rural Mississippi who aspired to becoming a professional singer, the business side of the music industry was a rude awakening. She would later confess to an interviewer from *Country Music* magazine that she got to see "a side of the music business that I never even guessed existed." Still, she was also learning what made the industry tick.

Key to her later success would be this basic understanding of what went on behind those closed doors on Music Row as well as a recognition of the most valuable commodity that was being passed around between the songwriters, publishers and recording artists. It was not money. It was songs. "One thing I learned very quickly," she recalls, "was the importance of good songs. For a song to impress me, it has to have a melody or lyrics that stand out." Further valuable lessons came from her observations of the image-making that went on in Nashville. As she later confided to a British journalist, "I also learned that it was vital to be myself. When I signed my record deal, I knew how I wanted to look. That was to my advantage."

Faith was also able to meet a variety of singers, songwriters, and executives, many of them intrigued by her beauty and bubbly, out-going personality. Many were eager to date her, including music publishing executive Daniel Hill. Faith and Daniel became an item, and on July 23, 1988, fifteen months after they first met, the two were married. Faith was 20 years old.

For some young women who move to Nashville to pursue their dream, becoming the wife of a Nashville executive has often been the route to recording a demo tape and getting signed to a record label. In Faith's case, though, it would be staff-songwriter David Chase at Gary Morris Music who got the ball rolling, not her husband.

That opportunity came only when Faith's talent, which she had hidden from the people she worked with, was discovered by Chase, just in the nick of time. Faith had become frustrated beyond belief. As she told *Chicago Tribune* critic Jack Hurst in 1993, during the promotion of her debut album, "I was thinking . . . Lord, have I ever got myself stuck! Maybe I'm going to have to be a secretary for the rest of my life . . . If I tell 'em I'm a singer, I may lose my job."

The story of her discovery goes like this. One afternoon, not long after she and Daniel were married, Faith, believing that she was alone in the office, was singing along with the radio. When songwriter David Chase came in, hoping to find someone hanging out who might cut a demo of a song he'd just written, he heard Faith singing. He was surprised, impressed, and asked *her* to cut the demo of his newly written song, *It Scares Me*. After being in Nashville for nearly two years, this was the first time anybody had asked her to record anything. She couldn't say, "no"—even though this would eventually mean that her boss, Gary Morris, would probably hear this demo, as he listened to everything his in-house writers came up with. But what did she have to lose? No doubt, the security of her new marriage and her burning desire to become a recording artist overcame her fear of losing her job as a receptionist, and the rest, as they say, is history.

It wasn't long before Morris heard the demo. "Gary approached me one day," she recalls, "with this serious look on his face." She prepared herself for the absolute worst. As it turned out, she was not exactly fired on the spot, although her days as an office worker would soon come to an end. Despite her fear and trembling, Morris merely wanted to know what she was doing wasting her talent sitting behind a desk. He thought she should be pursuing a career as an artist. "I think you need to get out there and get busy," he told her. "I'd been working there over a year," Faith told *Country Music News*, "always singing on the side, when a writer by the name of David Chase heard me and got me to do some demos. They reached Gary Morris a few weeks later and he had me work on that album. It was a big thrill." One of the first to enlist her services as a background singer for an album project was Gary Morris, and her first appearance on a record would be on Gary's 1989 album, STONES.

Faith soon found herself invited to record more demos. When songwriter Gary Burr took an interest in her career, the two became friends. Burr helped Faith put together an eight-song demo of her own, just in case some label rep came knocking. "The real breakthrough came when Gary Burr, he's one of Nashville's best songwriters, and a great friend, asked me to work a gig at the Bluebird Cafe with him," Faith has stated. The combination of Burr, who frequently showcased his songs around town, and Faith Hill singing harmonies, clicked. "One song led to two, then a whole set of songs, every time he played somewhere," she recalled during an interview with a reporter from *Country Music People*. "Gary was a *godsend* to me." One night when Gary and Faith were appearing at the Bluebird Cafe, Warner Brothers Records talent scout Martha Sharp was in the audience. Sharp had got her start working as Jimmy Bowen's personal assistant at Electra Records. With Bowen's support, she had become one of the most influential A&R executives on the planet. Among her many accomplishments, Martha is credited with discovering Randy Travis. Signed by Martha to Warner Brothers in 1985, Travis provided real momentum to the new traditionalist movement and sold several tons of vinyl records for her label the following year. Sharp had also been head of A&R for Warner Brothers in 1983 when Bowen produced Gary Morris's breakthrough record *The Wind Beneath The Wings*. "A killer song that got things started for him," Bowen notes in his autobiography, *Rough Mix*.

Which, in retrospect, was an interesting tangency or synchronicity, considering that Gary Morris was the first recording artist to enlist Faith's talent as a background singer on an official album release, and Bowen's 'ex-girl Friday' was the first A&R person to take interest in her as a solo artist.

Bowen would go on from his 1983 merger of Electra and Warner Brothers, when he had also promoted Martha Sharp from personal assistant to A&R director, to rescue MCA's Nashville division and become the major influence in Music City during the years leading up to the discovery of Garth Brooks, who ironically, Bowen initially passed on, then inherited when he took over the operation of Capitol Records . . . then sparred with during the unprecedented years of the early Garth era until Bowen retired to a life after country music in Hawaii. Martha would not stay with Warner Nashville throughout Faith's career, but during the crucial early years, she was a guardian angel.

Bowen had put his early career on the line during sessions with proven-but-faltering stars like Frank Sinatra and Conway Twitty, had steered the early career of Dukes of Hazzard actor and wannabee country singer John Schneider, and had survived half a dozen corporate takeovers, mergers, and garage sales. Martha had moved steadily upwards in an industry where few men other than Bowen were willing to give a woman the time of day, let alone promote them from personal assistant to A&R director. In another ironic synchronicity, it had also been Bowen who had chosen James Stroud to succeed the existing in-house producer at Capitol, providing Stroud with the clout he eventually wielded when asked by Byron Gallimore to intercede in the career of Tim McGraw. Not only is Nashville country music a family affair, it has become over the years increasingly incestuous.

Martha Sharp had signed Randy Travis and helped kick off the most successful new traditionalist career of all, but she was now looking for someone who might reverse that trend, a prospect with pop crossover potential. Martha believed that Faith Hill was that artist. "I was just fascinated with her," Sharp recalls, remembering that night in the Bluebird Cafe. "I thought she looked like a star. I felt there was no limit to what she could do. I thought she was a prime candidate for not just crossover but endorsements, those kinds of things."

By paying her dues, working with the people at Starstruck Entertainment and the people at Gary Morris Music, Faith had forged some valuable contacts. She was no longer the kid outside the candy store with her face glued to the window watching the action going on inside. Not long after the show with Gary Burr at the Bluebird, Martha Sharp noticed Faith at an industry barbecue. This time Martha introduced herself and mentioned that Bluebird showcase. "A publisher was giving a fish fry," Faith recalls, "and she came up to me and asked if I was working a solo career and that's when it all started. At the time that she asked me if I had a demo tape to give her, I told her that I was working on a little eight-track tape with Gary Burr in his apartment, we were just doing this little eight-track tape. And I said, 'That's all I have. It's not much. We were just going to pitch it around to see if I can get some demo work.' That was the purpose of that tape, and she was insisting on hearing it. So you know, we brought it by and she loved it and that's how I got signed, just from my little tape." Martha liked what she heard and became resolved to go to bat for the strawberry blonde from Mississippi. As Faith later explained to *Country Music News*, "A&R lady, Martha Sharp, got to hear some of my work on a demo tape that Gary Burr put together, and that tape worked its way up the line and everybody seemed to show interest and I ended up with the record deal."

Key to the signing was that Warner Nashville needed to fill a vacancy in their artist lineup. "The reason I signed with Warner Brothers," Faith told *Country Music People*, "was that they really didn't have a female artist and they wanted one. We felt there was space for me there and that's what I wanted, a company that was excited and had a vision." Once the deal was done, Faith pitched her friend Gary Burr as producer for her debut album. She would quickly learn that hiring your friends was not always the best course of action. Later, she would tell *Country Music People* that "what we were getting was good, but it probably needed an experienced producer and Gary had so many other things going down; his writing, his artistic aspirations, and that wasn't what I needed. I needed someone who would be focused on making this record and I needed an experienced producer. I couldn't risk my chance, my one chance. It was the hardest thing in the world to go to Gary and tell him I wasn't happy with the way things were going and I had to put a stop to it." From then on, Faith, who was still headstrong, nevertheless listened more carefully to Martha's advice.

At the time Martha Sharp was actually the senior vice-president of artists and repertoire development at Warner Nashville, which despite the long-winded corporate pecking order title meant that she was their top scout and talent coach, an A&R rep whose vision was respected throughout the corporation. In 1985, when Martha had been approached by Lib Hatcher, who had transformed Randy Traywick from an ineffective and somewhat tentative performer to a country singer with tremendous poise and potential, Martha had been in a unique position—the only other female A&R person working in Nashville had been Margie Hunt at Columbia Records. Having worked with Hatcher during the development and triumph of Randy Travis's early career, Sharp had become aligned with a women's network, which was coming into its own during the 1990s in Nashville. People like Bonnie Garner, a former label exec, and Pam Lewis, a former publicist, were now working in artist management with performers like Willie Nelson and Garth Brooks. It was not widely known to the public, but when Pam Lewis had signed on with Bob Doyle, the guy who had initially inked a publishing and recording contract with Garth Brooks, she had been faced with a daunting task. Also unknown to the general populace is the fact that Brooks' debut album nearly stiffed at the record marts and his singles were not immediately playlisted at radio.

"Everybody passed on him," Lewis told James Dickerson, author of *Women on Top.* "I had people I thought I could count on, and they didn't see it right away. They really saw him as a sort of Clint Black clone . . . Journalists wanted to pit the two together. Clint had won all the awards, and RCA had made him a priority. Everywhere you went, his albums were in the stores. Everywhere *we* went, there were no albums. It was ridiculous." As Lewis exhausted connection after connection, including Kim Spangler, host of the syndicated radio program *Pulse Beat* and the only female personality putting together a syndicated show, she grew more and more determined that she was right—Garth Brooks was a potential star, and the radio stations that rejected the *Pulse Beat* show featuring her artist were simply in error. As Dickerson explains, "Lewis overcame that type of resistance by simply refusing to give up. She was absolutely relentless in her determination to get Brooks the break she thought he deserved. She was everywhere, leaving no stone unturned. She became his shadow. 'Out on the road, a lot of people thought I was Garth's wife or a fan club president. It used to piss me off a little,' she says." In the end, Pam Lewis was successful in getting her artist accepted. She was stubborn to the core. "We didn't have any money. We didn't have a label that had the power of RCA. I started a 'hearing is believing' campaign. We did bumper stickers. We did advertising. I called the radio stations every week. . . . Garth never had a national radio tour. We set it all up ourselves. When the first single, *If Tomorrow Never Comes*, went Top 40, the label was thrilled to death. We said, 'No, this can be a Top 10 record.' They were going to let it go."

Garth took much of the credit due to his hardworking, behind-the-scenes co-manager, which only made the other women in this Nashville women's network more resolved to back promising new female artists like Mary Chapin Carpenter, Pam Tillis, Martina McBride, Shania Twain, and Faith Hill. As James Dickerson recounts in *Women on Top,* Sandy Neese at Mercury Records not only chose the title of Shania Twain's second album, THE WOMAN IN ME, but also called in every single favor she was owed in promoting the first single, *Whose Bed Have Your Boots Been Under,* which met initial resistance at radio. Twain's lyrics challenged the good old boy system, as did her saucy videos and strident comments to the press during her mall promotions and in a host of cover stories for women's magazines. The women's network intensified throughout the industry during this period, and when Faith Hill came out with her third album in 1998, an album well-stocked with top-notch songs written by women songwriters, like Beth Nielsen Chapman and Matraca Berg, this network went to work again to ensure that never again would women in country music merely be treated as 'girl singers'. Martha Sharp had picked her candidate to be the next Garth, and *she* was not a hat act.

These Nashville women were determined to make sure that male domination of the recording business came to an end. The next generation of women working in the music business would not be compromised. Women artists like Faith Hill and even enlightened male artists like Tim McGraw now joke about the dark old days when male stars used their 'headliner' power to make advances, most often unwanted, on *their* 'girl singers' performing as opening acts on *their* tours. Male executives at record labels treated their girls no better. For a female artist even making the rounds to radio stations where the programmers were almost exclusively male was a problem. The situation was not all that different in the rock music world in the 1980s, as Pat Benatar told James Dickerson: "I had all kinds of radio programmers saying, 'Come over here, and sit on my lap.' That sort of thing. 'Let's see if we can get that record played.' It was truly amazing. I felt like I was in a movie. You can't possibly allow that kind of thing to happen, but they have the power to make your life hell. You couldn't come right out and say, 'You fucker, kiss my butt!' You had to say, 'Oh, no thank you,' because they were in positions of power. It was very demoralizing. People say, 'What's the big deal?' But it *was* a big deal."

Working with Lib Hatcher to develop Randy Travis had been a special assignment for Martha Sharp. Now she had the opportunity with Faith Hill to develop a country woman superstar, even though Martha officially drew her salary from a record label and never got into the management side of things with either Travis or Hill. A&R people who sign an artist often look out for them, helping them secure suitable management and booking agencies, and continue to look out for them as long as that A&R person remains with the label. It can sometimes be a disaster for a newly signed artist if their A&R person who signed them moves on or is moved on before they can establish themselves as a successful artist. Like Pam Lewis, who had come to believe in Garth Brooks long before he become popular with country fans, Martha became heavily involved in as many aspects of Faith's career as she could, especially in selecting songs and picking Faith's single releases.

Martha's vision differed somewhat from Faith's because Faith had only the idea of becoming a Nashville star as a goal. Martha saw Faith not as the next Reba or Tammy or Tanya; in her heart of hearts, Martha saw Faith as the next Garth, an artist who could fluidly cross over into major record sales if she gradually slid into the pop market—a goal that was put on hold for a while when Shania Twain came along and Faith decided to have children. That goal would not be realized until five years after Martha's retirement from Warner, when Faith succeeded Garth *and* Shania— and, in the process, eclipsed her own husband's shining star, winning bushels of awards, selling kazillions of albums, and being featured on Hollywood film soundtracks.

Back in 1992, Martha Sharp felt that Nashville-based management might not cotton to sparking a revolution in a direction opposite to the ongoing new traditionalist and new country movement, which *had* brought economic recovery after the rise and fall of the previous 'urban Cowboy era' pop experiment. She had a hunch that a country pop revolution was not far in the offing, and she suspected that Nashville management "might have been limiting." As an alternative, Martha suggested Faith hook up with LA-based manager Gary Borman, who had worked with James Taylor and was currently handling Dwight Yoakam. Borman, it turned out, was interested.

For a producer, Martha thought that Scott Hendricks might be the right person. He was a busy guy. His clients included the California-based Restless Heart, the newly formed Brooks & Dunn, who were MCA label exec Tim Dubois' special project, as well as up-and-comer John Michael Montgomery. Both Faith and Martha liked the idea of Scott Hendricks producing her album because he was one of the last independent producers in Nashville—and he wasn't currently producing any female artists. Initially, Scott passed on the offer, but fate intervened when Faith made an unscheduled appearance on the *Nashville Now* show on TNN, filling in for an artist who had fallen ill. While flipping channels, Hendricks caught her performance. Right away, he liked her, which was too bad, because he had declined the opportunity to produce her when Martha had called. Still, he was intrigued by Faith's willowy figure, her radiant beauty, and her Tammy-meets-Patsy vocal power. He could hear real potential in her live vocal performance. If she was produced effectively, he was convinced she could sell tons of records. Live on television, Faith was so much better than on her demo cuts.

A few days later Scott Hendricks received a phone call from Martha Sharp. She was merely calling to request a "hold" on a song he controlled. Once they had got that item of business squared away, Scott mentioned to Martha that he had seen Faith Hill on TNN. "I want to say," he added, "I have never regretted anything more than I regret not taking this artist. Next time, I'll listen to you." Martha smiled. She knew they had their producer. Soon after that, Faith and Scott were in a studio working together. It would mark the beginning of a working relationship that resulted in sales of several million copies of her debut album, TAKE ME AS I AM.

During the time spent preparing for the recording sessions with Scott Hendricks, Faith began a search for her birth mother, prompted as she began considering that someday she and her husband, Daniel Hill, might have a child or two. She desperately needed to know her own biological background. In the midst of the hectic search for songs, her birth mother agreed to meet with Faith. "The first time I met her," Faith told *People* magazine, "I just stared at her. I'd never seen anybody that looked anything like me. It was the awe of seeing someone you came from. It fills something." Faith's world soon changed as a result of this meeting, as her husband explains. "That search," Daniel Hill would later tell interviewers, "consumed much of her energy. Meeting her birth mother was the most profound, altering experience for her. After that, her world turned upside down. I was part of her old world, and she had to let that world go. But there was no bitterness. I'm proud of her success." Their marriage soon after broke down.

No doubt, there were other reasons for the marriage breakdown. As Faith explained, "I was young. I just jumped in the fire way too soon." The Nashville gossip at the time was that Hill left her husband for her producer. As usual, history has blurred what actually took place. In order to clear up some of the scuttlebutt, Faith told one interviewer, "No beating or cheating took place. I just felt captured." Later, she would tell *McCalls*,

"He was a great, great, guy, but there was a lot going on in my life during that time. I just honestly didn't know who I was. Today, I know who I am." By 1993, Faith and Daniel felt estranged; by 1994, they were divorced. Telling her mother Edna that she was breaking off her marriage with Daniel Hill had been one of the toughest things Faith had to do in a year of tough decisions, during which she had also had to face Gary Burr and tell him he was not going to be her producer. Thankfully, Edna supported her decision.

Meanwhile, Faith's relationship with both Martha Sharp and Scott Hendricks was buoyed by the way things were going in preparation for the release of Faith's debut album. Both veterans were impressed with Faith's drive and involvement. "She was totally hands-on," Martha recalls, "and a perfectionist from the beginning." Sharp would tell and re-tell the story of the time that Faith arrived at the Warner offices at the end of a long day, utterly exhausted, yet summoned new energy and acted like a trooper. "The head of promotions caught her," Sharp told interviewers, "in the hall, and asked if she would come up and do some radio spots. I saw her do a complete turnaround. She caught herself and said, 'Let's go do it.' She always had the capacity to pull it out of herself." Both veterans also felt that Faith's pronounced Southern accent, her sultry stage presence, and her distinctive vocal warble qualified her as a candidate to become, at the very least, the next Reba. One crusty critic called Faith's debut, "the best little record Reba ever made."

But once Faith hit on the radio with *Wild One*, she rapidly became everything her idol had never been. It had taken Reba eight years as a recording artist before she overcame her timidity and took charge of her recording sessions, changing her label and producer and finding some independence working with Jimmy Bowen at MCA. Six years before she hit big on the radio with her first number one hit, *Can't Even Get The Blues*, in 1982.

*Wild One* was released in the fall of 1993. By January 1994 it was number one on the *Billboard* country chart. Reba had not sold significant quantities of her albums during the first ten years of her recording career. Her first multi-platinum album to be listed in the Top 40 on the *Billboard Hot 200 Albums* chart, which is based on sales, did not come until 1991, 15 years after her first release on Mercury Records in 1976. Faith Hill's TAKE ME AS I AM sold two million records in its first year of release. Scott Hendricks had handed Faith a number one hit. "It (*Wild One*) was one of the tunes that Scott Hendricks came across," Faith told *Country Music*

*News.* "He felt it would be a door opener. Boy, was I lucky to get that song." So far, Scott Hendricks was turning out to be everything that music publisher Daniel Hill had not been. Which was good. The chemistry was right. And miracles had kept on happening right up until the moment they had gone in to do the recording sessions. "You know," Faith confided to Larry Delaney, "as late as two weeks before the session, we were sill looking for material. We had most of the tunes picked, but we needed a couple more. The title song, *Take Me As I Am*, was found during those last couple of weeks. Sometimes, they turn out to be the best ones."

Scott Hendricks had by now risen to a position of power with Capitol Records, but he continued to produce Faith, working with her on her sophomore album for Warner Brothers. In February 1995, nearly a year after Faith's divorce, she and Scott announced that they were engaged. In London, England in August 1994, Faith confided to *Country Music People*, "Yes, he's met mom. ... I took him home at Christmas and she just loved him. I hardly got to sit beside him because she was always just right there. My two brothers liked him a lot, too, and that's good because if they hadn't it would have been all over. They're real protective of me."

*Wild One* held at number one for four weeks, the first time that a country woman had enjoyed such a long run at the top with a first record since Connie Smith's 1964 debut, *Once A Day*, which spent eight weeks at number one on the *Billboard* country chart. Since then only a handful of women had managed to stick at the top of the charts for very long at all. Lynn Anderson's *Rose Garden* had been at number one for five weeks in 1970. Tammy Wynette had enjoyed three weeks at the top with *I Don't Wanna Play House*, *D-I-V-O-R-C-E*, *Stand By Your Man*, and *He Loves Me All The Way*. Also during the 1970s, Jeannie C. Riley's *Harper Valley P.T.A.*, Donna Fargo's *The Happiest Girl In The Whole USA* and *Funny Face*, Jeannie Pruett's *Satin Sheets*, Barbara Mandrell's *Sleeping Single In A Double Bed*, Dolly Parton's *Heartbreaker*, Lynn Anderson's *How Can I Un-Love You*, and Sammi Smith's *Help Me Make It Through The Night* all held for three weeks at number one. In 1977 Crystal Gayle charted Richard Leigh's *Don't It Make My Brown Eyes Blue* for four weeks at number one, and Dolly Parton held at the top of the chart for five weeks with the first of her pop-flavored country singles, *Here You Come Again*.

During this same time period, male artists like Buck Owens, Johnny Cash, Merle Haggard, and David Houston often held the top spot for five, six, and seven weeks at a time. In 1963 Buck's *Love's Gonna Live Here* had spent a total of 16 weeks at number one. David's *Almost Persuaded* had held for nine weeks in 1966. Even novices like Jerry Reed with *When You're Hot You're Hot* and C.W. McCall with *Convoy* would hold for five or six weeks, once they hit the number one position. The key to success for a country artist was often the ability to crossover into the pop radio audience, either through novelty or 'countrypolitan' production. During the 1980s a glut of mediocre country releases and a plethora of country artists had meant that an artist seldom repeated for a second week. In 1990, during the heyday of the new traditionalist movement and the beginning of the new country era, Clint Black, Randy Travis, George Strait, Garth Brooks, and Alabama had begun to reverse that trend, all hitting with number one singles that held for four weeks or longer.

During the 1990s, women came to dominate sales and air play in all genres of music. Country music women would not drag their heels in the sand; in fact, some of them would lead the way. And in 1999 when Warner Nashville released Faith's controversial fourth album, BREATHE, the lyrics to *Wild One* would seem to have been prophesy of a time that had come, as battle lines were clearly drawn between traditionalists and others, like Faith and Shania, who dared to take their country beyond Nashville to the pop and even the rock worlds.

*She loves rock & roll*
*They said it's Satan's tongue*
*She thinks they're too old*
*They think she's too young*
*And the battle lines are clearly drawn . . .*

— *Wild One* (Jamie Kyle, Pat Bunch, Will Rambeaux)

The next single Martha Sharp selected had been a huge hit during the psychedelic era for a blues singer from Austin who had made it big in San Francisco. It was certainly not your usual country & western song or even a svelte 'new country' composition, though it was a cover of a proven pop hit. Faith Hill's version of the 1968 Big Brother & the Holding Company pop hit, *Piece Of My Heart*, which had featured Janis Joplin's legendary heart-crunching vocal, hit into the country Top 40 during the final week of February 1994. There was an initial smattering of controversy mounted by a handful of critics who said Faith's version was bland, watered down. In response, Faith would declare that she had never heard the original before she recorded *Piece Of My Heart*. She had been advised not to listen to Joplin until after she had recorded her own version. The version of the song she had learned was a demo cut by the daughter of the co-writer of the song, Cassie Burns. "I'm so glad I didn't hear the Janis Joplin cut before I made my recording," Faith told interviewers. "I'm sure my version would have been much different." When the initial criticism did not go away, Faith responded, "Critics, radio stations, Woodstock era fans—they were like, 'Oh great, here's this country crap singer trying to do this legendary song.'" Country fans, some of whom had never heard Joplin's "legendary delivery" either, didn't seem to give a hoot about what the critics and Woodstock generation folks were saying, because despite the controversy, or perhaps because of it, Faith's version would do very well on country radio, hitting the number one spot in May 1994.

While these two tracks off her first album were triumphs, there had been times that Faith had stood up for songs she really wanted on the album that were not being selected as singles. For example, Faith liked *I Want To Be Stronger Than That*, which Gary Burr had pitched to Faith from the stage of the Bluebird Café. "Gary played this one night at the Bluebird," Faith recalls, "saying it was a new song he had written. I was just in tears. It affected me so much. I thought, how could he have written that? How could that have come from a man, you know? It seemed so tender and real, so beautiful, and I remember promising myself that one day I would record it." Faith learned the song and pitched it herself to Hendricks and Sharp. "I sang it while we were sitting there talking," she remembers, "the whole song, and they said, 'Okay, you can do it.' It was one of the most magical moments of the whole album." But in the end the label did not select Burr's song as a single release. *But I Will*, the third single, stalled at number 35, but a fourth single, the title track, *Take Me As I Am*, caught fire in November and climbed up to number 2 on the *Billboard* country chart before Christmas. All in all, Faith Hill's album debut had been one of the most successful for a 'girl singer' in Nashville history. By comparison, Shania Twain's self-titled 1993 debut album had bombed.

Despite media inclinations to pit the two singers against each other, Faith and Shania became friends. Faith often defended the Canadian country singer during the days when Shania faced major criticism following her landmark 1995 release THE WOMAN IN ME and sold more records than Patsy Cline. In fact, there was often a feeling of solidarity among all of the women country artists who spearheaded the "new country" movement in the '90s. Patty Loveless, Mary Chapin Carpenter, Martina McBride, Pam Tillis, Trisha Yearwood, and Faith Hill had led the way in the early going. Shania had taken it over the top. Together, these women toppled the good old boy system, which had dominated Nashville since the day in 1925 when WSM debuted a barndance radio show to promote sales of insurance policies to audiences throughout the South. None of them forgot the crucial role that Reba had played before they arrived on the scene, and, even though McEntire's popularity would wane in the wake of their rise to the top, Reba continued to support all of them. Their sales began to equal, then to surpass, sales by male country artists—for the first time in the history of the genre. Although Faith's sales in the 1990s were not be as spectacular as Shania's were, a tip she received from Shania put her in touch with one of the producers who would eventually make her the top country diva by the time the new millennium rolled in. As sales of TAKE ME AS I AM continued to pile up, all the magazines were phoning for interviews. Larry Delaney at *Country Music News* wanted to know if she had expected such immediate reaction to her music. "Never in all my dreams," Faith said. "I was hoping that sometime in my career I would have a number one hit. And I had my fingers crossed that I'd get on the charts with some of the tunes from this debut album. But to have *Wild One* go to the top of the chart and stay there, week after week! I just had to keep pinching myself, just hoping that I wouldn't wake up from this dream."

In the fall of 1994, the Academy of Country Music in California named Faith their Favorite New Female Artist. *Billboard* listed her as their Top Female Country Artist. Then *Performance* magazine blessed her with a second Best Female Country Artist award. She appeared on *The Tonight Show: with Jay Leno* on the west coast and hobnobbed with David Letterman in New York. When pressed with questions about whether she saw herself as the next Reba, she answered much as Reba should answer similar questions about her fame. "Reba's my hero," Faith insisted. "I want 20 years from now to feel like I made a difference in people's lives the way she did with *Is There Life Out There*, sending people back to college. It's truly amazing what music can do, isn't it?" Throughout this time Faith had been on the road opening for Reba and John Michael Montgomery, then Brooks & Dunn. Another dream had come true. As she told Larry Delaney at *Country Music News*, "I'm looking forward to a series of concert shows with one of my idols, Reba McEntire. That's happening in February. We're on the road with John Michael Montgomery, too. Twenty-nine and single, I hear it . . . Just kidding. And this summer we're working with Brooks & Dunn." Opening for Reba was a profoundly moving experience. "I went out front to watch her final rehearsal," Faith describes her first show on this tour, "and sat out there and cried because I just could not believe I was actually going to open for her."

When Faith sang the national anthem at a Dallas Cowboys game, it was reported in the media that she was having a fling with star quarterback Troy Aikman. She was the "wild one." Members of the press was going to have their way with her whether this rumor was founded in fact or in fiction. When both Aikman and Hill denied these rumors, the tabloids began to imagine even less probable scenarios—none of which has ever hurt an artist's record sales. Faith had hit a vein that Tammy Wynette had taken advantage of during the 1970s and, although this country girl was not "gonna go bad," she did gain national press that she wouldn't have otherwise enjoyed merely by being the country artist who critics alleged had slaughtered Janis Joplin's signature song. As a consequence of the rumor mill, Troy, Scott, and Faith would eventually get to know each other, with Aikman providing Super Bowl tickets to Scott.

Faith soon made friends with other country stars. Alan Jackson offered her a song for her upcoming second album, and Faith toured with Alan in 1995. Then yet another dream came true as she opened for George Strait. Faith scarcely touched down in her sunny little condo in Nashville before she was off again, promoting her record and touring with the stars of country music. During this whirlwind period, she also had a chance encounter of a most intriguing kind, meeting fellow class of '93 country artist, Tim McGraw, at an artist showcase. It was the first time the Warner and Curb artists rubbed shoulders together at an industry event. Although neither realized it at the time, they both made lasting impressions on each other that day.

*Let's Make Love*
Academy of Country
Music Awards, 2000

Faith, 1994

Tim, 1994

Faith, 2000

Tim, 2000

Faith performs *Breathe*, Soul 2 Soul Tour

Tim performs *It's Your Love*, Soul 2 Soul Tour

Grammy Awards, 2001

# SPONTANEOUS COMBUSTION

When the phone rang, Tim McGraw rolled over and noted that it was 8:00 a.m. Real early for a country singer who had mostly been living on 'lonesome standard time'. He picked up the receiver. Bryon Gallimore was on the line. "It had to be important for him to call me at eight in the morning," Tim recalled during an interview with Nick Krewen at *Country Weekly*, "but he called me as I was about to get up and go out in the bus." Byron had a song that Tim just had to hear. He could take it along with him as he headed out to begin his Spontaneous Combustion Tour. By this time, Tim and Byron were fast friends. They would soon combine their talent in the studio working together as co-producers on sessions for Jo Dee Messina's first album. Tim told Byron he would wait there and check out the song when Byron arrived. It turned out to be a smart move. "I lived way out in the country at the time, and he came out and played me the song," Tim continued. "It was just an incredible song and right away we knew we were cutting it." That song was *It's Your Love*. The writer was a woman, Stephony Smith, but her lyrics worked very well for a male vocalist. During the second stage of the 1996 Spontaneous Combustion Tour, when Tim's opening act, Faith Hill, returned to the stage during his set to sing with him, Tim would sit at the end of the stage on a stool with just his acoustic guitar and their audiences would melt as pure vocal magic rang out through the big main speakers of the sound system. The merging of their voices on their harmonies would be an added bonus, but Byron had been right—this song had "hit" written all over it.

In country music the song is the thing. Which is why Faith Hill and

Scott Hendricks spent so much time searching out the songs for her second album. Because Faith was on the road so often, whenever she returned to Nashville, the time they shared together was spent re-acquainting themselves and listening to new demo tapes. So far, this liaison between artist and producer seemed to be progressing smoothly. Life was good. Even their personal relationship seemed to be progressing smoothly, despite Faith's reputation as a "wild one" among the press. In fact, Faith herself sometimes joked with interviewers about the fact she was often on the road with some of the hunks and hat acts who were regarded as the most desirable eligible bachelors in country music.

Dealing with minor tremors on the Richter Scale like media rumors was relatively simple in comparison with the trauma Faith faced when real disaster struck. Her heavy 1994 touring schedule had wreaked havoc on her vocal abilities. At first she was merely hoarse, then she couldn't sing at all. A dilated blood vessel in her throat was blocking her voice and causing considerable pain. But the real trauma came from her fear that she would never be able to sing again. When doctors examined her throat, she learned that they would have to operate. She had been singing louder than the choir since she was three years old. She had little formal vocal training and seldom practiced regular warmup exercises or any of the breathing techniques that take the strain off your throat and vocal chords. She'd been promoting herself and her music nonstop in the United States, Canada and the United Kingdom since the release of TAKE ME AS I AM in 1993, singing with her band nearly every night and giving what seemed to be non-stop interviews over the phone and in person during the day.

Before she went in for surgery, Faith said she was "scared to death"— a figure of speech, to be sure—but she did fear being no longer able to entertain her fans. The surgeons at Nashville's Vanderbilt Hospital were familiar with this sort of operation, having treated dozens of country singers, mostly women, in the past. Scott Hendricks stood by his woman, and once the surgery was completed, her mother's healing chicken soup helped her begin the road to recovery. For a person as talkative as Faith, not speaking for several weeks after her operation proved to be nearly as tough a hurdle to get over as the operation itself.

On February 14th, Valentines Day, 1995, Scott proposed marriage. He had to ask Faith to give him a sign because the doctors had forbidden her to speak aloud. Scott got the nod he wanted, that they both had said they wanted. If in retrospect this seems opportunistic—with Faith still in doubt as to whether she would ever sing with the same power and fluidity again—it was hardly an unexpected move. Faith had spoken of a "special person" to many interviewers and mentioned that she was awaiting a "proposal." What better day was there than Valentine's Day to pop the question? Now with her multi-platinum throat damaged and the results of her surgery not yet apparent, she was comforted by the fact that even if she could never sing again, she had her man.

Modern medicine has changed many people's lives and careers, extending life expectancy, and, in the case of professional athletes like Tommy John, extending careers. It's not all that different for professional singers. The name Tommy John, a starting pitcher for championship teams in both LA and New York, became synonymous with "Tommy John surgery." Sports writers joked that the left-hander had been equipped with a 'bionic arm', just like actor Lee Majors who played *The Bionic Man* in the popular television series. Country singers have been more reticent to speak of injuries to their throat or the growths called "nodes" on their vocal chords. In the past these injuries and ailments were usually kept secret. In 1992, Kathy Mattea had undergone a throat operation and survived to sing again. She had also decided the time had come to let her fans know what she had gone through and how she had become inspired to record the emotional vocals on two especially moving songs, *Knee Deep In A River (And Dying Of Thirst)* and *Seeds*. In the liner notes to her album LONESOME STANDARD TIME, Mattea spoke openly about the matter. "I've had the chance at the height of my career," she explained, "to stop and think about what I really want. I think I've found a nice balance. When I recorded the vocals for LONESOME STANDARD TIME, I sang with the knowledge of the possibility that I might not ever sing again. Thank God I can." These words had also been helpful for other country vocalists who took courage when they read them.

In the studio to record her sophomore album, Faith was nervous as all get out, but she scarcely needed to be. Once Scott and his crew of engineers and musicians heard her sing, there were smiles all around. Faith's voice came through loud and clear, and, if anything, a little bit richer and more mature—certainly as good as it had been before she had subjected her vocal equipment to the non-stop wear and tear. The sessions for IT MATTERS TO ME went very well. With unexpected extra time on her hands while she was recuperating, Faith had been able to apply herself to even more song-selection than she had undergone for her debut. She also summoned up the nerve to reject label-mate Alan Jackson's initial submission, a lite-country offering she simply could not relate to. Alan then came back to Faith and handed over the moving song *I Can't Do That Anymore*, a truly marvelous composition that stunned Faith when she first heard it. The song appeared to be written, remarkably, from a woman's point of view. Before handing over this 'tailor-made' song, Jackson told Faith that he had written it especially for her because "you pissed me off," a surly yet light-hearted comment. No doubt, Alan was fairly confident she would like this one. As she listened to Alan's demo with a fellow musician in the bus, Faith blurted, "I can't believe a man wrote that." Having courage enough to stand up to Alan Jackson and reject his first song had resulted in her getting a far better work to record.

Faith also had the courage to record a song that tackled the issue of spousal abuse. This wasn't the first time a contemporary country woman had recorded such a song. Martina McBride's *Independence Day* had broken down a lot of taboos. That song had been pitched to Faith but she had not recorded it. "I passed on it," she recalls, "it wasn't a song for me. I completely believed in what the song said, but I believe the song found its home, the right singer." Women had long been known to purchase more country records than men, and in the past Nashville labels had responded by pumping out tons of records by men, believing that women listeners wanted it that way. In the 1990s, female country fans were proving they wanted to hear more songs about real issues by buying more and more records by women artists. Martha Sharp pitched *A Man's Home Is His Castle* to Faith, handing her a demo tape and suggesting she have a listen when she had time. While driving in her car in downtown Nashville, Faith heard the song for the first time and was moved to tears. She knew she wanted to record it. When the album was released, there were detractors who put her down for being trendy and climbing on a bandwagon that was already rolling. Faith would simply say, "I don't care what people say. The bottom line is this song moved me. This song ripped my heart out when I heard it."

The label chose to release the light-hearted *Let's Go To Vegas*, written by Faith's backup singer Karen Staley, as the lead single. In August 1995, *Let's Go To Vegas* began its climb into the Top 10. In November a second single, the title track, hit into the Top 40. In the new year, *It Matters To Me* became Faith's third number one, enjoying a three week stint at the top of the country charts. *Someone Else's Dream*, *You Can't Lose Me*, and Alan Jackson's *I Can't Do That Anymore* were all Top 10 hits in 1996. Sales of IT MATTERS TO ME surpassed sales of her debut album, edging over three million before the release of her fourth album. Neither Faith, nor her producer Scott Hendricks, nor Martha Sharp at Warner Nashville knew then that Faith's personal life was about to take an abrupt left turn, which would also affect her recording career until 1998.

Three months after surgery Faith was back on the road, opening for Alan Jackson. During a swing through the Canadian maritime provinces, her performance was praised by *Country Music News* reporter Paul Kennedy. "I must tell you how impressed I was with show opener Faith Hill," he wrote in his June 1995 column. "She just returned to touring prior to this first Maritime visit. The sound wasn't as good for Faith as it was for Alan. It was obvious, however, that Faith had her powerful voice back after that three month break for vocal chord surgery." At an outdoor festival Faith encountered that guy from Curb Records again, Tim McGraw. "I thought she was gorgeous," Tim would say later, "but out of my league." Faith would subsequently admit that she had been attracted, too. Of course, Tim McGraw was not the only person who found her overwhelmingly attractive. There was Scott Hendricks, her fiancée, of course. Then there were the readers of *People* magazine who voted Faith one of the "50 Most Beautiful People of 1995."

Faith had begun to carve out a reputation for stunning performances. There had been times when she had been unable to move an audience of boisterous fans who merely viewed her set as something to endure until their favorite—George Strait or Alan Jackson or Reba McEntire—took the stage. But Faith had learned to deal with these disappointing moments, and she had got better at drawing in many of these established stars' fans, despite their initial indifference. Faith's experience back in Mississippi fronting a band and playing all manner of gigs turned out to be a huge advantage during this period of dues paying out on the road. She had also assembled a very good road band, headed up by veteran steel guitar player Gary Carter. Some artists endure a constant revolving door as musicians seem to enter and leave their band at will. Some artists would rather have it that way. In Faith's case, the original unit that was put together clicked, and most of her players stuck with her for years.

Gary Carter was a unique musician with 18 years of family band experience behind him before he first traveled with a Nashville act. After working with Lorrie Morgan, he had acted as a picker, band leader, and road manager for the first band put together for Randy Travis in 1986. It hadn't been glamorous. "In the early days with Randy," Gary recalls, "I drove Randy and his manager, Lib Hatcher, in a van while the other five musicians traveled in a bread truck with only four bunks and no air conditioner. That was rough." He next went on the road with Pam Tillis. By the time that he met Faith, Gary had settled-in to married life, enjoying cookouts when he was off the road and playing steel, slide, and dobro guitar whenever and wherever he was hired to do so. In addition to being influenced by the seminal steel guitar playing of Nashville cats like Buddy Emmons, Pete Drake, and Curly Chauker, he had also been influenced by jazz players like Cannonball Adderly, Chick Corea, and John Coltrane. His favorite morning listening with his first coffee is classical music by composers like Hayden.

Gary had pretty well done it all, from debuting on the *Grand Ole Opry* at age 16 to "doing a live show with Randy Travis in Liverpool with the London Philharmonic Orchestra," as he explains. In 1999, after six years with Faith Hill, he wasn't planning on leaving just yet. "Faith sets the pace for everyone else on the tour," he explains. "This is the first band I have ever worked with that knows and understands the music. I have been doing this for a long time and, believe me, understanding is hard to find."

Faith has said, "I feel that I've got the best band on the road. All of them great musicians. For some miraculous reason, we all get along great on the road. I've heard horrible stories about bands that don't . . . There's usually one or two people who seem to be sore thumbs in the crowd, and they make life miserable for the other band members—we don't have that. Everybody gets along great—they always have. It's really a special group of people. I feel very lucky." From drummer Trey Gray and bassist John Howard to lead guitarist Lou Toomey, steel guitarist Carter and fiddler Dan Kelly, this is a band that can lock in and provide Faith both the ambience and the groove that she needs in order to perform her shows. Lisa Gregg, who replaced Karen Staley in 1998, and Micah Roberts are equally in synch when it comes to singing background and harmony vocals. Being together year after year, they were a band of friends who also happen to be very talented. Faith's boast that hers is the "best band on the road" is not an idle one.

Another contender for this crown would be Tim McGraw's Dance-hall Doctors. In 1995, Tim was often lumped together as one of the new breed of Nashville outlaws. Journalists simply took the title of his hit novelty song *Indian Outlaw* and extrapolated their own headline making assertions. Tim wasn't always comfortable with the designation, especially during the controversy that followed its release, but he came to terms with his renegade label once he recorded his second album and the aura of a novelty act and any hint of blind imitation had dissipated.

It was Travis Tritt and Marty Stuart who had innocently set this '90s outlaw thing in motion when they tried their luck with a duet version of *The Whiskey Ain't Working* and triggered a reaction that clicked just like when Waylon and Willie got together during the "outlaw era" in the 1970s. Their newfound camaraderie in tow, Travis and Marty gleefully embarked on a "No Hats Tour," rocking their country together and having a fine old time. Critics and fans alike saw this as a reaction against the 'hat act' mentality that Music Row was endorsing. And the tongue in cheek promotion worked. It set Travis and Marty off from the rest of the pack. "I figured, it's funny," Tritt wrote in his autobiography *10 Feet Tall And Bullet-proof*, "maybe a speck controversial, but, hey, everyone can take a joke." Garth Brooks would not be amused. During the press conference that preceded his first television special, Brooks commented, "I just don't get it. I don't know what they are saying." Garth really loves his hat.

Nashville country music is the only music genre on the planet that is constantly politicized. Most experimental or fresh sounds coming out of Nashville will be met with a chorus of people harping on the tired old cliché, "That's not Country." Travis Tritt wasn't worried about that. He understood that southern rock sometimes ended up on rock charts and sometimes on country charts, as it had when Hank Williams Jr. had cranked up the volume and reinvented himself. Charlie Daniels had walked the line between rock and country for years. Willie Nelson had told Travis Tritt that "any time you do things your way you're gonna end up fighting the establishment." In his autobiography Tritt notes, "I hate those little boxes, little categories. I've seen them just about kill some of my good friends, strangling off their creativity until there was almost nothing left. It happened before in Nashville. I suspect it's going to happen again. . . . I like that image, outlaw. It's an old and venerable one, one that's carved out its own niche in country music. It started out as an insider's joke, a song written by a veteran Nashville songwriter that got great response at the picking parlors and guitar pullings that drive the Nashville star-making machinery." That song was Lee Clayton's *Ladies Like Outlaws* and, Tritt points out, the outlaw movement helped bring about country's "first huge boom. Driven by the likes of Waylon and Willie, the music was, for the first time, drawing in the kids, the young people, the rock audience."

Alan Jackson was emerging as a different kind of superstar, a country artist who could deal with mega sponsorships from Ford trucks for his tours and at the same time not forget to keep the two-steppers happy at his shows. Alan had hit first in 1990 with a ballad, *Here In The Real World*, which he followed with a string of number ones that included *Don't Rock The Jukebox* and the fun-times *Chattahoochie*, the 1993 CMA Single of the Year. Despite having declared "Don't rock the jukebox" in one song, he could deliver blistering rock versions of cuts like *Mercury Blues* and a re-make of Eddie Cochran's 1958 pop hit *Summertime Blues*, but he kept it country by also recording tracks like *Gone Country* and the George Jones and Roger Miller collaboration, *Tall, Tall Trees*.

Tim McGraw would run headfirst into these questions when he released *Indian Outlaw*. Concerning Tim's outlaw image, which journalist James Hunter said "puzzled Nashville," Jo Dee Messina once commented, "Tim was kind of heavyset back then . . . Really long hair and his longer-than-usual mustache. He's always fighting for the underdog." In the February 1995 issue of CMA *Closeup*, Tim pointed out that because he'd been on the road for 274 shows in 1994, he hadn't really come to feel that he had "made it" yet in Nashville. "When you're in busworld, as we call it," he explained, "it's hard to get a perspective on what's going on at home. Last year seems like three years, and at the same time it seems like it went by fast and it was all one big show. It's hard to let anything sink in. I still feel we're out there as the underdogs, always kicking around trying to make a living and prove something." For Tim the word underdog worked better than the word outlaw. Renegade was another word that stuck to Tim, especially after he recorded the Jeff Stevens and Steve Bogard song *Renegade* on his second album:

> I might ride with the wind
> I might follow the sun
> I gotta go where I've never been
> 'Cause my heart beats to a different drum
> It's just the way I was made
> I'm a renegade
> I'm a renegade

— *Renegade* (Jeff Stevens, Steve Bogard)

While Tim rode this new outlaw wave onto the radio and adopted a wide-brimmed black hat as his trademark image, his shows were not political statements. They were all about having fun. Tim had adapted a page or two from Garth Brooks' blueprint for his stage shows and would adapt ideas being developed by artists like Alan Jackson, too, often entering the building with a flurry of bodyguards or appear dramatically in the center of the room and stride to the stage like a relief pitcher come in to save the day.

In the 1990s Garth Brooks and his "friends in low places" had once again brought in the rock audience. Garth's high voltage live performances were drawing huge crowds. Performance was also key to Tim McGraw's early success. By 1995 Tim's production included three jumbo video screens and state-of-the-art lighting equipment. As James Hunter notes, "For McGraw, the show is the thing. His muscular sound, driven by a rangy tenor, has the rock-rooted energy of his hero Garth Brooks, but his delivery and choice of songs avoid the sanctimony of much of the new country."

"Garth said it best," Tim told Hunter. "When you go to a concert, you want to see a show, not hear a CD. The vibe is feel-good—I think Sawyer Brown and Hootie & the Blowfish have the same attitude. They're happy."

While Tim hung out with guys like Tracy Lawrence and Kenny Chesney and sometimes rubbed shoulders with Garth Brooks—such as the time when Garth, Tracy, and Tim acted as "bridesmaids" for Tammy Rose at her Nashville wedding—he was still labeled as a "novelty act" by many critics. Which had only made him more determined to put those allegations to rest for once and for all when he went into the studio to record ALL I WANT. As he told James Hunter, "After *Indian Outlaw*, I wasn't taken as seriously as I wanted to be. It never feels good when somebody writes off what you do as a whim or a fad. The reaction challenged me to prove that I was serious about being an artist." Rising to that challenge without compromising himself by making records that other people thought he should be making would be key to his success. Establishing individuality at a time when critics were referring to all of the new country males as 'hat acts' made the challenge especially tough. But there was no way that Tim was going to modify his music or take off his hat just to make a few critics happy. Ironically, when George Strait first showed up on Music Row in 1980, the first thing the people he met in Nashville wanted him to do was doff the stetson. As Strait has recalled, "When I came to town wearing a hat, that's all I ever heard. 'Take the hat off.' This is from people in the record business, 'man, you sounded great, but take the hat off. Trust me, take the hat off.' But I never would do it. They were trying to make me into something else but I was too hard headed."

But Tim wasn't one to politicize anybody's music. He wasn't as angry as Garth sometimes appeared to be, and he had never recorded a song as violent as *The Thunder Rolls*. Tim's adrenalin moments were less about venting anger and mass psychology, focused solely on having a great time. He might have depended upon that imaging a bit on cuts like *Indian Outlaw*, but with the release of ALL I WANT in September 1995, Tim had upped the ante several notches. As Alanna Nash wrote in *Entertainment Weekly*, "When McGraw hit big with 1984's *Indian Outlaw*, he looked like a commercially successful embarrassment, a la Billy Ray Cyrus. On his follow-up ALL I WANT, McGraw makes an astonishing leap to fully realized performer. His superlative song choice, emotional embodiment of a lyric, and persona, the loser with the heart of gold (on *All I Want Is A Life*)—make him this year's most deserving underdog."

The cut from ALL I WANT that put Tim over the top and provided him with an identity that nobody could say was mere novelty was *I Like It, I Love It*, which sounded like it had been recorded at one of the wildest parties of all time. Movie goers would soon hear Tim's record on the soundtrack of the motion picture *Something To Talk About*, starring Julia Roberts. Tim and the Dancehall Doctors had worked up the arrangement out on the road, and producers Stroud and Gallimore had taken their cue from Tim's live version. "The background singing on *I Like It, I Love It*," Tim says, "was recorded in Nashville when a big group of my friends, including the songwriters Jeb Stuart Anderson, Steve Dukes and Markus Hall, all gathered at a local studio to add the 'party' to the song." If you hadn't been to a Tim McGraw show yet, this record let you know exactly what you were missing.

> *Spent forty-eight dollars last night at the county fair*
> *I throwed out my shoulder but I won her that teddy bear*
> *She's got me saying sugar-pie, honey, darlin', and dear*
>
> *I ain't seen the Braves play a game all year*
> *I'm gonna get fired, if I don't get some sleep*
> *My long lost buddies say I'm gettin' in too deep*
>
> *But I like it, I love it, I want some more of it*
> *I try so hard, I can't rise above it*
> *Don't know what it is 'bout that little gal's lovin'*
> *But I like it, I love it, I want some more of it . . .*
>
> — *I Like It, I Love It* (Jeb Stuart Anderson, Steve Dukes, Markus Hall)

While this song set off a frenzy of screaming among his female fans at live shows, once he and the Dancehall Doctors finished the final ringing chord of their encore and he climbed down off the stage—Tim was still shy about asking girls out. Despite all those kegs he had "floated" along the way, he hadn't overcome the small-town boy bashfulness he has mentioned he felt when he first met Tug in Houston. He hadn't developed very many 'smooth moves'. In 1984 at a dance at St. Frederick High School in Monroe, he recalls, "My date said, 'I have to go to the bathroom.' She left and never came back. The only thing was, she left her purse in my car. So at one o'clock in the morning, I'm sitting on the hood of my car—the only one in the parking lot—waiting for her to come get it."

McGraw's anecdotes often conjure up such singular images. How much more hang-dog can you get? His sister is said to have had to dig up a date for him for his high school prom. "Even when he started touring," his mother says, "he'd have his road manager ask girls out for him." It wasn't like he'd never got lucky, and he *had* established a relationship with Kristine Donohue that has been described as an engagement, but he was by no means the sly romeo that you might have expected him to be by listening to his records or going to his shows. By the time that Tim suggested to his management that they get Faith Hill as an opening act for his 1996 tour, he had broken off his engagement with Kristine. He was at loose ends as far as a relationship went and in danger of spiraling into an oblivion of fun-loving party times, especially when he was on the road with the Dancehall Doctors. Tim was attracted to the blonde Warner Brothers artist, sure enough; as he has said many times since, "the first time I saw her walk onto the stage and start singing, I was mesmerized." He was as attracted to her talent as he was to her beauty. He had seen how a crowd reacted to Faith's performance and, whether he made any hay while the sun shone would not matter—together they would sell tickets and fill venues.

Before he heated up, Tim McGraw was still wide-eyed and innocent, a strong, well-fed farm-boy, so to speak, beneath his black, oversize stetson. Too many brewskies and Flash's Hound hot dogs consumed during long, soul-searching days spent in Printer's Alley, along with a party-down lifestyle, which he had settled into during his college years, had filled out his six-foot frame—perhaps filled it out a little too well. By the time that Tim began courting Faith Hill during the Spontaneous Combustion Tour in 1996, he would be lean and mean. In his promo photos and shots taken for magazine covers, his eyes would be staring intently into the camera lens. A relentless touring schedule helped trim off some of the extra pounds. Regular afternoon flag football with the Dancehall Doctors helped, too. Once his records began selling in the millions, he might have become a "fat cat" and an arrogant one, as well, which is often the biggest challenge an artist faces. That did not happen. Instead, he merely grew more confident. In 1999, he would tell *Knix* magazine's Sandy Lovejoy, "I've gotten more confident about everything I do, out of music and in music. Confidence breeds success and success breeds confidence."

As Tim McGraw and Faith Hill headed out to begin the Spontaneous Combustion tour, Tim was just coming off a five week run at number one on the *Billboard* country chart with *I Like It, I Love It* and the follow-up, Gary Burr's *Can't Really Be Gone,* had already climbed into the Top 10. Tim holds Gary in the same high regard as does Faith. "Gary Burr is one of the most incredible songwriters around," Tim had told *Country Weekly* in October 1995. "It's just one of those songs with a real beautiful melody and a simple lyric that really touches you in a lot of ways. It's one of those songs that doesn't have to say a whole lot." *All I Want Is A Life* would follow the first two singles into the Top 10 during the 140 city tour. On the eve of their departure, Faith's third number one, *It Matters To Me,* had been at number one for three weeks, and Warner Brothers had just released *Someone Else's Dream,* which would rise to number 3 during the spring of 1996. In May 1996 Faith, Time-Warner, and Warner Brothers Records announced Faith's Family Literacy Project, which would gain considerable momentum a few years later when General Colin Powell joined her in her efforts to collect and disseminate books during the Soul 2 Soul Tour 2000.

As Faith and Tim got to know each other, they began to discover that they had a whole lot in common, not merely the fact that they both regarded Gary Burr as one of Nashville's top tunesmiths. When Gary Burr first met Faith he had also taken to her immediately. He would later tell journalists, "That was the time of big hair, and, let's just say that Faith more than held her own—she looked like a small little thing you wanted to protect, and, you know, guide through life." No doubt, if he could make his way into her affections, Tim had more than protecting on his mind. Still, he knew for a certainty that—as Gary had learned earlier—she would more than hold her own on the road. Tim decided to call his tour the Spontaneous Combustion Tour, which turned out to be right on the money, once he and Faith and their two crackerjack bands hit the road in March 1996.

Critics who had not yet seen or heard Faith Hill live were surprised to find that she was not your usual rhinestone cowgirl. In fact, the image that Faith, Gary Borman, and Martha Sharp had developed was not all that country. A writer for *Good Housekeeping* magazine who went to one of the Spontaneous Combustion Tour shows in '96 later noted, "I was more wowed by her clothes than her music. As she strutted across the stage belting out her early country hits, *Take Me As I Am* and *Wild One*, she debunked every cliche about bad Nashville fashion. There were no sequins, no fringe, no ruffles. Instead this lanky blonde from Star, MS, came on like a betwanged *Vogue* model singing for an arena of cry-in-your-beer country fans while wearing gowns and pantsuits designed by Richard Tyler, high fashion tailor to the likes of Julia Roberts and Ashley Judd."

On May 30th in Knoxville, Tennessee, the forces of nature conspired with Tim and Faith to bring the house down, literally. They had just completed their show at the World's Fair Park Pavilion when a storm rolled in and hit the area with vengeance. Thunder and lightning and hail with hurricane-force winds that ripped the roof of the Pavilion from its moorings. Miraculously, no one was injured. Their set was ruined and their lighting equipment lay in a tangled mass of twisted towers and shattered bulbs. Damage was also sustained by some of the semi-trailer trucks parked outside. "It was scary," Tim told *Country Weekly*, "it just seemed to come from nowhere. The bus was really rocking. Thankfully, nobody was hurt." While the set was repaired and lighting equipment replaced, Tim played a show at the Chesapeake Country Music Festival in Baltimore using borrowed equipment.

When Faith and Tim sang *It's Your Love* at these shows, there was no denying that something special happened. To the fans it was George and Tammy all over again.

*It's your love*
*It just does something to me*
*It sends a shock right through me*
*I can't get enough*
*And if you wonder*
*about the spell I'm under*
*Oh! It's your love*

— *It's Your Love* (Stephony Smith)

It wasn't long before the word was out—there was something cooking between Tim McGraw and Faith Hill. "I used my power as a headliner to make sure she fell in love with me," Tim would later say in jest to Faith and a journalist during a limousine ride en route to one of the CBS "Divas" shows. Hill, not one to be put off by his light-hearted mock chauvinism, would counter with, "Yeah, right." Their ongoing dialog would differ from city to city, but journalists wherever they went would come to love their banter. It made very good ink. They would say that Tim spoke "mock boastfully" and they admired Faith's matter of fact put-downs. Tim's most often quoted line would be, "You can't meet Faith and not fall in love with her. I just got lucky." Faith eventually admitted that when she and her band first joined up with Tim and the Dancehall Doctors, she was already attracted to Tim. "Whenever I could," she later confessed to *People* magazine, "I would try to bump into him. I was so attracted to him, and, though I didn't know it at the time, he was feeling exactly the same thing." At the time, Tim had still thought she was way out of his league. "I didn't think I had a snowball's chance in hell," he told *People*. "It was very cat and mouse," Faith admits. "Very high school. My singers are going, 'He's walking in the hall, go, go, go . . .'" Their first kiss came shortly afterward with Tim embracing Faith and "planting a big old kiss on her."As Tim commented later, turning around the snowball-in-hell metaphor, "things started snowballing from there."

But Faith still had her engagement to Scott Hendricks to consider. She would later comment that "it obviously wasn't a rock-solid situation or it wouldn't have ended. There wouldn't have been someone else who could walk into my life. Tim is not the reason I left. If someone is going to judge my character, because I was engaged to somebody and then I left him for somebody else—'Oh, okay, now she's a slut and a bad person'—I can't control that. But I wasn't about to let Tim slip through my hands. And I had more self-worth and self-respect to not stay in a situation just because someone else thinks I should. I have to be happy, too."

"She hadn't been happy for a long time," Tim explained to *People*. "You don't feel bad, but you realize the other guy knows he's lost."

When Faith was invited to sing during the closing ceremonies of the 1996 Summer Olympic Games, she was seen and heard by an estimated television audience of 3.5 billion viewers. For the promoters of the Spontaneous Combustion Tour, this event provided a huge boost for ticket sales at their shows. For Faith, her Olympic performance was a key projection of her image that helped sell records and remained lodged in many of those viewers minds for several years down the line, preparing the way for the eventual success of her breakthrough album FAITH and the triumph of her super crossover success with BREATHE.

During a break in the tour schedule, Curb Records staged a party in Nashville to celebrate Tim's fourth number one single, *She Never Lets It Go To Her Heart*. Industry insiders invited to this event could see first hand that the rumors, which had filtered back to Music Row from the tour, were not merely rumors. Faith and Tim had become more than merely friends, although at this time just what their status was would remain in the realm of speculation. Once they were on the road and over the initial hurdles, Tim had proposed marriage. He cooked meals for Faith in supplication for her answer. By the time they got to Montana in the fall of '96, he had the answer he wanted, scrawled on a mirror in the dressing room trailer.

The more Faith and Tim talked, the more they discovered they were like two peas that had grown in the same pod, or very similar pods, the towns of Star and Start. They had more than their Southern accents in common. What they both missed most, now that they had ignited their careers in the country music world, was the warm camaraderie of family life. Tim had bonded with his band—being one of the boys in the band had become a substitute family—but it wasn't the same. Faith had bonded with Scott Hendricks, but she didn't feel the same electrical tingles and bipolar attraction that she now found herself feeling when she was with Tim. Tim just plain liked kids—and he was good with them. Faith had considered having a child and had set out to search for her birth mother, but she had not chosen her first husband to be the father of her children. Tim would make a very good father. She was convinced of that. As they spent more and more time with each other, going to movies together, cooking meals together, and learning just how many experiences, likes, dislikes, and beliefs they shared, Faith became more and more sure that Tim would be the father of her children. "It was the way he handled children," Faith explained to *Country Weekly*. "I'd seen him on the road with young fans. I thought he had this incredible ability to communicate with a child. But more than just liking children—they had his attention and had theirs. At this point, it was like, 'this guy's *it!*'"

But Faith had already acknowledged her love for Scott Hendricks publicly in the liner notes to her second album, where she wrote, "Scott, you have taught me patience and understanding, but most of all you have taught me love." Her fiancée would be forced to summon forgiveness from

95

his stock of virtues. He had taught Faith love but he had lost her just as quickly as he had discovered her while casually viewing his television set one night in 1992. Perhaps Scott had already witnessed Faith and Tim on one of the gigantic video projection screens at one of their concerts, Faith slow-dancing in Tim's arms during a musical interlude in their duet segment of Tim's set on the Spontaneous Combustion Tour. If he hadn't seen any of those images, he couldn't miss the photo of Faith and Tim kissing on stage that ran in the November issue of *Modern Screen's Country Music* magazine.

This affair was not the first time in the history that a headlining male star had bedded his girl singer opening act, but Faith Hill in 1996 was scarcely the stereotypical 'girl singer' of days gone by. Everybody who knew her admired her fiercely independent spirit. If you weren't prepared to *Take Me As I Am*, then you were not likely to get to play tiddly winks or checkers with Faith Hill, let alone sing duets and plant any further kisses, however lovingly macho yet tender. Nor was Tim McGraw a male country star mired in the fabled past of cheatin', hurtin', lovin', and leavin', either. Tim was serious and sincere.

The Spontaneous Combustion tour played 140 dates that year, and before it was over the two stars had got hitched in Rayville, Mississippi, not that far from Star and Start, the two little towns where they had started out in life and attended elementary school. "There is the big old oak tree that we used to hang out under all the time as kids," Tim says, "and that's where we got married."

For Dancehall Doctor Keyboard player Jeff McMahon, the most memorable moment of the Spontaneous Combustion tour was "finding out that Tim and Faith were getting married on the way to our benefit softball tournament! The first pre-game wedding I've ever experienced." The band had not been told of this ceremony, but had been lured to Tim's aunt Barbara's backyard in Rayville to attend a pre-game family breakfast in order to insure privacy for family members and friends. The Dancehall Doctors were not the only guests dressed in their softball uniforms. The hardest part of all for the guys in the band would be to keep the union a secret throughout the charity softball game that followed and right up until Tim made an official announcement that night from the stage of the Tim McGraw Sports Complex during their Swampstock set.

"It was a big secret," Richland Parish county clerk Ramona Haire told *Country Weekly*. "Only the immediate families, his band, and closest friends were there. I had to come up here on Saturday, type the license, and help get the judge to wave the three-day waiting period. It's no big deal. In little towns like this, we do things like that." In order to ensure that the wedding was not invaded by hoards of curiosity seekers, Tim had wisely enlisted the services of sheriff's deputies from Richland Parish to secure the area surrounding Barbara Harper's house. "It was a beautiful day," Ramona Haire remembers. "The weather forecast had a 40 percent chance of rain because Hurricane Josephine was headed this way, but it passed to the east. It was sunny and in the 70s. It was a perfect day. Stunning floral arrangements decorated the spacious yard. Strains of a string quintet played as the guests arrived. Tim and Faith were married at noon—in front of an ivy-covered trellis under a beautiful spreading oak tree. Faith wore a real pretty, simple, white dress and veil. And she was barefoot. Tim wore blue jeans, a long black jacket, and boots. It was all very casual. It's what they wanted because they were all going to play softball as soon as it was over."

Although Tim has said that he had come from a "fractured" family situation, he has also been a uniting and healing force, which was obvious at this breakfast wedding where the 75 family members and friends included both Tug McGraw and Betty Trimble, Betty's husband Joe Trimble, Tim's step-dad Horace Smith, Betty's mom, and Faith's parents Ted and Edna Perry. Tim's best man was his college pal, Ricky Hooter. Faith's bridesmaid was her home-town friend Gaye Knight. Reverend Adrian Pater, who had baptized Tim way back when, performed the ceremony and came up with the one-liner of the day when he saw the two rings, especially Faith's "stunning emerald-cut diamond," which is a five-karat yellow diamond set in platinum. "When the bridesmaid gave me the rings," Pater recalls, "I looked at them and said, 'It's very obvious these were not bought at Wal-Mart.'" Pater also told *Country Weekly* that "I have to admit, I've never done a wedding like that. They obviously didn't want publicity and I honestly understand. They didn't want a zoo over there."

When Tim and Faith arrived at the softball field, they were greeted by country artists Tracy Lawrence, Jeff Carson, Kenny Chesney, and Mark Collie. Word of their nuptials was spread further but no public announcement was made. The charity ball-game, auction, and concert that followed added another $70,000 to the $90,000 collected during the 1994 and '95 Swampfest fundraisers, all proceeds being donated to the management of the Tim McGraw Sports Complex and the scholarship fund Tim had started in memory of his deceased school pal, Steve Colvin. Tim's team led in the early going, but Faith's team soon overcame the early lead, going on to a 30 to 15 drubbing of her husband's team. "I think it's unfair that Faith's team has Tracy, Jeff, Kenny, Mark, and my family members," Tim said. Tug had opted to play on Faith's side, as well. Tim had hit a home run, but during another at bat Faith had tagged him out. As the jesting continued during the auction, Jeff Carson delivered another memorable one-liner when he said, "My favorite sports are baseball and softball. Tim's performance today didn't much resemble either one of those games."

As the concert began, Kenny Chesney almost let the cat out of the bag when he introduced his song *Fall In Love*, saying, "Tim's taken. You can't fall in love with Tracy (whose engagement was public knowledge). So do you want to fall in love with me?" Mark Collie dedicated his song *Born To Love* to Tim and Faith, and added, "Have you ever seen anyone so much in love? They're definitely in love." Faith took the stage next and told her audience, "Today has been a very, very special day in my life." But it was Tim who made it official. As Tim introduced *It's Your Love*, Faith joined her husband and the newlyweds closed off the night with the power ballad that would soon become one of the most popular songs at weddings throughout the South and just about every place else where people were being united in holy matrimony.

The Spontaneous Combustion Tour would not fold its tent until New Years Eve when Faith and Tim played the new hockey rink and entertainment complex in downtown Nashville. It went off so well that New Years Eve gigs in Nashville would become an annual event. Many of those who attended could not help but think of George and Tammy as the newlyweds welcomed in the new year. There were plenty of tears in everyone's eyes as the strains of *Auld Lang Syne* rang through the arena. Looking back on this night, it seems supremely appropriate that they had seen fit to bless Nashville—where they had first met, and where they had been treated so well by their label executives, producers and session musicians, without whose help none of this would have been possible, on this auspicious ending of a very special year. The first couple of new country then consummated the occasion with a kiss. It would not be long before they were celebrated as the male and female 'artists of the year' by the Country Music Association itself, as George and Tammy never were during their long and winding careers.

# THIS KISS

"**M**y life, you know," Faith told *TV Guide*, "began when I met my husband." Tim McGraw was now a husband, and before 1997 had run its course, he would become a parent, which was exactly what he needed to take his career to the next stage. "My family life," he says, "keeps me focused. Before them, it was just about making music. Then I saw the responsibility that comes with being a husband and a father. It required me to make some major adjustments." For Faith, marriage meant putting her touring career on hold for a spell. Tim and Faith's first daughter, Gracie Katherine, was born on May 6, 1997, an event which changed both of their lives, but did not shut down either of their careers. When Faith went into the studio in early 1998 to record her third album, she was pregnant for a second time and filled with the love and inspiration that such a connection to the heavenly gate through which new beings enter this life brings. She would surpass her previous efforts and come up with a career album, self-titled simply FAITH. Marriage would be very, very good to the McGraw-Hills.

Likewise, when Tim began recording his fourth album with James Stroud and Byron Gallimore, he was inspired by the happiness he had found in his marriage to Faith and buoyed by the impending birth of his first child. During those sessions, he really hit his stride, which the world learned in May 1997, when Curb Records released EVERYWHERE. Stephony Smith's *It's Your Love* was the song that Tim and Faith had honed into a sparkling gem while on the Spontaneous Combustion Tour, with Faith joining Tim to sing background parts and harmonies in a style that has come to be called a "vocal collaboration" by the country industry.

Technically not a duet, their presence together was nevertheless viewed as one by their fans.

Tim recalls the genesis of the arrangement. "I started doing it acoustically during our show just to see how the reaction would be," he told *Country Weekly*. "The reaction was great! When we cut the record, we cut it as a song just for me. The night before we mixed I got a chance to put Faith in to sing on it. And her voice was just magic. Nobody can match her." In the studio that day, with Faith nearly come to term with their first child, she had to exert an extra effort during the vocal session, but once she and Tim and James and Byron listened back to what they had on tape, there were high hopes for this cut to be a single release. Curb Records agreed. *It's Your Love* would be the lead-off single. In order to debut the song in the highest profile situation possible, Tim and Faith performed Stephony Smith's song during the Academy of Country Music Awards that spring. This strategy worked. With Faith modeling her designer fashion maternity wear and beaming with the healthy glow of an expectant mom, their performance provided the release with an enormous push toward the top of the charts. *It's Your Love* would set a modern era record for a country track, spending six weeks at number one on the *Billboard* country chart and winning the couple the CMA Vocal Event of the Year award in September. Tim would quip, "I'm sure glad I got that blonde to sing with me on that song."

Tim won four CMAs in all, including Album of the Year. EVERYWHERE set other records, being named *R&R* or Radio and Records magazine's top album in both 1997 and '98. *It's Your Love* was Tim's biggest single to date, and when it began to cross over onto pop charts, resulted in two Grammy nominations.

Country fans have always loved duets, so it wasn't a total surprise when Tim and Faith's first record together did so well at radio. The real surprise came in 1998 when Tim's *Just To See You Smile* once again stuck at number one for six weeks on the *Billboard* country chart and hung around for a total of 42 weeks, the longest by any country single tracked by *Billboard* magazine. Most surprising of all was that all five singles released from the album held at the top of the chart from more than the usual one week. *Everywhere* for two weeks and both *Where The Green Grass Grows* and *One Of These Days* for four weeks. But it was no surprise at all when the voting members of the CMA chose *Just To See You Smile* as their Single of the Year for 1998. One of the fringe benefits of these award-winning times was that Tim's handlers secured a Bud Lite sponsorship for his tour dates, which helped out when it came to promoting ticket sales and paying the gas bills for the semi-trailer trucks that hauled around Tim's lighting gear, sound equipment, and the Jumbotron projection screens he used in his shows. His father Tug would join Tim for the filming of a Bud Lite tv commercial

What enabled Tim McGraw—who has acknowledged that there are people who work at 7-11 stores in Nashville who can sing rings around him—to create such an astonishing album was, once gain, strong song selection. Tim has an ear, there is no doubt about that. Early on he had learned that test-marketing a song in your show was a very good way of learning whether or not you should record it or whether to release it as a single. "I remember doing *Don't Take The Girl* in Houston," Tim told Nick Krewen at *Country Weekly*, "and the fans started singing it and were drowning us out. The band and I looked at each other and thought 'Well, this is going to be a hit.'" Tim also credited his label, noting that Curb Records hadn't given up on him after his first album bombed. "Labels don't do that anymore," he pointed out. "If you don't have a hit off the bat, the label drops you. I had a great label with Mike Curb who stuck with me and allowed me to do another record. I was determined to make it work."

EVERYWHERE was like a country SGT. PEPPER'S LONELY HEARTS CLUB BAND or Fleetwood Mac's RUMOURS—you could just stick it on your CD player and let it spin. There wasn't a bad song or track on it. And contrary to most contemporary albums where fiddles were either mixed into the background or not used at all, the album began with a fiddle solo that proved irresistible to four million record buyers and countless millions of fans who heard *Where The Green Grass Grows* on their radios. "This is the first song we found for the album," Tim says. "It reminds me of summertime and little league baseball. I really dig the fiddle intro." Everybody could relate to the lyrics.

*I'm gonna live where the green green grass grows*
*Watch my corn pop up in rows*
*Raise our kids where the good Lord's blessed*
*Point our rockin' chairs toward the west*
*And plant our dreams where the peaceful river cools*
*Where the green green grass grows . . .*

— *Where The Green Grass Grows* (Jess Leary, Craig Wiseman)

This vision of paradise appeals right across the board, to everybody who has ever lived in the concrete jungle of a city, that is, and plenty of folks who never have. And while Tim may knock himself as a vocalist, everybody in the radio audience loved the way he sang, better, some thought, than ever before. The second verse is key, a home-town reference and a jump into the frying pan pavement of the big city.

*Well I'm from a map dot*
*A stop sign on a blacktop*
*I caught the first bus that I could hop from there*
*But all o' this glitter is gettin' dark*
*There's concrete glowin' in the city park*
*I don't know who my neighbors are*
*And there's bars on the corner and bars on my heart . . .*

— *Where The Green Grass Grows* (Jess Leary, Craig Wiseman)

This same universal appeal can be heard on Mark Nesler and Tony Martin's *I Do But I Don't*, a very nearly perfect cut, as Byron Gallimore notes. "The vocal you hear was the first one from the original tracking sessions where everything synced up—artist, musicians, producers. Wow!" Up tempo tracks seemed to crackle and pop like never before. *Ticker* really really works. "This record takes me back to my teenage years," Tim acknowledges. "For some reason I think of *Grease*. We let Dan Huff loose on the guitar. His playing is amazing."

Tim's personal favorite was the title track. Once again, small town nostalgia plays a large part in hooking listeners in during the opening lines of the song.

*. . . I've been out here on the wind*
*And baby you would be surprised*
*All the places you have been*
*I've seen you in . . .*

*Albuquerque*
*Waitin' out a blizzard*
*Arizona*
*Dancin' 'cross the desert*
*Watchin' the sun set in*
*Monterey*
*Girl I swear just the other day you were*

*Down in Georgia*
*Pickin' them peaches*
*In Carolina*
*Barefoot on the beaches*
*No matter where you choose to be*
*In my heart I'll always see you*
*Everywhere . . .*

— *Everywhere* (Craig Wiseman, Mike Reid)

Most incredible of all, everyone of these "everywhere" and "every-man" songs resonates as being eerily reminiscent of Tim McGraw's own life, even though he did not write a single line or note. Of course his vocal interpretations of the songwriters' creations *were* bordering on the transcendant. Tim McGaw, you might say, had learned to "emote." McGraw, Stroud, and Gallimore and team could also smile when they listened to their final mixes. There are breakthroughs here, too, and not merely more of the same old same old loud approach. Lonnie Smith's drums are mixed in such a way that they never ever step on Tim's vocals, which is a tricky dance. Guitars and fiddles and keyboards enter and leave seamlessly. The dynamics often begin with no more than a single acoustic guitar and Tim's vocal, then swell to crescendos, then gliss and hiss back down to not much more than acoustic and vocal and a hint of percussion. Tim had stepped it up several more notches on EVERYWHERE. "Tim was a very active co-producer song-wise," Byron Gallimore remarks. "His influence is heard everywhere on this record. I couldn't resist."

During this time, Byron and Tim also held out a hand to their friend Jo Dee Messina, who had been signed to Curb Records in the summer of 1997. Now that he was receiving co-production credits with Byron and James on his own records, Tim felt confident he could co-produce Jo Dee with Byron. Their initial efforts in the studio yielded radio hits galore for Jo Dee, who certainly had been through the washer and dryer and several extra spin cycles when it came to record deals and the shifting sands of corporate music making. After 18 months of song selecting and recording, Jo Dee's self-titled debut was finally in record stores and she was finally heard on country radio stations.

Tim didn't wait until the singles from EVERYWHERE had run their course before going into the studio to record his fifth album. Having become more involved in the recording and producing process, he saw that you didn't have to follow the old Nashville rule of thumb that you put out a record in the fall, toured till you dropped, then went back in and scrambled to put out another album the next fall. Too many poorly chosen songs had been recorded too hastily over too many decades by one too many artists who had stiffed at both radio stations and record stores since the days that this procedure had first become routine. Which was a lesson to be learned. Plus, with his new family commitments as a father and husband added to the many requests for personal appearances and all of the above added to his usual touring dates with the Dancehall Doctors, he really did have to learn to manage his time more effectively. And he did.

"I have learned over the making of the first four albums how important it is to give yourself the time to make a record," Tim explains. "With all the commitments an artist has, you just can't wait until the last minute. We started looking for songs right away. I have a team that works. We know each other so well, personally and professionally. They work really hard with all the publishers and writers to find what's right for me."

For a while during the time Faith Hill was in the studio cutting her third album, her husband was on the tour circuit along with two supporting acts, the Mavericks and Canadian country artist Charlie Major. By this time, the mere rumor that Faith might join Tim for a "date" was headline news, and if Faith showed up to sing It's Your Love with Tim and they kissed on stage—their fans went bananas. "She'll be flying into Edmonton," promoter Ron Sakamoto of Gold and Gold Promotions told the Calgary Sun when the tour swung into western Canada. Everyone wanted to hear them. As the days, weeks, and months of 1998 rolled slowly by, it became apparent that the album EVERYWHERE was aptly titled because Tim McGraw and Faith Hill seemed to be everywhere, performing to stadium audiences of 50,000, featured on the covers of glossy magazines in racks by supermarket checkouts, and accepting awards on national television shows. And everywhere either one of them traveled, they stayed in daily if not hourly contact.

With this third album completed and Warner Brothers Records poised to release FAITH, Faith Hill returned to the tour circuit as one of several acts featured in George Strait's Country Music Festival, playing these weekend dates throughout the spring of 1998 and early summer months. Mid-tour, on April 15th, Faith also made a little country music history when she became the first artist to perform a live concert for CMT. Faith had baby-proofed her bus so that Gracie felt right at home as they rolled down the highways and byways into the artists compounds, the areas fenced off and protected by security guards, near the stage door to the stadiums. Also featured on these shows were John Michael Montgomery, Lee Ann Womack, Lila McCann, and Asleep At The Wheel.

Tim would fly in from his own tour when he could for these weekend shows to join Faith and Gracie in the bus. "The bus is babied out," Tim commented, with a smile. "It's the family bus. And I do my shows, I take off with my band bus and do a couple of shows and fly back and meet with them for three or four days. And then I go back. I'm the one who does all the flying." Other times he would catch a red-eye flight into Nashville between shows to be with his family. "We can only make it a couple of days apart," Faith told interviewers. "It means a lot of traveling, but it's worth it. Home is where our family is. Gracie just brings a joy and peace to my life and Tim's life that didn't exist before."

Faith began to sport a new, shorter, more practical hair-style, blonder than during her big hair days when she appeared as the barefoot country girl on her first album. She seemed more focused, more businesslike, perhaps even more determined to win everybody over with her music, especially in the photo her fans would soon discover displayed on her upcoming album cover, where her hazel eyes gazed right back at you. Warner Brothers Records released FAITH on April 21, 1998. Right away critics noted that it was an exceedingly happy outing. *Calgary Sun* reviewer Anika Van Wyk wrote, "Hill's new album is a wonderful offering of mostly happy songs." Faith told Van Wyck, "I have no reason to be depressed. The fact I had time to do it made it more fun. Usually, you do a record between coming home and doing shows and it's difficult. The fact I was off the road, got married, had a baby—all those things helped make it fun." Also mentioned in nearly every review of the album was Faith and Tim's duet *Just To Hear You Say That You Love Me.* "We didn't try to find another *It's Your Love,*" Faith explained to Van Wyk, "because it's not possible. The song is too special."

While critics and fans alike loved the new directions that Faith was exploring on this third album, some interviewers queried her on her choice of specific songs, such as Sheryl Crow's *Somebody Stand By Me.* "My management is out of Los Angeles," Faith explained. "I've got connections in New York. It didn't matter where the songs came from. I'm a fan of Crow's and I just love that song. It fit me, totally. It's got a gospel color to it and that's the kind of song I sang when I was growing up."

Replacing Scott Hendricks, who had put her on the map with his radio-friendly productions, had been both a challenge and a blessing because Faith would gain more control over the direction in which she wanted to take her music. "I had been on the road four years," she related, explaining that there had been more to her three-year hiatus from recording than merely her pregnancy, "and decided to take a break between albums. I wanted to make some production changes and needed some time to live and get inspired. I think that gave me time to grow and catch up with myself." Tim suggested Byron Gallimore as a co-producer, and that combination clicked right off the bat. "I just love what he does," she said at the time of the album's release. "He's incredibly talented. We get along so well. We fight like brother and sister, but we love each other completely." Faith also got a tip from a fellow recording artist that led to a second collaboration. "Shania and I were visiting," Faith told Janette E. Williams for an article in *Country Song Roundup*. "We were talking about what I was gonna do as far as producers. She said, 'Did you know that Dann Huff produces?' She said that Mutt Lange said that he had incredible talent and was a 'diamond in the rough'. So, I took her advice and called up Dann, and that's where all this madness started."

That "madness" entailed working with two producers in separate studios, because for this experiment Gallimore and Huff didn't collaborate. Altogether 28 tracks were laid down, so there were plenty of decisions to be made before the final cut. This also meant that unlike days gone by when Nashville albums were merely ten tracks from which three singles might be culled for radio play, there would not be a bad apple or a clunker left when they had made their final decisions. In the process they would also end up delivering a convincing autobiographical portrait. "I think FAITH is a mirror reflection of where I am in my life," Faith suggested. "Musically, for sure, there's no question about it. I could not have gone deeper to find what this record is. As far as the personal side, there are a lot of positive songs. And that's because I found it hard to sing about something sad and then go home where I was exuding happiness all of the time. I felt I had to sing about things that were about the way I was really feeling." Finding these songs became a grueling experience, as Dann Huff relates. "Faith knew me. Obviously you don't hire me because you want to make a traditional country album. When we started we probably passed on about a hundred songs. All of them sounded like her previous albums, and she rejected them all. She was very firm that she wanted to go in a new direction." "It worked magically," Faith told *Billboard*. "It really came together. I had to not be afraid to dig deep within myself and pull out this person that's in there musically. I do it in my show, every single night. But for some reason I had never done it on record. This is the best musical experience I have ever had."

"My idea for the record," Faith explained, "was to focus a little more on the music that I do in my live shows, which is a lot livelier than anything I've ever put on record." She was referring to the sometimes pedestrian productions that Scott Hendricks had come up with during their three-year association, productions that were more in line with the country pop and country rock Reba was known for, rather than the sleek, driving, power-pop tracks Shania Twain was known for. On FAITH, country elements are treated much in the same way Mutt Lange uses them, as textures and color instruments to be faded up and faded down as the final mix is flavored. "Because I don't write," Faith continued, "I really had to rely on songs that were out there. Miraculously, it all came together better than I had ever dreamed." *Billboard* magazine agreed, applying accolades like "an intoxicating blend" and "an overall sonic delight" and predicting that programmers and radio listeners would find *Love Ain't Like That* "instantly appealing."

There are indeed some very good songs on this package, written by such well-known women songwriters as Sheryl Crow, Gretchen Peters, Diane Warren, and Bekka Bramlett—and one that had "crossover" written all over it, a song called *This Kiss*. It would turn out to be Faith's greatest radio hit so far. The song had been written by Beth Nielsen Chapman, Robin Lerner, and Annie Roboff. Chapman had previously recorded a pop version for one of her own Warner Brothers albums. Beth, Robin, and Annie's lyrics provided Faith a woman's point of view for her country rendition, a very romantic point of view, as Beth relates: "We were three girls out at the beach, a widow, a divorcee and a single woman talking about love; the ups and downs of it, how daunting it can be, and how that sometimes all it takes is just one special person to come along and, with one kiss—'this kiss'—all resistance melts away." She could have been talking about Faith Hill and Tim McGraw and their spontaneous combustion in '96.

"Beth is such a fantastic artist," Faith told journalists, "and is so respected by her peers. Because she co-wrote *This Kiss*, we invited her to sing on it and she ended up creating a completely new harmony section, which totally changed the sound. We already had a great song, but Beth was capable of taking it even further. It was really incredible!" Beth Nielsen Chapman had become known for her ability to add that something extra. In 1989, Beth had recorded moving background vocals for

Tanya Tucker's record of *Strong Enough To Bend*, a song that she and Don Schlitz had co-written, and Tanya's record had shot to the top of the country charts. That same year, Beth had experienced a similar studio magic when she had written *Nothing I Can Do About It Now* for Willie Nelson, then played rhythm guitar and "framed harmony vocals" on the sessions for Willie's number one record of her song.

Faith Hill was not the only person heaping praise on Beth's ability to write great songs and contribute emotionally moving vocals. Science fiction author Orson Scott Card put it this way: "Beth Nielsen Chapman is to music what Anne Tyler is to fiction—she goes straight for the heart and breaks it and makes you love her for it." The combination of Beth's song and Faith's ability to render an indelible vocal performance resulted in an irresistible record that would lodge itself at number one for three full weeks on the country charts and eventually peak at number 7 on the pop charts. Although it's not widely known, the Top 40 Seattle deejay who first playlisted *This Kiss* and started a domino effect that spread across the continent had been acting purely on a tip he got from his wife—not in response to any high pressure phone campaign conducted by Warner Brothers, which is more usually the case when a country song crosses over onto the pop charts.

The next time Faith touched down in Seattle, she spoke with this deejay. "He said that his wife was watching *The Tonight Show*, when I was on," Faith recalls, "and she told him he had to hear this song. The next day a gentleman who works for the station brought in the song and said, 'We've got to add this to our format.' They put it on the air and within the hour, the phones were jammed." While this initial response proved exciting in the Seattle area, there was an entirely different initial reaction on Music Row. "My record company wanted to pull it, because they were afraid of losing my country fans," Faith relates. "But the station said, 'You have got to listen to these phone calls.' Then a lot of other Top 40 stations followed suit."

*This Kiss* would become Faith Hill's signature tune and her first million-selling single, a breakthrough record that lifted her career to the elevated cruising altitude where Shania Twain, Mariah Carey, Celine Dion, Whitney Houston, and Alanis Morrisette were selling tens of millions of albums and being called "divas." In earlier interviews Faith had named her influences as being Reba McEntire, Tammy Wynette, Amy Grant, and Emmylou Harris. Now in her 30s and no longer worried that a more complete list might alienate her country fans, Faith listed Reba, Tammy, George

Jones, Aretha Franklin, Elton John, and Rod Stewart as her favorites.

Since Faith Hill made her first record for Warner Brothers, song selection had been key to her success as a country artist, and being in love and being a new mother had inspired her to choose to record the joyous celebratory song that would take her new life to the next level. "*This Kiss* changed my life," Faith told Wendy Newcomer. "It's amazing that a song can do that. It's the true power of music." Before the release of *This Kiss,* she had been regarded as no more than one more country singer with a few hits to her credit. Now she was poised to become an international superstar in her own right. As she told Wendy Newcomer, "I believe the more people that can hear my music, the better. I'm certainly not going to sit here and say, 'I don't want anybody except country music fans to hear my work.' As an artist and an entertainer, I want to reach as many people as I can." Echoing this sentiment, Beth Nielsen Chapman pointed out in a 1998 website diary entry, "The song *This Kiss* has crossed over from a three week run at number one the country charts to the CHR pop singles chart . . . It's picking up steam! This will further confuse when I say I'm not a country artist and then a country artist has a huge pop hit on the pop charts with a pop remix of a country version of a pop song. But who cares? I'll be thrilled when they just put artists in alphabetical order! That way I could write my jazzcountrypoprockbluesfolk songs and not have to ever explain categories."

The video for *This Kiss* was directed by Steven Goodmann, who had been involved with several of Shania Twain's spectacular video productions. Featuring some highly innovative special effects, this video would go on to win several awards. During the video, Faith undergoes a metamorphoses and becomes a butterfly, which in fantasy terms is a fairly accurate biographical metaphor. Where Faith had felt uncomfortable during the filming of her earlier videos, she now appeared to be right at home on the small screen. CMT viewers loved the show. A whirlwind tour of the television talk shows, where Faith appeared with everybody from Letterman to Leno and Rosie O'Donnell to Regis and Cathy Lee, helped push sales of FAITH into multi-platinum sales figures.

*The Secret Of Life*, a killer song written by Gretchen Peters, was selected as the next single. The lyrics presented a scene more familiar to country audiences—two men talking in a bar; however, it also seemed to fit Faith's outlook on life to a tee. Writing *The Secret Of Life*, Gretchen explains, "was really a matter of wrapping music around a simple philosophy: don't listen to the tv gurus, don't waste your time searching for happiness. It's not a big Cecil B. DeMille moment, anyway. It's usually waiting for you when you're not expecting it—in a cup of coffee, at a baseball game, or while you're driving and your favorite song comes on the radio. The secret of life is just recognizing it when it happens."

Faith Hill seemed to grasp this secret of life, at least when choosing songs for this album. Another song was brought to her by co-producer Dann Huff. "Dann Huff found this great Diane Warren song called *Just To Hear You Say That You Love Me*," she explains. "After listening to it, it was obvious that Tim should come in and sing, because the song says so perfectly what we both feel. It's just a sweet love song that talks about how important those three words are in a relationship."

Dann Huff was already familiar to Tim and Byron, having been pulled in by James Stroud to do guitar tracks on Tim's albums in the past. But Dann's remarkable guitar work on Shania Twain's COME ON OVER album— which has now sold more units than any country album by any artist, male or female, and more than any female artist in any genre—put Dann into an enviable position. If he wanted to do sessions, he could pretty well call the shots. As it was, he was getting a little more interest in his solo albums on Giant Records. But he had begun to produce a few artists and wanted to get into producing on a full-time basis.

Born into a musical Nashville family, Dann had first experienced the studio environment while tagging along with his father, an accomplished arranger of contemporary Christian music. Picking up the guitar while he was still a pre-teen, Huff discovered his vocation. In LA for a few years, he played on sessions for the top acts of the day—Michael Jackson, Celine Dion, Whitney Houston, Amy Grant, Wang Chung, Fine Young Cannibals, and Chaka Khan. "Whatever was going on in the pop world in the 1980s," Dann says, "I played on at least one song by everybody." After moving back to Nashville, he began to play on sessions for country artists like Clint Black, Tim McGraw, and Reba McEntire. While working with Mutt Lange on Shania's sessions, Lange encouraged Huff to get into production. "The first thing I did was Chris Ward," Dann recalls, "which I co-produced with James Stroud. I was nervous. Then I did one I'm extremely proud of—John and Audrey Wiggins' second album THE DREAM. . . . Then I got a call to do Megadeth. Mutt and Shania recommended me to Faith, and because of that she looked at me as a producer, because the label sure as shootin' wasn't looking at me as one!" He would later credit Faith's album project as being the one that put him on the map.

In addition to recording this duet with Tim for her record and asking Beth Nielsen Chapman to harmonize on another cut, Faith realized a long-standing dream when she invited Vince Gill to sit in on a vocal session. As early as August 1994, when she had pondered possible duet partners during an interview with a reporter from *Country Music People*, Faith had speculated on the possibilities and then said, "Wouldn't it be absolutely marvelous to sing with Vince Gill!" Faith's intense involvement with Tim McGraw had put that possibility off for several years, during which time Vince had sung with just about everybody who recorded on Music Row, especially the girl singers. He would later quip that he was just a "boy singer." When Vince agreed to sing along on the Steve Diamond-Dennis Morgan song *Let Me Let Go*, he did not let Faith down. "From the moment he opened his mouth," Faith relates, "we knew it was more than just harmony. Vince has such a distinctive style that he brought pure magic to the song."

Faith would not waste any time in hunting down songs for a follow-up album while she was still out on the road promoting her third album. When she found some songs she liked, she would go in and lay down several tracks at a time during breaks from her touring schedule. Her instinct to do this would prove to be right on the money when her performance of *Breathe* on the 1999 CMA Awards created an immediate demand for a whole new album, an album her label wanted to ship before Christmas.

Back in April 1999, Cover Girl cosmetics announced that Faith had been added to their roster of celebrity spokesmodels, which already included Niki Taylor and Brandy. Faith would meet Brandy several times during west coast jaunts where she also worked with the world's most successful record producer of all time, David Foster, on a remix of *Let Me Let Go*. Faith and Brandy met at a party that Foster hosted, then they met again at a photo shoot for the cosmetics giant. At first Faith was irritated that Brandy kept playing *This Kiss*. "She played that song five or six times during our photo session," Faith explains. "I said, 'Brandy, please, I hear this all the time. Can you please turn it off?' But she kept playing it. We sat there during that photo session, and she was singing *This Kiss* to me over and over. Then we were both singing Aretha Franklin songs together. The next week, we get a call from VH1. They were doing this duets thing, and all the divas were bringing on a special guest. Brandy chose me, which was really cool." Faith's debut on the *Divas Live '99* show, where she shared a stage with Cher, Tina Turner, Whitney Houston, and Brandy, would be a duet with Brandy. They did not sing an Aretha Franklin song but chose instead Mutt Lange and Bryan Adams' *Everything I Do I Do For You*.

Tim McGraw was not content to rest on his laurels either. He would co-produce Jo Dee Messina's sophomore album I'M ALRIGHT with Byron, and he would continue to credit both of his mentors when accolades were showered on him for his production genius. "I love producing," he told one interviewer. "I try to bring an artist and fan perspective to the studio. But I really rely on Byron Gallimore. He and James Stroud have been my teachers in the studio. Any success I have had as a producer, I owe to them."

The initial team of James Stroud, Byron Gallimore, and Tim McGraw, now rated as the hottest production team in Nashville, was founded solidly on a basis of professional respect and ongoing friendships. These friends had simply networked with their pals—singers and musicians who had come in to work with them in the studio. Now in 1998, this close circle of friends had begun to lead the way on the contemporary country scene. Dann Huff would go on to produce new acts like SheDaisy and Lonestar. Mutt Lange would see his songs recorded by Nashville acts. And Faith and Shania, although often pitted against each other in the media, would also remain friends. It was similar to the days during the 1970s when Billy Sherrill produced Tammy Wynette, Charlie Rich, David Houston, George Jones, Tanya Tucker, Lacey J. Dalton, Marty Robbins, Barbara Mandrell, and Janie Frickie. When Sherrill needed a hit song, he would roll up his sleeves, sit down at the piano with his artist, or a pal, or both—as he did with Tammy and George Richey when they wrote *Stand By Your Man* one afternoon in 1968. When he became too busy to collaborate, he enlisted a whole stable of writers and friends to write songs for Jones and Wynette and his other artists. Dann Huff fit perfectly into this inner circle that spun out from Stroud and Gallimore, and he soon formed his own production company with tracking engineer Jeff Balding, the engineer who had worked with Mutt Lange on Shania's COME ON OVER.

The story of how Jo Dee Messina got her deal with Curb Records is well known to country fans. Invited to Fan Fair by Tim, who also provided a backstage pass to his showcase, she met Curb Records A&R Director Phil Gernhard backstage during Tim's showcase set and delivered one of the more memorable one-liners in Nashville history: "I was thinking y'all need a redhead on your label." Tim had been pitching Jo Dee's talents to the Curb executives, but he remembers with a chuckle that "she wasn't afraid of telling them herself." Since that time Jo Dee has made a career out of being a cheeky, yet vulnerable, red head.

Beginning with her Curb Records debut single, *Heads Carolina, Tails California*, Jo Dee, Byron, and Tim have come up with great records, but it seems that cheeky redhead careers can sometimes be somewhat vulnerable to implosions and explosions. The implosions began back in the days when Byron was first working with Tim, before Jo Dee had any kind of record deal at all. Raised by a single mom in Holliston, Massachusetts, Messina had chosen Nashville over LA because, in her words, "I could relate a lot better to *Leavin' On Your Mind* than I could to *Hit Me With Your Best Shot.*" Winner of a talent contest at the Pink Elephant Club in Nashville, Messina, who was hard up for cash at the time, accepted one of the fringe benefits, which was to sing on a radio station in Kentucky. She became a regular on that radio show, which also paid some of her rent and bought her a few boxes of 'corn flakes' from time to time.

"I was singing on the show one night," she recalls, "when they told me I had a phone call. This guy says he's a producer and he wants to get together. It's December 19th and I'm going home the next day, because I'd missed Christmas with my family the year before and it about killed me, so I wasn't in the mood for the runaround again. I was thinking, 'Oh, great, now I gotta go meet with this guy!

"He starts in with 'You got a little Dolly in your voice, and a little Reba.' He's running down all his plans: make a demo, shop it to a couple labels, maybe do a showcase . . . Finally, I said, 'Hey, that's great, but I don't have any money'. He looks at me at me like I was nuts. He said, 'I don't want your money.' . . . And we went down in the basement of this publishing company he was with and actually put some stuff on tape."

That "guy" who thought she had a little "Dolly" and "Reba" in her voice was Byron Gallimore. He and Jo Dee made demos and began shopping them. Messina was eventually signed to RCA, but a changeover of label personnel kept delaying her record project—a sweet deal had gone sour and Jo Dee was left out in the cold. "Just about every label in Nashville offered us a deal," she recalls, "but by the time my deal fell apart, they'd all signed women and the slot was full." It would be several years down the line before Messina met Gernhard at Fan Fair and signed with Curb. Bonding with her pals Byron and Tim in the studio, Jo Dee made an immediate impression on country radio programmers, and both her first single, *Heads Carolina, Tails California,* and her second release, *We're Not In Kansas Anymore,* hit into the Top 10 on the national charts. Then, just as everybody believed she had a genuine chance to make it as a Nashville star, her management company blew up and she found herself exploring the possibility of filing for bankruptcy.

"It's all life," the plucky singer would tell interviewers, "and you can't take anything for granted." Tim and Byron thought she deserved better. They pitched in and began all over again. The 18 months the three friends spent putting Jo Dee and her career back together would be rewarded by multiple platinum sales, awards, and a bright future for country's favorite red head. The first two singles from I'M ALRIGHT hit the top of the chart. Both stuck—the attitude laden *Bye Bye*, which hung there for two weeks, and the survivalist anthem *I'm Alright*, which stuck at number one for three weeks. "These songs are very survival oriented," Messina acknowledged after winning the CMA Horizon award in 1999. "As I sing 'em and as people hear 'em, it's a strength thing that you hear in my music. When I'm down, I listen to *I'm Alright* and the energy lifts me up." By the end of the year, Jo Dee would be the highest played female artist on the *Billboard* country chart for 1999. "I'm really happy for Jo Dee," McGraw says. "She went through her own tough times. She almost lost it all. We knew that the only answer was to go in and make a great record."

With the release of her third album, BURN, Jo Dee was fully healed and ready to move on. "It took us two years to make this record," she says, "and I thought with I'M ALRIGHT 18 months was a long time! It was about finding the songs, because the music is everything. There's a lot of great material out there . . . It just didn't feel like what we were going for at the time. I'm in a very different place in my life from I'M ALRIGHT. So much has happened in my career." The title track was unique. "Once you've been burned," she declares, "you never forget that. It also comes with living and learning. And I think my albums seem to reflect where I am in my life, because I need to relate to my songs on that level." She also recorded a duet with Tim McGraw. "Tim loved *Bring On The Rain* so much he wanted to sing on it," Jo Dee says, explaining how their decision to record a duet had taken place. "I think we both gravitated to that song because we both truly understand what it's saying. I mean, he's been there; I've been there—and it's one of the common bonds that we have. After all, we've always had the same dreams. We had the same struggle in a lot of ways with relationships and our careers. I've always wanted to sing with him, but obviously for us, love songs weren't going to work. This song seemed to be the perfect song for us."

While the careers of Tim and Faith had been blooming during 1998 and 1999, their family had been growing. When their second daughter, Maggie, was born on August 12, 1998, they became known as the 'first' family of country music.

# GEORGE STRAIT'S
# COUNTRY MUSIC FESTIVAL

The George Strait Country Music Festival got its start in San Antonio, where for five years Strait and Texas promoter Louis Messina had staged a much smaller annual festival. In 1998 they took their festival on the road for the first time. "It's a huge undertaking," tour coordinator Scott Kernehan explained to journalists, "and of course there are risks and uncertainties, but we figured, hey, it's George Strait. If it's going to work, he's going to be the one to do it." Tim McGraw came along for the ride in the company of an all-star lineup that featured his wife Faith Hill at some venues. Texans seldom do things half way, so naturally people expected this road show to be big, but when the trucks began to arrive and roadies and carnies pitched in to set things up in the stadiums and parking lots, the mix of country music and midway was surprisingly corporate, even more so during its second and third incarnations when Chevy Trucks and Bud Light became major sponsors. Straitland, with its midway atmosphere and cotton candy plastique, complete with hawkers, pitchmen, and food booths, opened at 11 a.m. Stadium gates opened at noon. The first artist hit the stage an hour or so later. Sometime before midnight, George Strait strolled onto the stage to go to work.

There is no doubt about it, George Strait is the man. "He's the man," Tim remarks. "He's the star everybody shoots to be. He's been around 15 to 20 years and he's still at the top." Every artist who has played one of these package shows has nothing but good memories and good things to say. "I mean," Tim explains, "you're on a tour with George Strait, so you can't go wrong there. And he has to pay for it all." The fans have been pleased as well, save for a few dissenting souls. One woman wrote, "If you don't mind crowds, tiny little chairs for the field seats, and bad sound quality, check out the George Strait Festival. I certainly didn't blame George for the quality of the experience. I just don't like big crowds and I have a big butt. For someone who isn't bothered by that, doesn't mind waiting in line for bathrooms for up to 30 minutes at a time, they would have a great time." Another disgruntled fan complained, "It seemed like a cheap flea market, with booths of silver and turquoise jewelry, and booths where you can win stuffed animals." But others were wowed by this sideshow. A small stage in the Straitland midway featured up-and-comers like Big House, Keith Harling, and Jesse Dayton performing between sets on the main stage. "The concept was," Scott Kernehan explained, "if we've got people in the stadium for ten hours, let's give them something to do during those intermission periods. More bang for the buck."

Tim McGraw, now heralded as the "hottest artist in country music," shared a star billing with George Strait. Asleep at the Wheel, Lila McCann, Lee Ann Womack, Faith Hill, and John Michael Montgomery appeared on stage before Tim, and in turn, Tim was kind of like the set-up man for Strait, who had sold so many records and won so many country music awards for so many years that he had lost count. Tim would continue as George Strait's set-up man for these spring season stadium tour shows until the new millennium.

For the first Strait Fest shows in 1998, Faith Hill pitched a few innings of middle relief of her own before Tim took the stage. To keep the family together, she had made modifications to their bus to accommodate Gracie. What might have been a challenge to many a working mother was not a problem for Faith. She was also beginning to "show" during the early legs of the tour. That this carnival didn't touch down in seven cities on seven days of brutal non-stop touring was a relief. The production—with a fleet of semi-trailers hauling Jumbotron projections screens, lighting gear, and sound equipment, plus all the nuts and bolts and screws that held Straitland together, and the midway carnies tagging along, setting up and tearing down their tents, rides, and booths—could not be done night after night. It took five days to set it up. For Tim and Faith, this was the best of both worlds—they got to spend time with their daughter and perform with the impressive line up of talent assembled for each show.

The George Strait Festival started out on its journey across America on March 14th in Phoenix. By the April 17th weekend, they were cruising into Pontiac, Michigan to play the Silverdome. "This is the biggest tour that country's ever had," Tim told journalists. "It's just a whole different deal. And it's very cool." He was right. The show reminded people of the days when George Jones had toured with Buck Owens and Johnny Cash for many years along with artists like Melba Montgomery, Stonewall Jackson, 'Little' Jimmy Dickens, Faron Young, and Merle Kilgore. Farming families from miles around would attend these shows as much to witness the camaraderie among the performers as to listen to their music. In those days, country audiences numbered in the hundreds, not anywhere near the 60,000 fans who came out to see George Strait and his friends or the half million people who crowded into New York City's Central Park to see Garth Brooks perform. Even by rock music standards—where this sort of traveling minstrel show had been going on since Bob Dylan embarked on his Rolling Thunder Revue tours in the 1970s, which eventually spawned Lapalooza tours and Lilith Fairs—the George Strait Country Music Festival was impressive. Country music was catching up—"Y'all appaloosa, now."

At the end of the road in 1998, George Strait celebrated by staging a wrap-up party at the Hard Rock Cafe in Houston. Asleep at the Wheel backed up everybody who had been on the 1998 stadium tour. "I looked out on the dance floor, and there was George," Ray Benson of Asleep at the Wheel told *Ottawa Sun* writer Rick Overall, "two-stepping with Norma, and doin' the 'Cotton-eyed Joe.' Then he got lubricated enough to get onstage with us. We were doin' stuff that we used to do in the '70s honky tonks. Tim McGraw and Faith Hill joined in. He made us stay till the bitter end. It was, like, four in the morning and he wouldn't get off the stage! Whenever we'd stop to figure out what we were going to do next, he'd grab the mike and belt out the first line of *How Do I Live*, that song by Trisha Yearwood and LeAnn Rimes that was all over the radio. Then he'd just laugh."

Tim McGraw has said that this rare moment of jamming with George Strait is among his best memories. "We were up there for six hours, actually," Tim recalled during an interview with *Knix* magazine's Sandy Lovejoy, "he and I and Faith. We did his songs together, we did my songs together. He did my *Indian Outlaw!*" Lovejoy was intrigued. "Did it astound you that he knew your *Indian Outlaw?*" she asked McGraw. "Yeah, it did. He did it great!" Tim said. "It was about midnight and everyone was up singing. I wasn't going to, then I had a few beers and figured I'd get up there. And I thought, I'm gonna get up there and sing *Unwound*. And just as I was fixin' to start the second verse I hear this voice and he came up and started singing with me. That was about 11:30 or 12:00, and we walked off stage at 5:45 in the morning with about 20 people left in there. Ray Benson was draggin', we all were. George wouldn't let us leave the stage. Faith was pregnant. It was three in the morning, and I said, 'Baby do you want to go on home?' And she said, 'Are you kidding me? George Strait's up here on this stage, singing with me, I'm not going to go anywhere!' So, she was sittin' in the chair, I was laying down on the floor with a microphone and George was standin' up there and just going. He was great!" Later that summer, on August 12, Faith Hill gave birth to her second daughter, Maggie Elizabeth.

Tim McGraw staged his own Place In The Sun Tour in 1999, but on weekends throughout the spring, he would reprise his role as set-up man for George Strait. Tim always had high praise for George. "George Strait is the king of country music to me," he told the *Boston Herald*. "He's a great guy, he's a good friend, so to be out on the road with him it's all candy to me." Tim McGraw and Asleep at the Wheel were the only artists returning for the second year, which Tim took as a major endorsement from the Texan and for all the right reasons. As Tim told Kyle Munson, "The crews work so good together, the bands work so good together, it's pretty relaxed. There's no tension at all, which is pretty amazing when you get so many artists working together."

By 1999 the promoters of the George Strait Country Music Festival had picked up a major sponsorship from Chevy Trucks and an additional one from Budweiser, which made for an even more impressive production for their second tour. There would still be plenty of those ugly, uncomfortable, white-plastic folding-chairs, and some fans would continue to complain at numerous internet websites, but the sound would be better and many of the sets would border on the spectacular, not merely because of the lights and the Jumbotron Screens, but because when Tim McGraw dropped in to play the Strait Fest shows, he brought along his opening act, which just happened to be the red hot Dixie Chicks. Add Kenny Chesney, who had just enjoyed a six-week number one run with *How Forever Feels*, Mark Wills, who had hit with *Wish You Were Here*, and Jo Dee Messina, who was hot, hot, hot, George Strait had himself darned near a royal flush of young, superstar acts who were selling themselves tons of records every month, even if the full title of the show that pulled into Las Vegas to play Boyd Stadium was a little long and sometimes confusing. "Nokia Presents The George Strait Chevy Truck Country Music Festival."

Just a little 'corporate country jargon' most people thought when they heard it, but nobody complained about the music. With the Chicks along for the ride, cresting on a wave that had begun a year earlier when they had released their multi-platinum debut album WIDE OPEN SPACES, there was a strong made-in-Texas country spirit to these package shows. Tim was happy to be part of the action and had begun to refer to Ray Benson as "our spiritual guru." That fall, Ray Benson and Asleep at the Wheel played Tim's Swampstock festival. That's what friends do.

*Ottawa Sun* music journalist Rick Overall described George Strait's Chicago show with his 11-piece Ace in the Hole Band as being "as smooth as butter." Then he lauded Strait's many accomplishments, which include 50 million records sold, 24 gold and platinum and multi-platinum albums, and 43 number one country hits. "Despite his popularity," Overall pointed out, "Strait is as mysterious as Howard Hughes." Like most writers who attended these package shows, Overall settled for interviews with Strait's supporting cast, an approach that produced an immediate crop of revealing quotations. Tracy Byrd commented, "In Texas, he's the king and always has been. He's got the ability to pick these amazing songs and over the years his voice has just gotten stronger. George is the real deal. He is confident and comfortable without being extravagant or tacky. Strait's like Elvis in that way, it's more than just talent—people get all choked up over him."

"After the Chicago show," Overall noted, "Strait met with fans backstage as a huge black limousine and a breath-taking pearl-white tour bus sat as silent symbols of his superstardom. But Strait himself is dressed in a ball cap and comfortable golf duds, looking like a father in a department store catalogue. It's typical. After all, understated elegance is what he's all about." As Ray Benson, commented, "My favorite George Strait quote is when they asked him why he won Entertainer of the Year at the CMAs. He said, 'Cause I got more votes.'" Benson and Strait go back a long way, to the times when Asleep at the Wheel was an established act in Austin and George first joined the Ace in the Hole Band. "We've played golf," Ray told Rick Overall, "and he's a very good golfer. He gets mad at himself, but not like Vince. And we both love pro sports, but we're not really rabid fans. He lives right next to David Robinson, the big center for the San Antonio Spurs. Socially, we're very compatible, we like to sit around with a drink, smoke cigars, and tell stupid jokes."

George Strait was not the only performer who received high praise during the tours. *Washington Post* music journalist Mike Joyce prefaced his review of Tim's set with a quote from Natalie Maines, who "confessed that the best thing about being part of the tour was watching 'George Strait and Tim McGraw walk away from you.'" As Joyce continued, "Wearing his trademark black hat, fashionably shredded jeans and a tight t-shirt, McGraw generated one earsplitting ovation after another as he and his crack band casually moved through a hit list that included a quiet rendering of *Everywhere*, a crowd-fed reprise of *Indian Outlaw*, and a house-rocking *I Like It, I Love It*." *Cleveland Plain Dealer* critic Chuck Yarborough praised both Martina McBride and Tim McGraw for their supporting roles. "McGraw and McBride—appearing back to back in a sort of 'country Big Mac attack'—were excellent scene setters for country music's king (sorry Garth). McGraw himself has admitted that he has not been blessed with the greatest of voices. What he has is stage presence and charisma, a star who comes across as your best friend." Yarborough saved his awe for Strait. "Strait showed why the festival bears his name in a set that ran over an hour and included 25 songs from his trademark *The Fireman* to *I Can Make It To Cheyenne*. Hanging from rafters and bellowing trite phrases like 'Hello Cleveland' to get a response isn't necessary when you've got this kind of gift. You stand in front of the microphone and you sing, you sing and people live, laugh, love and cry. *Amarillo By Morning, Blue Clear Sky, Write This Down* and the wonderful *Does Fort Worth Ever Cross Your Mind* had a weather weary stadium crowd trying to decide whether to live up-wind or down-wind of Ft. Worth's celebrated stockyards." Nic Spinelli, writing in the Jacksonville *Time Union* noted, "When McGraw came out, the crowd went insane. One rabid fan rushed the stage with a camera, but was quickly detained by security. Every lyric to every song sent the crowd into screaming fits. McGraw just smiled and went through his set with ease."

In the first week of May 1999, Curb Records released Tim McGraw's new album, A PLACE IN THE SUN. His last album hadn't fallen off the chart yet—in fact, EVERYWHERE was still in the Top 10. One interviewer wanted Tim's opinion on reports of sagging record sales for just about everybody else, except for the Dixie Chicks, of course, who had sold five million copies of their debut album. "There are always peaks and valleys in every kind of music," Tim replied, "and there always will be. I'm not worried. Country music is very strong—my family's records are doing good." When he said things like that, the writers glanced back for a second look at the charts and noticed that FAITH hadn't exactly fallen off, either. While commenting on the Dixie Chicks' demand to play their own instruments on their records, Tim told *Las*

*Vegas Review Journal* critic Mike Weatherford, "Since the beginning of my career I've had pretty much free reign over what I did. A lot of people can't say that. I think it's one of the best things an artist can have when they are cutting records and making music. Let them do what they want to do, and what they feel they've got to do, to be the best that they can."

The first single, *Please Remember Me*, was pop country, Beatlesque. "I always do stuff a little different," Tim said. "It's always going to sound like me no matter what I do, but I'm always looking for different songs. I don't want anybody to get bored. I'm going to change things up a little bit. A PLACE IN THE SUN probably is the most different thing I've ever done. It's got a little Sgt. Pepper's sound to it, which is a little different for me. It's not really psychedelic, it's just got that kind of feel."

> ... *You'll find a better love*
> *Strong as it ever was*
> *Deep as a river runs*
> *Warm as the morning sun*
> *But please remember me* ...

— *Please Remember* Me (Rodney Crowell, Will Jennings)

Written by Rodney Crowell and Will Jennings, *Please Remember Me* does evoke the same sort of Beatle-chord nostalgia that had worked so well for Crowell as a solo artist in the late 1980s. It had also worked very well for his former wife Rosanne Cash, especially on cuts like *Runaway Train* and the Rosanne-Rodney duet, *It's Such A Small World*, on her classic KINGS RECORD SHOP album, which Rodney had produced. Rosanne had also covered the Fab Four's *I Don't Want To Spoil The Party*. So it wasn't as if Tim was committing a cardinal sin and straying from country traditions; he was an innovator, one of a long line of country innovators who had all born their share of criticism from reactionary traditionalists. Country music may very well owe its long running success to this very tension between innovation and traditionalism. The vocalist harmonizing with Tim on *Please Remember Me* is none other than Patty Loveless, providing those 'blue-side-of-town' harmonies, one of the best there every was.

As he took to the road to promote the new album, with the Dixie Chicks as the opening act, Tim faced more questions about his allegiance to traditional country music, but in comparison with the Chicks, he seemed more country than pop. As one critic noted, "The Dixie Chicks are sassy and chic in dress and in song, while McGraw is stern with his wide-brimmed hat pulled down to his eyebrows. In a way it was the perfect pairing of country western styles: new and old, feather boas and Wrangler jeans." Tim's penchant for striking dramatic poses was noted in nearly every concert review, and while some of these reviewers seemed grudging in their admiration, some even claiming that he wasn't country at all, and that Tim and the Dancehall Doctors played classic rock all night long, all of these reviews acknowledged Tim's undeniable popularity with his fans. As one reviewer observed, "McGraw sang to thousands of screaming girls holding carnations and roses out to him, and to young cowboys in their Justin boots and cowboy hats, shamelessly singing along in adoration."

What Tim McGraw had discovered was that a combination of intimate confidences on the verses of his ballads and Wagnerian pomp on the choruses, followed by up-tempo feel-good music, then another soulful ballad, then another southern fried country rocker, was simply the very best recipe for success. It was what the people wanted, the medicine that healed their souls and animated their soles, so to speak. That's why his band is called the Dancehall Doctors. "We just have fun," he says. "My guys in my band and me have been together for my whole career, pretty much. We're all best friends and we love being on the road together and playing together on stage. We're entertaining each other and ourselves as much as we are anybody else. So we try to keep it fun for *us*. That's what makes it fun for everybody else."

Because Tim was also performing sets at the George Strait Country Music Festival shows, where audiences preferred Strait's new traditionalist approach, Tim was sometimes called "Bruce Springsteen with a cowboy hat." Tim's response to this country vs. rock debate was simple. "I know what I do is country," he told one interviewer, "but I grew up with a lot of influences in music and maybe that shows in my music a little bit. But when it's all said and done, it's definitely country." Another time, he told journalist Kimmy Wix, "I don't even consider that at all. I just try to make good records and record good songs. I sing the way I sing and however it falls, it falls. Just play it. I don't care where you play it, but just play it!" With passing references to "The Boss" and "The King," Tim reiterated this position in yet another interview on the subject. "There's so many different styles of entertainers, and people do it so many different ways," he said. "I think people like Bruce Springsteen, for instance. That's a great entertainer. Elvis was a great entertainer. There's just so many people that do it different ways. I think that just connecting with the crowd, I think that's the main thing—just being out there and connecting. And that's not as easy to do as it sounds, especially in a room with 20,000 people." Whether he liked it or not, he *was* crossing over from country to rock and pop.

By now Tim was being treated as a veteran country artist, asked for his advice on how to launch a career in country music. Neil Pond, respected senior editor of *Country America* magazine, sidled into the issue obliquely. Did Tim have any advice for this year's newcomers? How can they avoid letting their careers consume their lives? "Everybody's trying to sell their product, their can of beans," Tim told Neil. "Just don't get caught up in being the can of beans. Have a good sense of your partner, your family, and your friends. I've been lucky to have a lot of friends who knew me way before. My road manager, Robbie, was my roommate in college. How can I throw an attitude on someone who knew me back when I was borrowing money from him? You wake up every morning and make a conscious decision that you're a person, first and foremost, and then you go out and go to work." As Pond added, "Tim, who was burned a couple of times in management situations that turned ugly and messy, told me he would caution newcomers to stand their ground and not be afraid to be vocal." "The way things are set up in the music business," Tim confided to Neil, "it's like jumping into a pool of sharks. There's only so much you can do to defend yourself. You just try to be as smart as you can, ask as many questions as you can, and don't be afraid to speak up. I'm not one of those people who knows everyone in the industry, who hangs out with everyone in the industry. I'm not an 'industry person.' I've got some good friends within the industry, but it's the fans who have been the glue that's held my career together from the beginning."

Also key to understanding Tim McGraw's successful superstar career is to recognize that when he is wearing his cowboy hat, he is in the office, and when he's not, he's not. Like George Strait, Tim can doff the stetson, put on a baseball cap, shop at a 7-11 store, and not be recognized by anybody. He has learned to keep his business life separate from his personal life. Sprawled on a couch in the lounge of a Nashville recording studio, Tim was described in a recent *TV Guide* article as "neither sad nor pensive, but warm as the summer evening. He's even a bit silly, laughing behind his hand, when daughter Gracie, who is helping water some plants, douses her sister Maggie instead. The difference between the pained young man in the photos (in the booklet that accompanies A PLACE IN THE SUN) and this happy fellow in a t-shirt and clogs, McGraw explains, is simple. 'It's the hat. If I don't have the hat on,' he says. 'I'm not working.

That's part of being able to leave it at the door.'"

While on tour, Tim and Faith had adapted cell phone technology to their purposes, not just for keeping in touch with each other privately but also for appearing in public. While Tim might be at work in a studio or in the midst of an pre-sound-check interview with a reporter from the *Los Angeles Times* or the *Cleveland Plain Dealer*, he never really left his home because he never turned down a call from Faith or Gracie. At times he and Faith seemed to live in a sort of celebrity cyberspace, both aware of each other's movements throughout each day even though they might be thousands of miles apart. It worked so well that Tim had effectively adapted this family phone fun to his shows, singing *My Best Friend* to Faith as he held his cell phone in hand, and he got a great crowd response when he introduced Faith to his audience, her image displayed on huge video screens as he sang.

Tim's domestic life had indeed become so well known across the nation by this stage that it played a central role in the Bud Light tv commercials he taped for the new sponsor of his tour. Set in a bar, Tim is identified by beer drinking patrons as "Mr Faith Hill," and when he protests that *he* sings, too, he is met with remarks like, "well, bless your heart." These 30-second spots were aimed at all beer drinkers, country, rock, or whatever—including millions of sports fans during television coverage of the biggest sports events of the year. Faith's profile indeed rose into the stratosphere during 1999 as she filled arenas across the nation on her "This Kiss" tour and garnered country and pop music award nominations. When asked if he felt he was being eclipsed by his wife's star, Tim responded, "Are you kidding? . . . That means that I can retire early. I got me a fishing boat picked out already on the coast of Florida." Fielding a similar question from another interviewer, Tim said, "She's had a great year and to just be able to sit there together is great. It would be *really* cool to win Female and Male Vocalist together. That would be really cool!"

Faith Hill's "This Kiss Tour" began on Friday, April 9, 1999 in Minneapolis, interrupted briefly the following Monday and Tuesday while Faith was in New York City taping the VH1 Special, *Divas '99 Live.* When people from all walks of life had first heard her crossover hit *This Kiss* on different radio formats, country and pop, they had gone out and purchased her new album. Now on her 50 city tour, droves of new fans were showing up every night. Faith had called 1998 the "year of the woman," referring to the fact that Shania Twain had staged a successful arena tour and erased the age-old Nashville taboo that women couldn't sell enough tickets to fill

GEORGE STRAIT'S COUNTRY MUSIC FESTIVAL

the larger venues. In 1999, Faith's tour would gain a similar momentum.

What was working for Faith was a savvy publicity campaign that linked her tour to her hit single and its video. Before and after Faith hit the road, she fielded interviewers questions non-stop for weeks at a time. She spoke with journalists while cooking a Mexican food snack for a nephew, while doing her housework with her children playing next to her—while biding her time during "hurry up and wait" photo shoots and video productions—and backstage at television studios, or merely while she was riding in her SUV or relaxing on her bus. This tour marked the first time she had assumed to the role of headliner in her six-year career. Faith would be up to the challenge. "I've been the opening act for just about every working headliner out there, it's just time to do something myself," she explained. In order to achieve all of her plans and aspirations she had become masterful at multi-tasking. When preparations gave way to rehearsal, and the moment of departure arrived, she gushed like teenager as she responded to media inquiries. "I'm excited, nervous, oh gosh I could go on! . . . When I saw the stage the other day, I just cried. I can't believe all that stuff is mine. And I get to tell it when to move, you know. There'll be some surprises, but I'm not going to be flying from the ceiling or that sort of thing." This reference to scenes from the Steven Goldmann video, in which she does fly and also sits a-swingin' on a studio prop swing that is obviously attached to some ceiling somewhere above her, reassured everyone that there would be no attempt to reproduce the *This Kiss* video production in her live shows. With a laugh and a chuckle she added, "That would be fun, but I'm not going to do it this time around."

Faith fielded numerous questions as to why she hadn't headlined before this. "I wanted to do it right, you know what I'm saying?" she explained. "And that's why we waited. Now I can have the things I've always wanted. I've never even had my own backdrop in all the years I've been working. Isn't *that* funny." Faith would be starting out in theaters, not arenas or stadiums, a prudent plan. There is nothing worse than playing to half-empty houses night after night, nothing except perhaps the realization that you will end up owing big time at the end of your tour instead of counting at least some profit for your efforts. Responding to each new flurry of phone inquiries, Faith improvised upon this basic theme. "I'm nervous, but it's an excited nervous, I guess. I want to do a good show; I want to entertain. I thought Shania Twain's show was fantastic; she's such a great entertainer, and crowds just go crazy for her. My show is quite different. Our music is very different. And this is my first headlining tour, so we're going to be doing all sorts of things—playing my hits, playing songs I haven't recorded yet, playing songs that are just favorites of mine." Not having toured as a headliner up until this point, she pointed out, was an unproductive way of looking at things. Having toured with the artists like Reba McEntyre, George Strait, John Michael Montgomery, Alan Jackson, and Brooks & Dunn, as well as her Spontaneous Combustion tour with Tim McGraw, had been great exposure to far larger audiences than she might have achieved on her own playing far smaller venues. "Last year," she noted, "I was part of the George Strait Festival that played stadiums. I've been able to play in front of a million people or so in the five years I've worked."

While promoting her tour, Faith continued to benefit from the cross-over success of *This Kiss*, which was totally mind-boggling. Co-songwriter Annie Roboff, vacationing on a beach in St. Thomas, heard two girls singing lyrics that sounded vaguely familiar. "I was waist high in the ocean," she recalls, "behind me I heard these two 11-year-olds saying, 'Oh, that's my faaaavorite song!' Of course, as a songwriter I leaned back to hear what their favorite song was because, if I hadn't already heard it, I'd probably wanna go out and buy it. One of the girls started singing . . . 'It's the way you love me' . . . I couldn't place it but I knew I knew it—then I realized they were singing *This Kiss*. I was so honored that it had made their favorite list. I turned around and told them I had written it and they of course were in disbelief, like, what are the odds of that?" Annie admits that she loved the song at the time she and Beth and Robin wrote it, "but I had no idea how huge it was gonna be. Faith simply nailed the song, and it was clearly the right song with the right artist at the right time."

Unlike some other records that have crossed over, it had all happened quite naturally. Faith's *This Kiss* record and video had been in heavy rotation on country stations and on CMT. Her breakthrough had come when a pop station in Seattle began playing *This Kiss* and then stations all over the country began to pick it up. Faith Hill and *This Kiss* had become "household words." But Faith would never forget just how important a role her fans had played in her success as a recording artist—a role that continued to be crucial when she went on the road. "This tour and the success of *This Kiss* is the culmination of a dream," Faith told *Loveequine*, an aol.com webzine. "I may have had the day-to-day responsibility for keeping this tour running, but it's the fans who made it work. It's been a great tour."

When people learned that Faith and her Family Literacy Project team had joined forces with General Colin Powell and his "America's Promise: Alliance For Youth" to collect thousands of books during a campaign that coincided with her concert tour—books that would be donated to needy schools—they wondered how she could survive the hectic pace with so much poise. "The response we've had from the fans," she admitted, "has been overwhelming and humbling. So far, we have collected more than 25,000 books. It's blown my mind. The fans keep giving and giving. And to me, the best part of this program is that it produces immediate results. One of the things that I insist on is that the books that are collected at each show must be distributed by the end of the next working day. It's amazing the places that I have been—hospitals, schools, day cares that don't have books for children to read simply because they can't afford them."

For working moms, Faith's ability to balance career and family life was exemplary and inspiring. She is much admired by her fans for her strength of character and her ability to reach down inside herself during her shows and give unselfishly during her performances. But her most remarkable feat of all is that she and Tim kept on showing up at each others' shows throughout this period of time, honoring, they told the press, their vow to not be apart for more than three days at a time. Both had come from "splintered" family situations; their decision to have children was something they took very seriously. She and Tim had made a pact, when they first married, and they kept their promise. They would sink or swim together as a family.

This resolve had come to them in the days they spent together in 1996 before they decided to tie the knot. As Faith told *People* magazine, "I saw that we had some of the same goals in life. Our careers were important, but we wanted a family. We wanted that stability." Tim remembered one moment in particular. "A conversation we had in a Jeep in Pennsylvania is one of my favorite memories. It was a conversation about our future. That was the point where we realized we wanted to be together for the rest of our lives." But as Faith admitted to *People*, "putting our tour schedules together is like trying to solve a Rubik's Cube. When one is on one coast and the other's on the other one, and there's only two flights a day and you've got to go through Timbuktu to get there, it gets very difficult." Tim did most of the flying. "I love my wife more than anything in the world," Tim told *People*, "But, boy, when she had our babies it quadrupled." As he told *Star* magazine, "Right after our first baby was born, I knew I wanted to give my children what I didn't have when I was growing up—a father who was there for them." He admitted it was hard for himself to tear himself away. "If I'm gone from home for three days in a row, it almost breaks my heart. I just can't imagine not being with them and not being there for everything they do and being a part of their life. That's more important than anything in the world to me." The arrival of their second daughter in the days following the final date on the first George Strait Country Festival tour in the summer of 1998 had only made these logistics more difficult. When Faith launched her own tour, both Gracie and Maggie were with her in the bus, which had been further modified to include bunks and a playroom.

When Faith cleaned up at the 1999 Academy of Country Music Awards, winning four major awards, country fans viewed her with an ever increasing reverence. Which helped sell tickets during her first tour as a headliner and placed her in the forefront of the nominees for the even more prestigious Country Music Association Awards in the fall of the year. The combined "teams" that Faith Hill and Tim McGraw had put together to make their careers hum were also heavily nominated in several categories for this 33rd Annual CMA Awards Show. Faith was scheduled to perform on the show, but in the weeks leading up to the awards, a snag appeared in her otherwise seamless supermom and superstar existence. The CMA Awards committee had laid down the law and told her she couldn't perform the song she had chosen on their show. Before this situation was resolved news began leaking out—like George Jones, who had declined to appear on the show because this committee had cut his song in half, Faith had also declined to perform.

"It was a case of artistic difference," Faith said. Her fans were dismayed and devastated as they waited anxiously for news that someone would come to their senses and this decision would be reversed. Jones had refused to alter the length of his current single *Cold Hard Truth* when the CMA Committee overseeing the show told him he'd have to do so. What dictate had Faith refused to obey? Her manager, in a rare display of diplomacy and public statement, was quoted by *Billboard*. "We don't normally go into something like this," he told the magazine, "but to set the record straight, the show's TV Committee informed us of their concept for Faith and we declined. For artistic reasons." Song selection, it turned out, was indeed the issue that had artist and committee at odds. The CMA TV Committee liked it better when artists performed their hits. They hadn't been amused when Shania Twain had used their show as a platform to launch new singles, and they were not going to let Faith perform an unfamiliar song. Faith wanted to sing a track from her upcoming fourth album release, a song called *Breathe*. They wanted her to sing *The Secret Of Life*, her most recent radio hit. It was their way or the highway. Trouble was . . . Faith was already on the cover of *TV Guide*, touting the awards, so to speak, and Cover Girl had purchased a sizeable block of advertising minutes during which Faith was their spokes-model.

In years past, most country artists had towed the line and gratefully accepted this opportunity to gain international exposure, unless they were George Jones, of course, who has never had a good working relationship with the people who headup the Country Music Association. George and Tammy had hosted the notorious foundation of the rival organization ACE in 1975 in Tammy's living room, during the controversy that had stemmed from pop crossover artists Olivia Newton John and John Denver being acknowledged by the association in 1974 during an earlier 'country-goes-pop' conflict. Denver was deemed to be a folk artist, not country, which merely meant that he recorded in LA and not Nashville. Newton John, like Shania Twain, had often experienced opposition, which some attributed to their foreign citizenship, because they had sold too many records to too many pop music fans. Which was not the Nashville way. Better to keep it so country that nobody except country fans bought your record. Ironically, Jones and Wynette, with their producer Billy Sherrill, would make records in the ensuing years that were so countrypolitan that their fans only forgave them because they also kept it country on a few other cuts. Dolly Parton was at that founding meeting of the rebel association against pop in 1975, but by 1977 Dolly was cutting records like the crossover hit *Here We Go Again*, which was a whole lot like the records that Olivia Newton John had been making in 1972, '73 and '74. In this current controversy, the fact that Faith Hill had been suspected of having pop aspirations and was riding the success of her crossover hit *This Kiss* into these awards just might have been a factor in the committee's decision. There were other dynamics at work, no doubt. For example, Warner Brothers didn't have anybody sitting on the committee at this time to defends their artist's position.

As Faith herself would comment, "The people in country today are getting younger and they didn't listen to George Jones or Tammy Wynette, unfortunately. To be totally honest with you, the first record I listened to was Elvis Presley and it wasn't country. In this day and age, I wish the younger generation—the ones who are behind me and Tim—we're 30 years old and have been doing this professionally for years—I wish they had the opportunity to study the greats, and I wish we still heard them on the radio. I really do. I wish there was a way to insert George and Tammy and Merle and Loretta on occasion. Just for the listener to hear what country music is. I think it's a crime that they don't. I believe there's some really great country music coming out of Nashville today, but I hope we don't go so far that we forget about the legends that came before us."

In a show of support for his artist's wife, Mike Curb resigned from the committee, citing conflict of interest as his reason and suggesting that the other label executives on the committee should follow his example. All of which served to point out to people reading about this in the press just how much of an ingrown toenail the Music Row establishment still was after all these years. Then in an unanticipated fit of retro bullying that harkened back to the days when rural musicians were first called hillbillies by business men wearing suits, CMA executive director Ed Benson delivered a most politically incorrect jab. "Anybody who tells you there shouldn't be politics in this process," he asserted, "just fell off the turnip truck." Some people were reminded of the time that Chet Atkins had been blacklisted by Red Foley because he wouldn't accept Foley's dictate that he not record on other artists' records, a political power-play that had kept Chet from recording in Nashville until he returned under the protective wing of Mother Maybelle Carter a few years later. Sure there were politics, but were they helpful in any way? Or productive? Or were Faith and Shania merely being punished because they had upset the male-dominated apple cart? Despite her million-selling records, which by this time had begun to rival the top pop divas of the day, Twain had not been awarded so much as a paper rose by the CMA, let alone one of their hoarded and coveted awards.

"Faith was very happy to accept the committee's decision," Warner Reprise Nashville President Jim Ed Norman said, "and she planned to be at the show to support Tim and to support her nomination. She equally felt that she should perform what she feels best doing. It was never a boycott as some media reports claimed." As the final hour for a decision neared, it seemed incredible that this CMA committee still held its ground. There was considerable face to be lost if their stubborn attitude kept one of their most visible stars from appearing. It was a no win situation. Faith held her ground, too. She may have believed that she was holding the trump card. In the final hour, the more sensible-minded CBS

GEORGE STRAIT'S COUNTRY MUSIC FESTIVAL

executives stepped in and instructed the CMA committee to "let her sing whatever she wants." "We want the best show possible," Nancy Carr, a CBS spokeswoman and a superlative spin doctor, stated to the press. "If Faith isn't in the show, everybody loses. We gently encouraged the powers that be to resolve whatever was going on." As Jim Ed Norman explained, "CBS stepped in and said 'We really want Faith on the show.'"

Faith's performance of *Breathe* would be cited as one of the most spectacular highlights of the 33rd Annual CMA Awards show. And BREATHE, her fourth album release in her short, seven-year career, would soon debut at the top of the *Billboard* Hot 200 albums chart. In preparation for the release of her fourth album and in anticipation of the demand that would begin when she debuted *Breathe* on the CMA Awards Show, Warner Brothers had wisely burned some 500 CD singles on the day of the show, and these were quickly dealt out to key radio stations where *Breathe* was immediately played in heavy rotation.

Tactfully, neither Faith nor Tim let this agony-and-ecstasy political power-play move them to making public the no doubt exceedingly politically incorrect stuff that was said around the breakfast table. Or, for that matter, what was said out on their 175-acre spread where they planned to build their dream home and where Tim would jostle journalists over a makeshift road to that site on an all-terrain vehicle from Hell. Tim was a veteran of issues management, an easygoing guy. Why spoil the fun of walking into the Opryland Theater to join all their friends and fellow artists in the audience at the number one media event of the year?

Songwriter Annie Roboff was excited to be going to the Awards Show with her co-writers Beth Nielsen Chapman and Robin Lerner, but they didn't think they had much of a chance of winning the Song of the Year award for *This Kiss* because, as she recalls, "it had won Record of the Year and Single of the Year a lot (at awards nights staged by other organizations) but it hadn't won for 'Song,' so, we didn't expect it now." She would soon be standing on the stage and doing her best not to forget to thank everybody who had helped them. "We were up for the first award," she remembers, "and the Dixie Chicks started off the night so cool with that great opening number. They called out our award and . . . BOOM! It's us! Wow! We were all stunned." Annie accepted for Beth and Robin because the CMA preferred to have one writer go up to accept rather than all three or four or five writers who often collaborate on country songs. Then, she recalls, all three were "whisked backstage. We did an hour and a half of press. All the TV shows, local news, *Entertainment*

*Tonight*, photographers, print press like *People* and *TV Guide*." Which was cool. "It was really something," she emphasizes, but they did miss Faith's performance in the meantime. "We had heard that Faith was going to sing a new song called *Breathe*, but we didn't make it back to our seats in time," Annie explains. "We were disappointed. Afterwards, we were still reeling from winning and since then we've all received *so* many congrats and flowers and just plain warm wishes. Shania Twain sent all three of us flowers! We were quite surprised and thrilled."

Later in the show, Tim was named CMA Male Vocalist of the Year and picked up a second trophy for A PLACE IN THE SUN, the CMA Album of the Year in 1999. Tim had his first repeat award, having already won the best album award in 1998 for EVERYWHERE.

It would continue to be an evening for precedents to be set and a moment in time for the changing of the guard as the newest wave of Nashville artists succeeded the entrenched. Shania Twain hauled in her first ever CMA Award for International Achievement, then accepted as Entertainer of the Year, with former winner Reba McEntire presenting her the CMA's most prestigious honor. Jo Dee Messina won the Horizon Award. And Dixie Chicks Natalie, Emily, and Martie were named the winners of both the Single of the Year and Video of the Year awards for their number one hit, *Wide Open Spaces*. Everybody in the building was tickled when Martina McBride was named Female Vocalist of the Year.

Annie, Beth, and Robin won another award for their collaboration on *This Kiss*, this time from the Nashville Songwriter's Association. At the same ceremony, Shania Twain won several awards for her songs. The common link that tied all of these award-winning songs, songwriters, and artists together, with his hand in production on FAITH and his fingers picking up a storm on COME ON OVER and on Tim's projects, was Dann Huff. At the Nashville Music Awards their song would win again, as would Steven Goldmann's video of *This Kiss*. Goldmann was unable to attend and sent a prepared video clip in lieu of an acceptance speech. In this clip, the director superimposed his own head on Faith's body. The effect created was hilarious as Goldmann became a butterfly nestled in a flower in different scenes of his speech. Faith claimed her own award at the Nashville Music Awards when FAITH was named album of the year.

Tim McGraw knew he, too, was on a roll in 1999, but it was *Billboard* magazine that made it official when they named him their top ranked solo country act (based on sales and radio play). He was cruising at the same altitude as Garth Brooks, Alan Jackson, George Strait, and Vince

Gill—very elite company indeed. Each one of these artists had brought his own unique abilities and talents to the country music world. All five of them have proven to be exceedingly generous with both their time and their interest in their fellow artists, musicians, and songwriters. Garth Brooks called Beth Nielsen Chapman up one night with an idea that they might write a great song together, if they collaborated. His call could not have come at a better time—that August Beth had been diagnosed with breast cancer, and three months of chemotherapy had confined her to her home during the Christmas season. "One afternoon," she explains, "I got a call from Garth Brooks! He wanted to speak to me about writing a song with him—which I was honored to do, but I told him I would have to wait until January or February because I was still going through chemotherapy. Well Garth had no idea I was dealing with breast cancer. We spoke for a few minutes about it and then he said, 'Hey, guess what. Tomorrow I'm flying out to LA to be on *Hollywood Squares* and Whoopie Goldberg is going to give me $100,000 to give away to charity . . . with your permission I'll just turn that over to you Beth, to donate to breast cancer!' It was the coolest Christmas present I could have gotten!" Beth has made a complete recovery, she reports.

This same year Vince Gill had been invited to go into an LA studio with Barbra Streisand to help out with a record she was making with David Foster. Vince was quick to oblige. This was a unique acknowledgement from someone who knows what good vocals and sweet harmonies really are. Vince had become one of the most influential people in Nashville, but he still walked softly and spoke quietly, even though he had won a bushel of CMA Awards and sold millions upon millions of records.

Alan Jackson and George Strait would be going into a studio together, too, recording Larry Cordle and Larry Shell's *Murder On Music Row*. Alan had stood up for George Jones when he had sung a chorus of the Possum's song—the one that George had declined to perform—during the CMAs, which had pissed off the powers that be but had certainly honored their peers, revered artists like George Jones and Merle Haggard.

Tim McGraw had now been brought into this league by the *Billboard* editors. When your peers acknowledge your accomplishments, it's time to learn a little humility. Tim has. "Tim wears the crown at the moment," *Billboard* chart manager Wade Jessen said in an official press release. "Tim's music and touring activity have pushed him into the position of the premiere artist for the country format. It doesn't mean that other male artists haven't been active and viable. But if you look at his airplay and sales, it was definitely Tim McGraw's year."

When Tim teamed up with his wife to stage their Soul 2 Soul Tour 2000, they were sitting on top of the country world. Their fans eagerly gobbled up every single ticket that became available, making their first ever tour as Mr & Mrs Country Music the top-grossing tour of the year. It would be a fitting way to celebrate the coming of the new millennium.

# BREATHE

On November 9, 1999 Warner Brothers Records released Faith Hill's BREATHE. The album debuted at number one on both the *Billboard* Hot 200 Albums chart and the country albums chart, selling a total of 242,229 records in its first week of release. A world radio premiere the day before and an exclusive closed-circuit broadcast of Faith Hill live in Nashville shown in 100 Wal-Mart stores on the day of release were key ingredients in the coordinated marketing push provided by Warner Nashville. Initial reactions to Faith's new album were mixed. Critics were stunned. Diehard traditionalists were numbed. And Faith Hill fans felt blessed. She was singing better than ever—and singing great, great songs.

There was no doubt that Faith Hill, Byron Gallimore, and Dann Huff had come up with a forward-looking album, but the reactionary crowd in Nashville simply did not get it—just as they hadn't got it when Olivia Newton John had transcended her early country hits like *Let Me Be There* and *If You Love Me Let Me Know* with a series of multi-platinum albums, blockbuster movies starring alongside John Travolta, and planetary superstar status with global hits like *Magic* and *Physical*. Yet this was very the direction in which Faith appeared to be heading. She had already made her acting debut on an episode of *Touched by an Angel,* and confirmed as fact a rumor that she had been reading a movie script or two. "I would love to do a film at some point," Faith told Wendy Newcomer. "But it would have to be a role that I really felt I could pull off. I would never allow myself to be put in a situation where I couldn't contribute or handle it. I think a drama would be easier for me than a comedy, but it's hard to say."

The tracks on BREATHE benefited from a Motown meets Memphis

approach with Owen Bradley's trademark 'cross-over' production style in the mix. The first track opens with a Hammond organ swell that threatens to burst forth into something resembling Procol Harem's *Whiter Shade of Pale*, then Stuart Duncan's incredibly nimble fiddle riff breaks the mood, the band track kicks in, and Billy Burnette, Bekka Bramlett, and Annie Roboff's *What's In It For Me* begins to melt down your home entertainment system.

> *Thought we had a good thing baby*
> *You pulled the wool over my eyes*
> *I should've seen it coming baby*
> *Now all I see is a cool love dyin'*
> *Honey I don't want to hold you down*
> *Why you gotta own the lock and the key (tell me baby)*
> *A good thing don't just come around*
> *And you just can't have it for free (not me) . . .*

— *What's In It For Me* (Billy Burnette, Bekka Bramlett, Annie Roboff)

At first the listener is reminded of Aretha Franklin, harkening back to the days when Faith sang at gospel services in rural Mississippi. Then as soulful track after soulful track plays, notably Bob DiPiero and Annie Roboff's *I Got My Baby* and the sleek *Love Is A Sweet Thing*, the country-flavored '70s records of Rita Coolidge and Ry Cooder spring to mind. It's "bop till you drop" all over again. By the time the title track arrives, you realize you are listening to a *country* singer performing authentic *soul* music—not what you get when a Whitney Houston or a Janet Jackson gives material like this their standard urban treatment. There's no hip hop or jive here. This lady sings country soul like Barbara Mandrell did when she hit a similar groove in the 1980s and like Reba McEntire has on occasion. This music has roots.

"I just need to stay true to who I am," Faith comments. "I could never just go out and make a pop record or, for that matter, a traditional country album." As she told *Entertainment Weekly*, "I can only do what's real to me. I would never be able to do a record like Loretta Lynn. I did lots of her songs when I was growing up, and Tammy, oh Lord, I did everything of hers. But I couldn't go out and make a pop record if I tried. And I couldn't make a traditional country record either, because I'm inspired by too many things: deep gospel, R&B, Soul . . ."

Faith Hill has pioneered an expanded vocabulary for country music, singing lyrics like "perpetual bliss" and "centripetal motion" on *This Kiss*, breaking new ground on BREATHE with unusual images like "just like a fossil / frozen in time, I could not move" in songs with even more unusual titles like *Bringing Out The Elvis*. The allusion in the uptempo, upbeat tune *Love Is A Sweet Thing* is to a Paul McCartney album title, not to something recorded by George or Tammy or Donna Fargo:

> She shot out of Texas like a bullet from a gun
> With a van full of hippies and a band on the run
> She didn't wanna be famous, she just wanted to play
> At old dive bars and pool halls, she got up on stage
> And she sang . . .

— *Love Is A Sweet Thing* (Brett James, Troy Verges)

As her husband Tim McGraw suggests, "country's a more urban music than it used to be. I think that what country has turned into—and rightfully so—Americana music. It's not talking about plowing the fields all day. It's talking about real-life situations." Which explains why Faith sings about homeless people pushing shopping carts.

The *Tennessean* labeled *Breathe* as "distinctly un-country," and a Nashville-based *Billboard* critic declared that "there's no effort made here to adhere to any country music guidelines or standards." While Faith endured other critics who labeled her music "pro-wrestling," "Vegas," and "soft-rock schmaltz" for expanding the language and subject of country music, she was also defended by other writers like *Nashville Scene* columnist Beverly Keel. "I think too many people put a negative spin on her pop sound," Keel suggests. "Her music is a natural evolution. And I think her music is fun. That's why people like it. Why do you have to have a dark side? What if you're just a happily married mother of two who loves to sing?" Viewing Faith's BREATHE as a "natural evolution" proves to be far more productive than dismissing her outright as a "pop" artist, someone who should be cast off country radio, as one reviewer suggested.

This evolution can be traced back to the late 1950s and early '60s, when Owen Bradley's little Quonset hut studio pumped out great country, pop, and rock & roll records by Patsy Cline, Brenda Lee, and Loretta Lynn at the same time that RCA's Nashville Sound Studio released equally effective productions by Hank Snow, Jim Reeves, and Elvis Presley. Chet Atkins also worked at Columbia Records studios on sessions for the Everly Brothers' early hits. Great music had come out of these Music Row studios during the early rock & roll era when rock still had roots. Owen Bradley didn't give a hoot whether his session with Brenda or Patsy was destined to be labeled country, pop or rock & roll; he just made the best records he could at the time. When he handed the final mixes over to the executives at Decca Records, they could decide for themselves how to categorize their artists' releases.

Brenda Lee started out country, then spent ten years in the Top 10 regions of the pop charts with *Sweet Nothin's, I'm Sorry, I Want To Be Wanted, Emotions, Dum Dum, Fool #1* . . . and many, many more that helped drive her record sales over the 100 million mark by 1980. Ironically, when Brenda began to chart once again on country radio in the 1970s, all of the above would be regarded as country classics. Patsy started out country, too, with *Walkin' After Midnight, I Fall To Pieces, Crazy,* and *She's Got You*—all huge country hits as well as Top 10 crossovers on the pop charts. Same deal over at RCA with Elvis breaking out when he started working with Chet Atkins and cranking out his first chart-busting number one hits—*Heartbreak Hotel, Don't Be Cruel, Hound Dog, Love Me Tender* . . . Elvis never lost his country. As Beverly Keel has suggested, it was a natural evolution—Faith Hill was just bringing out the Elvis in herself.

"I'm just growing," Faith suggested to Gary Graff. "I'm not trying to be Shania. I'm not trying to be Whitney Houston or anybody else like that. I'm just being who I am. And I have an incredible respect for country music and what it's all about. It molded and shaped who I am today. But so did a lot of other sounds." As Faith told *Country Song Roundup,* "I just want to be respected as an artist that's trying to do great music. I don't want to be pegged as anything. Just an artist. I don't see a crime in that."

Faith was also proud of the combined input of the many women she worked with on her fourth album. The title track, for example, was written by two women who had not seen each other since they both graduated from the same high school in Georgia 14 years earlier. When Stephanie Bentley and Holy Lamar bumped into each other, quite by accident, they discovered they had both moved to Nashville. They got together one afternoon to write a song and merged two separate ideas into one that Faith Hill immediately recognized had hit potential. "We got together and, like, boom!" Holly recalls. "She sang me a bit of the melody, it was so sensual—and I'm, like, 'I've got the title! We need to really play on the chorus, raise it up melodically and just rock the chorus out a little bit.'" As Faith proudly declared, "This very original song speaks for itself, and to be written by two incredibly talented women and recorded by a woman is pretty cool, right?"

Holly Lamar and Stephanie Bentley's *Breathe* found a home in Faith's heart. "Boy, did this song strike a chord in me," Faith says. "Besides needing more time to breathe, there is nothing like that moment when you can lie there and watch someone sleep and watch someone breathe. It's ecstasy, a drug, that quiet peaceful moment, the calm, the contentment." She was not speaking of sex, drugs *or* rock & roll—she was speaking of lying awake in bed watching your husband breathe, a moment of tenderness that indicated just how much she was in love with Tim. This cut begins with gentle finger picking as Faith floats her vocal over an acoustic guitar. As the second verse begins, drums and bass enter with a gentility that equals the acoustic, then as Faith begins the lyrics to the chorus, you get big drums, explosive guitars . . . But as each verse comes 'round, the dynamic dies away to just enough. No doubt, as she sang these lines, she had someone special in mind.

> *I can feel you breathe, it's washing over me*
> *Suddenly, I'm melting into you*
> *There's nothing left to prove, baby all we need is to be*
> *Caught up in the touch, the slow and steady rush*
> *And baby, isn't that the way that love's supposed to be*
> *I can feel you breathe*
> *Just breathe . . .*

— *Breathe* (Holly Lamar, Stephanie Bentley)

Then there was that song that had the same rollicking lilt that people had liked so much when they first heard *This Kiss*—a new song called *The Way You Love Me*, written for Faith by Keith Follese and Michael Delaney. "Byron brought this one to me," Faith says. "And I especially loved the background vocal. It felt like two songs in one." Byron Gallimore liked the background vocal arrangement so much that he invited the singer of the demo, Stephanie Bentley, who was also the author of their title track *Breathe*, to recreate her vocal parts on Faith's version of the song. It was the most complex moment on the album, with a "double chorus that gave the song a different twist and an array of dazzling musical hooks that sweetened the song's appeal to radio," Delaney explains. "We knew that our song had a lot of commercial potential. It was a puzzle to put together—three different musical keys and so many overlapping lyrics." With Faith's and Stephanie's vocals overlapping as the track bubbles gleefully upward, this track turned out to be one of the most optimistic, fun-loving cuts since Cyndi Lauper's 1984 sing-a-long girl anthem, *Girls Just Want To Have Fun*. Some critics said "bubble gum." Faith's fans said "double yum!" Chalk another one up for Missy Gallimore.

When Faith began to accentuate her sensuality in her videos and photo shoots, she was attacked, just as Shania had been, for using sex to sell records. Faith's naked form writhing beneath satan sheets in the video for *Breathe* was in heavy rotation on all the music video channels. Teenage boys were hiding the booklet from Faith's CD beneath their pillows. Their favorite pose was being referred to as the "sports illustrated" pose. When journalists attacked Faith's choice of poses and outfits, it seemed that morality issues were dredged up to reinforce a country versus pop philosophy, as if country traditions of lyin', cheatin', hurtin, and leavin' were morally righteous church-going values. Frustrated by this puritan backlash, Faith spoke out during an interview with *People*, perhaps the most often cited comment she has made to date. "Do you want to sell or do you not want to sell, period? Whether we want to believe it or not, this is a business and I'm a businesswoman. I'll probably be crucified because my music has crossed over." But she was not going to compromise herself. Not now when her goal of being heard by as many people as she possibly could was within grasp. Martha Sharp, long since retired from the fray, told *People*, "Faith wanted this in the worst way and was willing to do what needed to be done. She had her own ideas from the very beginning about how she wanted to do it." Many years ago at the Bluebird Cafe, Martha had been the first to envision a future for Faith where she would not only crossover but would be a candidate for corporate endorsements. Faith's involvement with Cover Girl Cosmetics, AllTel, and Pepsi, not to mention numerous other endorsements and promotions, now helped her win over many, many fans from all demographics and age groups as her image proliferated, and became synonymous with health, happiness, and family values.

The *Breathe* video had been one of the most effective promotional tools the executives at Warner Nashville had at their disposal during the push to market Faith's fourth album during the Christmas spending frenzy of 1999, a coordinated effort also involving Warner Brothers' New York and LA operations that resulted in sales of 1,433,520 copies of BREATHE in the remaining seven weeks of the year. This all-out effort had not usually been mounted for country artists in the past when they had been considered a niche market that the Music Row divisions of labels should handle themselves. Garth Brooks and Shania Twain had changed that perception. Garth and then Shania Twain reaped and then harvested more dollars singing country music than had been made in the entire previous seven decades of country. Faith Hill and Tim McGraw followed suit. They took their music to as many people as humanly possible, and, although they had made it look easy, they had fought for every inch of ground they had gained. As Faith had told Jeanne Wolf, "I'm a tough girl, raised with two brothers, you better believe that I know how to take care of myself."

Faith was also speaking her mind to her new audience in online chats at AOL.com, taking full advantage of the opportunities available throughout the internet community. Tim McGraw had been one of the first country artists to hire skilled website designers and invest in sizeable chunks of cyberspace real estate. By the time the Y2K dilemma arrived on January 1, 2000, both Faith and Tim already had strong presence on the net. There was a Faith Hill screen-saver available in both Mac and PC formats. Spinner.com offered streaming-audio downloads of *Breathe* and a live in Vegas version of *I've Got My Baby*. Warner Nashville had also released this dance remix of *Breathe* and this same live cut as a spin-off CD, but the free, limited time-frame, digital downloads were a much-appreciated gesture. Spinner.com had also put together a 100-song playlist of Faith's favorite rock, pop, country, and R&B tracks for her fans's listening pleasure. "Tuning into Hill's playlist," a Spinner.com spokesperson suggested, "is just like tuning into Hill's own personal radio station on the internet."

On January 29, 2000, *Breathe* rose to number one on the *Billboard* country chart. It would hold at the top until Valentine's Day. Then on January 30th Faith wore the famous flawless 15-carat Ashford Diamond during her Super Bowl XXXIV performance of the U.S. national anthem in the Georgia Dome. The million-dollar, pear-shaped gem was the focal point of a national fundraising promotion. "I'm thrilled to have the opportunity to work with both Ashford.com and the NFL Youth Education Town," Faith said prior to the game. "It gives us the chance to give kids the tools that they need to learn and grow in an environment that is all their own. I couldn't think of a better combination." With the David Foster mix of *Let Me Let Go* included on the movie soundtrack of *Message in a Bottle*, featuring Paul Newman and Kevin Costner, due for a February 12th premiere, a Faith Hill photo calendar in the works, and cover stories appearing in *Country Weekly*, *McCalls*, *Glamour*, *Red Book*, *In Style*, *Vogue*, *Entertainment Weekly*, and *TV Guide*, Faith's affiliation with Cover Girl Cosmetics had taken on a healthy glow. She would soon be featured in *Time* magazine and as a fashion model featured in *Gucci* ads, one of Mr. Blackwell's ten best-dressed of the year.

On February 14th Warner Nashville released *The Way You Love Me*, an appropriate radio-friendly Valentine. There were several more singles yet to be pulled from BREATHE. *Let's Make Love*, perhaps the most sensual country duet of all time, was next. These lyrics *were* explicit. "No beating around the bush," Faith admits "I immediately thought of Tim and saw this song as a duet." "My husband and I are very much in love," Faith told veteran Hollywood reporter Jeanne Wolf. "That song we perform, *Let's Make Love*, is pretty direct. It just flat out says, 'Let's make love, get over here, take your clothes off, and let's get right to it.' We were completely at home with the whole idea when we recorded it together for the first time." In concert, *Let's Make Love* would bring the house down.

In the studio, things got awfully darned steamy while they were recording their vocals. "We didn't grope or anything," Faith confided to interviewers, but everybody could hear the heat that they had generated by listening to their vocals. On the record, Byron Gallimore and his mixing engineer Mike Shipley skillfully color Faith's verses with piano, organ, and faint hints of pedal steel. When Tim enters on the chorus, Aubrey Haynie's fiddle is heard for the first time. Tim's verses feature electric guitar, ringing tremolo soaked guitar chords, and pedal steel. Piano and organ are faded back or laying out. "It's cool," Tim told *Country Now*. "It's the first real duet that we've ever done together. I've sung harmony on her records, and she's sung harmony on mine, but we've never really done a duet together. It's the first time I actually sang good at all on anything we've ever done together. She's worked really hard this year—we've both worked hard. She's a great mom, a great wife, the perfect wife, the perfect mom, and she's also a great artist and a hard worker. She's the smartest person I've ever met."

Long before it was released as a single, Annie Roboff's *If My Heart Had Wings* seemed destined to become some sort of country-rock-pop spin-off anthem. It had this irresistible driving rhythm, then a soaring melodic line so strong it might be used in movie soundtracks to depict a hurricane of love or a country singer stuck out on the road far from home and missing her man way too much—a country singer who just might dream that she could fly home and be with her man for a while. Annie had written the tune with Fred Knoblock. "We wanted it to be a really rockin' kinda outside-your-normal-country groove," Annie recalls, "more like something like a cross between an Irish/African/Rock groove. Lyrically we thought it would be great to write a song about being on the road from a woman's perspective. There had never been one in country music that we knew of before and we knew that it was quite an issue. Not only for all the female singers but to some extent even for myself."

As Faith confesses, "I can definitely say, I have laid on a pillow at night wishing that there was some way to jump into the sky and fly home. . . . This is definitely autobiographical. I've lived this track."

*Damn these old wheels*
*Rollin' too slow*
*I stare down this white line*
*With so far to go*
*Headlights keep comin'*
*Loneliness hummin' along . . .*

*If my heart had wings*
*I would fly to you*
*And lie beside you as you dream*
*If my heart had wings . . .*

— *If My Heart Had Wings* (Annie Roboff, J.Fred Knoblock)

Beyond these obvious hits, there was an array of subtle melodies, rhythms, and lyrics on BREATHE that, taken together in the mix, wove a rich aural tapestry that included both a big production gospel number and a tender, heartfelt, and eventually triumphant rendering of Bruce Springsteen's *If I Should Fall Behind*, a song, Faith relates, that "the boss" played especially for her as an encore at one of his shows. "I got to meet him backstage before the show," she recalls, "and I told him that I was going into the studio to record this song. Tim and I had a great visit and when he came out for the second encore, just he and his Telecaster, he dedicated the song to us. I went nuts. It was really incredible." Most incredible of all on this new record was Faith's vocal performance. She was singing as soulfully as Aretha, as sensitively as Streisand, and with an uplifting melodic spirit that also brought Patsy Cline to mind. With her new-found confidence, she was able to ease into tender areas, then power up toward fantastic finishes and deliver rare moments of intimacy with crucial sincerity. Her vocalizing had become so subtle, easy, and fluid, and—above all—entertaining.

Faith followed Shania Twain's lead in providing her fans with bonus tracks. With a total of 13 tracks, BREATHE is in your headphones for a grand total of 52 minutes and 28 seconds. Longer cuts and longer albums had also proven successful for the Beatles and the Rolling Stones, Bob Dylan, too, and Fleetwood Mac. For several albums running, Tim McGraw's cuts had run well over three minutes and up to four and five, and his fans had begun buying four, five, then six million copies of each new album release.

On February 19, 2000, the Lifetime channel aired *An Intimate Portrait of Faith Hill*. "Tim and I were watching it," Faith told Associated Press reporter Beth Harris, "and were laughing so hard! They had access to all these photos and there were some I wish they hadn't." She wasn't merely talking about some of those bad hair days in high school when she had been a curly locked brunette. The Lifetime channel program is a showcase for profiles of American women who have distinguished themselves in their endeavors. Over the years *Intimate Portraits* host Meredith Vieira has featured a wide variety of subjects who range from Minnie Driver, Celine Dion, and Holly Hunter, to Lauren Bacall, Katherine Hepburn, and Rosa-lynn Carter. When speaking about the women's revolution in country music, Faith would often refer to 1998 as "the year of the woman." On another occasion she told Dixie Reif, "I think our music speaks for itself. Women brought so much diversity to the listeners, it's hard for it not to be successful. I think a fan could own albums by six or seven female artists, and no two would be the same. My husband records some of the most incredible music. I might be a little prejudiced, but I believe his records are great and timeless. And other male artists do the same thing. But I don't think if you were to own albums by seven male artists that they'd be very different from each other."

Faith Hill's "portrait" included interviews with a high-school friend and a high-school teacher. Faith spoke of her adoption, her father's illiter-acy, and how she came to be stuck with her last name. "That's a sore spot," she related. "Radio knew me as Faith Hill and I was divorced before my first single ever hit the airwaves. To change my name in the midst of all this . . . we didn't have a chance. Hopefully, someday I'll be able to just be 'Faith'. That's a goal of mine."

Two days later on February 21st, Faith performed her nominated song *Let Me Let Go* on the Grammy Awards broadcast. Then Pope John Paul II invited her to come to Rome and make a record with him, to be called WORLD VOICE 2000, high tribute to a country artist, even if she had been raised as a bible belt baptist. "Basically," Faith explained to *Launch.com*, "it's an invitation that Tim and I received from the Pope to be a part of this special reading of prayers he has written and kept in this book for several years. The book is of prayers that he has read in different cities around the world. We're going to have the opportunity to go to the Vatican to meet the Pope and then to read a prayer from the book." Faith and Tim made the trek to the Vatican, where they met with the exalted leader of Catholic Christians, received his blessing, then laid down their tracks. The other artists invited included LeAnn Rimes, Vince Gill, Britney Spears, 'N Sync, Monica, 98 Degrees, Jennifer Love Hewitt, Celine Dion, and Brooke Shields. The weather was good in southern Italy.

Faith and Tim had slipped away to vacations on tropical islands several times before this Mediterranean jaunt. For something a little different in the fall of 1999, they had left Gracie and Maggie with their nanny and spent some quality time together in Paris, France. Autumn in Paris had proven to be a nearly perfect way to celebrate their third anniversary. "Faith and I wanted to go somewhere by ourselves," Tim told *Blender*. "So we got on the Concorde—neither one of us had ever been to Paris. We'd sleep 'til noon, get up, walk around, shop . . . We stayed at the Ritz in the Coco Chanel Suite. We'd have crepes in the afternoon, go out, eat dinner, drink a couple of bottles of wine and come back and crash. It was, like, 'Remember why we got married now?' "

In March 2000 they returned to Paris to film a video for *Let's Make Love* with director Lili Fini Zanuck. Zanuck and Faith were pals. They had previously filmed the breathtaking music video for *Breathe* in the Arizona desert. Lili was familiar with Faith and Tim's family first, career second, way of doing things, although it had caused her moments of concern at times. On the set of the video shoot for *Breathe*, for example, where Faith was wearing that filmy one-of-a-kind Donna Karan gown, the video director had experienced several moments high anxiety. The fabric was delicate, it was pale, a stain would have been disastrous. "Although we had only one of that dress," Zanuck told *McCalls*, "Faith would pick up the kids and play with them between takes. I was afraid they'd spill something on her. But that's what's most important to her—family. She's not defined by her career. Her value system is so solid." Faith's hands-on approach to child-rearing meant that while she did have a nanny to help out when she was "at work," she often spent her coffee breaks and time outs between video shoot takes "at home," so to speak, being the loving mother she intends to continue to be. Mica Roberts has recalled times when Faith has changed a diaper mere minutes before taking the stage at her shows.

These behind the scenes moments were not often seen by the fans who watched Faith Hill's glamorous videos, television specials, and awards show appearances.

For the first video from her 1998 album FAITH, she had worked to create the distinctive, award-winning *This Kiss* video with Steven Goodmann. The choice of Lili Fini Zanuck for the first music video from BREATHE was also a decision based upon finding someone who could create a unique production. A little Hollywood glamor from the co-producer of *Driving Miss Daisy* and the forthcoming Academy Awards Show might just do the trick. "I could tell from the music that she was trying to crossover, and I don't do country videos, so I saw it as an artist with a pop tune," Zanuck told *Entertainment Weekly*. "I wanted to do something you used to see in movies all the time, which is putting a woman on a pedestal. When they used to make girls dream-girls, I thought that was pretty wonderful for men *and* women." The Los Angeles-based director had good raw material to work with in Faith Hill, who has been described as a "statuesque five-foot-nine blonde" possessing "radiant beauty."

As Faith recalls, "Lili Zanuck directed the video, the same director that directed *Breathe*, and it was so romantic, everything was perfect—except the weather. Everything else was just like you would imagine it to be, just like you would read in a romance novel." Artists who make music videos must master the art of lip-syncing, which both Faith and Tim had down pat by this point in their careers. However, they would also be required to put to film many takes of their famous on stage kiss, which they had rehearsed often enough while singing *It's Your Love*, even before they exchanged marriage vows. Oddly, in the shadow of the Eiffel Tower in the midst of the romance capital of the world, once the cameras began to roll, Tim became reticent. As Lili Zanuck recalls, "Tim thought they were kissing too much, and I had to laugh. They're very affectionate, they're kissing all the time."

March 2000 would turn out to be one of the busiest months of Faith Hill's busy life. Late in the afternoon of March 25th, she received a phone call from Lili Zanuck. With only hours to go before the broadcast of the Academy Awards Show, Zanuck's best laid plans were blowing up all around her. During rehearsal that afternoon, one of those high maintenance pop divas had come unravelled. Whitney Houston could not go on. Lili needed help. As Faith recalls, "I had just gotten off a plane from New York and I was so excited about spending Saturday with my family at home. We were going to hang out and just do fun things. Then we got the phone call from Lili Zanuck and Burt Bacharach, to see if I could fill in for Whitney on the Oscars Sunday night. I said I wanted to think about it and talk about it with my husband. So Tim and I talked, and we decided to do it, and we jumped on a plane about two hours later."

"When we called her at the last minute and asked her to rescue the show," Lili recalls, "Faith immediately said 'yes' and jumped on a plane. She was about to perform in front of 800 million people, but never once did she seem nervous." "It was a whirlwind, to say the least," Faith remembers. "It was one of those moments that I had to be so focused on what I was doing that I didn't really have time to enjoy it. I certainly would have liked to have had more time to prepare, but sometimes it's great to go into a situation like that, because you don't think about it so much and you just have to do it." Faith performed a segment of *Somewhere Over The Rainbow* during a tribute medley to past Oscar-winning songs along with Garth Brooks, Isaac Hayes, and Ray Charles, and a duet version of *The Way We Were* with Queen Latifah. Burt Bacharach would later have very kind words to say regarding Faith Hill. "She pulled it off flawlessly with two rehearsals," the show's arranger told *People*. "She's the real thing. She's totally musical. She ain't bad looking either." Faith had saved the Oscars. She had also gained more exposure than any other single artist or actor simply because—in one of those odd synchronicities—Pepsi had scheduled a world premiere of their 30-second tv commercials featuring Faith and "Pepsi Girl" Hallie Eisenberg singing the familiar *Joy Of Cola* theme for this same night on this same show. These commercials were in "heavy rotation" during the broadcast.

On April 5th, Tim and Faith were featured in an episode of *Sesame Street*, the most popular children's tv show on the planet, singing *Take Your Turn*, a song specially written for them by the show's writers. The lyrics have the McGraws teaching Elmo, Herry Monster, Telly Monster, Cookie Monster, and Lulu, all decked out in cliche country & western garb, about sharing. "We sing all day, every day, at our house," Tim told Sesameworkshop.org's Molly O'Connell. "Faith likes to dance around with music playing. And right now Gracie loves *Lucy In The Sky With Diamonds*." His fantasy for the perfect Father's Day? "To be awakened by my three girls (Gracie, Maggie, and Faith) and stay in bed in the morning hours playing and watching cartoons." The show had been taped back in December 1999, but not before Continental Airlines pitched in big time to help out and averted what could have become an international crisis. The story goes that Tim had left his hat on his tour bus, which he discovered was somewhere between Knoxville and Nashville. Yes, the driver confirmed, his hat was on board, but the bus would never make it to an airport in time—it was a time-zone thing. As Tim's people at RPM Management in Nashville scrambled to come up with a solution, the hands on the clock were ticking down to zero hour for the scheduled taping in New York. Quick thinking soon had McGraw's housekeeper rushing his back-up hat from their home to the Nashville airport. Continental had graciously agreed to hold their 11:10 flight until the housekeeper arrived. Once the hat was in the hands of a flight attendant in the terminal, the captain was informed. "We have Tim McGraw's hat . . . 10-4 . . . on its way." Even so, without Tim's tour manager rushing the hat cross-town from JFK International Airport to the studio, the crisis would not have been averted. Just in the nick of time, as rehearsals were concluding and the floor director was calling for a take, Tim's hat came through the door and onto his head. During the week in April before the show was scheduled to air, Tim told journalists, "We have a tape of it, so we've already watched it with the girls, and they loved it. Of course, I had a cold, I'm not the most in-tune singer to start with, but trying to sing with Elmo—that'll really kill you."

On April 11th, 2000, VH-1 aired their *Divas Live 2000: A Tribute To Diana Ross* Special. The show was marred by behavior that the word "diva" had stood for in the past—rich, petulant, ego-driven, self-serving stars of the opera and stage. No doubt this was merely some rub-off karma from the past history of the Supremes, which had been fraught with internal turmoil from the time that Florence Ballard, Mary Wilson, and Diana Ross first signed with Barry Gordy's Motown Records in the early 1960s. Ballard left in 1967 and died of cancer as a poverty-stricken single mother several years later. She had been replaced by Cindy Birdsong. Ross had left the group to pursue a solo career in 1970, replaced by Jean Terrell. After that, personnel changes became a regular occurrence. On the eve of this VH-1 show, Diana Ross and other former members of the group were involved in a display of public bickering because the diva being honored at Madison Square Gardens had announced an upcoming tour for which she had billed herself as Diana Ross & the Supremes, even though she would employ hired backup singers and none of the remaining actual members of the fabled Motown recording act. With this dark cloud of controversy looming over Madison Square Gardens, the 2000 edition of the divas show fell well short of the magic created on the initial show, held in a much smaller off-Broadway venue in 1998.

Mariah Carey kicked things off by saying, "I'm feeling devalicious tonight." Faith Hill performed *Breathe* and *Love Child*, her long, blonde hair blowing in a wind generated by an electric fan. Former disco queen Donna Summer sang the 1967 Supremes' smash *Reflections* and her own 1981 blockbuster hit, *Bad Girls*. At 52 years of age, Donna looked like she had been taking care of herself. The same could not be said for the frizzed, frazzled, be-wigged Diana Ross. Between sets, jumbo video screens displayed Elton John singing *The Bitch Is Back* as well as performances by divas featured on the previous two shows, where artists like Aretha Franklin, Whitney Houston, Cher and Carole King had performed.

Faith recalled being invited to the second Divas special. "I was a little awestruck that I was invited to be part of it," she confided to Deborah Walker. "I hold so much respect for Tina and Cher as well. When you think about how long they've both been doing what they do, it's inspiring. I'm not even sure I even know what a diva is. But I'm very glad I was there. . . . Being on the *Diva* show and singing on the same stage as some of the greatest singers in the world was great." It was the fan in Faith speaking here as she added, "I don't know where else I could have gone in one night to meet all those people and share the stage with them at the same time." As a result of her performance on the second and third divas shows, Faith Hill would now be referred to as a "country diva."

On May 3, 2000, Tim McGraw and Faith Hill performed *Let's Make Love* on the 35th Annual Academy of Country Music Awards. Some folks back in Tennessee may have reached for the smelling salts, but the bulk of the North American audience survived the torrid mono a mono make-out session without resorting to medication. Tim also performed his current single *Some Things Never Change* on the CBS network show. Faith hauled in a couple of "hat" awards for the California-based Academy's Female Vocalist of the Year and Video of the Year for the *Breathe* video, which she shared with Lili Fini Zanuck. Tim added another hat trophy to his collection when he was named the ACM's Male Vocalist of the Year. Tim and Faith's duet on this show in Los Angeles marked the first time in three years, since the 1977 ACMs, that they had performed on television together. It was an omen of things yet to come once they launched their Soul 2 Soul 2000 Tour.

Faith Hill and Tim McGraw have so far survived the slings and arrows that destroy most celebrity marriages, a survival both attribute to their ability to separate career from their private lives. As Faith told *Loveequine*, "We have a life outside of our celebrity, we're real people. If our celebrity was the only thing that kept us ticking, then it would not work. It would be impossible. That's what's so special about Tim. I never thought that there would be anybody else within this industry was actually a normal person and had normal goals besides selling out a show."

While she was careful not to let her career ruin her marriage, it was alright if her marriage helped her career, which had been the case when she had begun to work on her third album. "I think being in a good marriage gave me a kind of confidence I'd never had before," she relates. "My priorities and my perspective on my life and career have changed dramatically. I'd always been a little intimidated by the recording process, without realizing it. But this time I went in feeling different. It was the most sure of myself I've ever been when starting a record." This confidence was even more apparent on her fourth album. "I reached a certain place last year," she said during the promotion of BREATHE, "a certain level of success, and now it's time to go to another place. In order to succeed you can't be afraid to fail. I consider BREATHE a mixture of musical styles that reflects my love for country, pop, gospel and rhythm and blues. Yes, I decided to take some chances here, musically—as an artist that is who I am. I've always tried to achieve and do better."

# SET THIS CIRCUS DOWN

I n the summer of 2000, Faith Hill and Tim McGraw planned to tour together on a show to be called "Soul 2 Soul." Since they fell in love and married during the Spontaneous Combustion tour in 1996, the first couple of country had concentrated on raising a family and developing their individual careers, appearing together now and then when one of them made a guest appearance during the other's show, but resisting what George and Tammy had done before them when they had married and toured together almost exclusively until their Mr & Mrs Country tour bus ran out of gas and they divorced. Of and on, Faith and Tim had both joined the reigning King of Country during the George Strait Country Music Festival tours, but they had pledged not to be apart more than two or three days at a time, despite separate tours and dueling agendas. The longer they resisted touring together, the more their fans wanted to see them on the road. By the spring of 2000, the time was more than ripe. And when they announced their Soul 2 Soul Tour would kick off in Atlanta on July 12th, ticket sales were brisk for the initial 23 dates that would take them from Georgia through Alabama, the Carolinas, Florida, Louisiana, Tennessee, Colorado, Utah, Nevada, California, Arizona, Oregon, Washington, Idaho, North Dakota, Missouri, and Michigan.

"We always wanted to tour together," Tim told *Country Weekly* magazine's Wendy Newcomer, while piloting his '49 Chevy truck down a road outside Nashville that led to a recording studio, "but the timing with our careers was never right. Now, it's perfect. We've got enough songs under out belts. People want to see us together doing a show, and we want to be together." Tim recalled that first Spontaneous Combustion tour as they sped along, passing Faith in her Suburban, then reversing and pausing while the two stars exchanged greetings and endearments. "When we started touring together, I wasn't involved with anyone, but she was. But you can't be around Faith and not fall in love with her. Things just kind of happened. When two people are meant to be together, there's nothing that's going to keep them apart. . . . Nothing's hard when you have your priorities right and you know what's important."

The world was ready for a little more spontaneous combustion. "It will be more visual, more dynamic than any show we've done before," Tim said during the days leading up to the kick off date. Tim's manager, Scott Siman, the former chief of Sony Music Nashville, provided a more detailed description of the production: "Totally new stage design, new lighting rig, new sound system—everything brand new, from top to bottom. They were both really hands-on, working hard to give us their visions and their ideas of what they wanted to accomplish with their individual sets and with their duet set." As Siman explained, the reason this gala event had been so long in coming was because "there was so much going on for each individual career and so many opportunities to deal with, from making records to sponsorships, to advertising, to tv. We had to figure out whether we could create a realistic window to make it happen—and we did." Whatever problems arose because two separate management companies would be involved were quickly overcome. "Clearly we got the message from Tim and Faith, 'This is what we want to happen. You guys are great, you each have your skills and your talents. We want you to take those and focus 'em on this tour.'"

For some dates there would be an opening act. Phil Vassar, Keith Urban, and the Warren Brothers would fill that slot at various stops along the way. But the main show every night would consist of Faith's set, Tim's set, and a duet set. The focus would be on the music. "It's not all about how many fireworks we can set off at the front of the stage," Scott Siman noted. "We've got the fireworks with Tim and Faith. All our production elements are designed to make that the magic moment. This is a 'couples' tour. You're going to get a lot of Tim McGraw fans, you're going to get a lot of Faith Hill fans, but you're going to get a lot of people who want to come to see the couple."

On May 30th Faith was seen on the cover of the new issue of *Country Weekly*, named the number one choice in the magazine's poll of the "Top 25 Sexiest Stars." Shania Twain was second, George Strait third, Alan Jackson fourth, Lorrie Morgan fifth. And Tim McGraw sixth. "No other country star emits a sexier signal," the editorial copy declared, "whether gracing the cover of a high fashion magazine or posing with nothing more than a sheet for her *Breathe* video. For the stunning blonde with a model's figure, sexy comes easy. Her look has evolved from pretty, small-town girl to sophisticated sex symbol, eye-poppingly demonstrated in her ads for Cover Girl Cosmetics and her new calendar. And how about that glittering, low-cut number she wore for the Oscars?" Faith's *The Way You Love Me* rose to number one on the *Billboard* country chart on June 10 and sat there for the entire four weeks leading up to the summer tour.

Tim continued to appear on the George Strait Country Festival shows, and Faith made an appearance on the final show in Houston where she dressed up in a borrowed Houston police officer's uniform and "arrested" Tim on stage, hand-cuffed him, and led him away. The allusion was clearly to the June 3rd "horse incident" in Bufflalo where charges were brought against Tim, Kenny Chesney, and Mark Russo for assaulting a police officer. On and off again for the next year, Tim would be summoned away from the tour to appear in court.

Following his set during George Strait's Country Music Festival at Ralph Wilson Stadium near Buffalo, Tim saw a police cruiser speeding through the secured back stage parking area toward a knot of people that included his wife and two daughters. Leaping forward, he ran toward the scene where Kenny Chesney was being pulled from a police horse by two uniformed officers. "I didn't know it was a police horse," Kenny later told Jay Leno on *The Tonight Show*. "A policeman wasn't riding the horse. I was with my road manager and we were going into the bus compound where all the buses are, and I said, 'Man, wouldn't it be funny if I got on this horse and rode into the compound,' because Tim McGraw and Faith were up there with their kids and Martina McBride was up there with her kids." As Tim recalls, "I was just coming off stage in Buffalo, when I saw a police car burst into the private artist area going incredibly fast. My first thought was for the safety of my children who were playing there. I saw two officers leap from their car and run toward Kenny who was riding a horse. Kenny raised his hands as if her were surrendering, yelling he had permission to ride the horse, when they reached up and began to rip him from the horse. Fearing for Kenny's safety, I ran over to offer assistance. At no time did I ever throw any punches or put anyone in anything remotely resembling a choke hold. One of the officers pulled his night-stick and hit me at least three times on my leg. The other officer kept saying, 'This is all a misunderstanding.'"

The tussle that ensued involving Chesney, tour manager Mark Russo, Tim, and several sheriff's department deputies made headlines that reverberated in the national media throughout the following 11 months until the charges laid against the two entertainers and their road manager were finally resolved. On June 5th, the day before McGraw, Chesney, and Russo were due to put in an appearance at a court house in nearby Orchard Park, it was reported in the media that "McGraw faces a felony charge of assaulting a police officer and three misdemeanor charges: obstructing government administration, resisting arrest, and menacing. He was freed on $2,500 bail." Buffalo attorney Thomas Eoannou had been hired to represent McGraw. The charges against Chesney and Russo were said to be less serious than the felony charge against McGraw, which could bring him up to seven years behind bars. The news shocked Faith and Tim's fans who knew Tim as a fun-loving, happy-go-lucky entertainer and a model husband and father.

Tim's attorney argued that the incident was "a complete misunderstanding," caused by overreaction by law enforcement officers. Tim, Kenny, and Mark were "not guilty" and "absolutely under no circumstances" would they take any kind of plea bargain arrangement. In the days to come, comments made by these officers, the local Erie County Sheriff's office, and a county prosecutor painted a portrait of Tim as a rich, arrogant superstar with no respect for the police officers and no regard for the law. Erie County Sheriff Patrick Gallivan was equally determined to hold his ground. "They won't consider any kind of plea bargain?" he said, "That's fine with me. Let the case go to trial. Just because Tim McGraw is a millionaire and a famous country singer, that doesn't mean he stands above the law. It doesn't give him the right to assault a police officer. . . . Tim McGraw essentially attacked him, he had his arm locked around Litzinger's neck, in a head lock, then one of McGraw's managers, Mark Russo, jumped in." In another statement issued by the Erie County Sheriff's office, Gallivan added, "Much has been said about the recent arrests of country music performers Tim McGraw and Kenny Chesney, along with a member of their entourage, following an incident at the Ralph C. Wilson Stadium. No one—not even a country music performer, not an elected official—is above the law. There is no justification for or circumstances that permit anyone, no matter who they are or what they think, to approach a uniformed officer from behind, then wrap their arms around their neck effectively in a choke hold/headlock and refuse to let go and having to be forcibly pulled off, ultimately injuring the police officer. Nor is it OK to approach a uniformed police officer from behind, put their hands on his shoulders and pull him back. Tim McGraw is not above the law. Tim McGraw is fully responsible for his actions and, as the law requires, must be held accountable for them."

Through his lawyer, Kenny Chesney issued a statement in which he said, "unfortunately, what was meant to be a totally innocent and fun gesture was blown a way out of proportion. Tim McGraw and I have been friends for a very long time. When he saw me in danger of being harmed, he simply came over to help out his friend." Tim followed suit, issuing a statement through his lawyer and his manager Scott Siman prior to his appearance on the TNN Awards show at the Gaylord Entertainment Center in Nashville. "I am confident," Tim stated, "that once the district attorney has had the chance to fully investigate, all the charges will be dropped and justice done. If it's necessary, then I welcome the opportunity to go before a jury who I know will agree neither Kenny or I did anything wrong." Tim would not alter this statement throughout the long, drawn-out controversy.

On Music Row Tim was soon being referred to as the 'NashVillain', a sort of macho Nash Bridges gone country. There were no shortage of horse jokes precipitated by Tim and Kenny's brush with the law, but none so entertaining as the old Nashville line, "What do you get when you play a country record backwards?" Simple. "Your pickup truck gets fixed, your dog comes home, and your wife comes back." In his statements, Tim said that he was disturbed that people "were making light of the incident," which he saw as a "very serious matter." No doubt the possibility of spending several years in a state penitentiary had proven to be a sobering thought that might have been difficult to put out of sight and out of mind as he and Faith walked into the Gaylord Center and took their seats at the TNN Awards show that evening. Still, a circus show atmosphere seemed to spin around this event as Kenny Chesney saddled up and rode onto the set of *The Tonight Show: with Jay Leno*.

Meanwhile, Faith and Tim made their final preparations for their Soul 2 Soul 2000 Tour. Rehearsals were held in the Gaylord Entertainment Center in Nashville. The primary needs of a tour like this would be "money and trucks," Tim's agent Ron Essig explained. The set, lights, and sound crew numbered more than 100 seasoned roadies and technicians. On the night of Monday July 10th, a convoy of trucks headed out of Nashville, their destination the Phillips Arena in Atlanta, Georgia. A fleet of buses carrying the road crew and performers would follow in their wake. On Tuesday morning, the trucks backed up to the loading bay doors of the arena in a preordained sequence. Sections of the set were wheeled inside and rapidly assembled. This was the first time out of the box in an unfamiliar arena, but these roadies had rehearsed as long and as hard as the performers during the two weeks spent in the Nashville arena. While the lighting grid was being assembled, a catering crew that had just come off the Bruce Springsteen tour began setting up for the first of the three meals they would prepare and serve each day. By dinner hour on the day of the show, lamb kabobs would be charring on the big grill behind the arena. Following this Wednesday evening opener, the crew would do it all over again, tearing down, packing the trucks, and driving non-stop to Birmingham, Alabama.

Among the many stipulations in the technical rider contract were a clean, empty arena floor for load in. Chair set-up on the floor could not begin until after the stage was assembled (approximately 12:30), and chair removal would begin immediately following the show to provide floor space for the load out. A large tent supplied by the venue would be assembled in the parking area behind the building; the buses would be parked in a circle around this outdoor food service area; and the gaps between the buses would be closed by portable fencing. Security guards would be stationed around the perimeter. Camera policy stated that no cameras with interchangeable lenses would be allowed. No video cameras. But "instamatics," small pocket cameras, and "the like" would be acceptable. There were also stipulations as to the size and number of production offices, management offices, electrical outlets, phone lines, and no less than six dressing rooms. By clearly laying out all of these ground rules, Gary Borman and Scott Siman and the tour promoters had minimized the risk of staging their shows each night. When setting up and tearing down and loading out and driving night and day for four to six months at a time, with maybe a few weeks off between the first and second stages of such a tour, time is money.

Percussionist and backing vocalist Dave Dunkley, who joined the Dancehall Doctors in 1995, speaks warmly of the camaraderie that developed among everybody on the road with Tim and Faith during the Soul 2 Soul Tour. "All the guys on the bus are great," he says. "It's kind of a locker-room atmosphere. And the crew is just as much a part of the band as we are." His insights into the character of his famous boss don't pull any punches. "Tim can be kinda ornery," Dave suggests. "He's a practical joker . . . You don't fall asleep in the dressing room. But he's a really good guy. He makes sure he takes care of all of us."

Ticket sales were brisk for all of the announced dates and "behind the stage seating" was being arranged for so that additional fans could be accommodated. Some of the cities on the tour had experienced near record sell-outs: it took only 30 minutes for their show to sell out in Ana-heim and a mere 15 minutes in Phoenix, Arizona. The tour opened in Atlanta on July 12th.

Faith Hill opened her set with *What's In It For Me* and *Wild One*. CNN Interactive reporter Mary Jo DiLonardo was one of the first to file a concert review, posted on the web at 1:30 a.m. Eastern Standard Time on Thursday, July 13th. "Hill started the show, rising dramatically from a sunken stage," DiLonardo reported. "Dressed in a blinding, sequin-encrusted dress—cut up to here and down to there—she belted her way through her biggest hits. 'This is opening night!' she exclaimed when the show was still young. 'You know how long we've waited for this tour? A long time!" Faith ended her one-hour set with *This Kiss*. Mary Jo DiLonardo was also one of the first to note the length of the intermissions. "The show lost steam during a lengthy intermission, a period made even longer by ceaseless bleating from AllTel and Bud Light, the show's spon-sors. It came to a sudden end when a taped, pulsing dance version of McGraw's *Indian Outlaw* filled the air. Fans roared in anticipation. They weren't disappointed, either. Clad in black like a young Johnny Cash, McGraw leapt on the stage, not even pausing as he rocketed into the rol-licking *Something Like That*." Another Atlanta journalist had remembered in his preview story that Faith had joined Tim on this same stage back in 1996 to sing Tony Rich's R&B hit *Nobody Knows But Me*: "From stage left, Hill appeared, in skintight, black leather pants, grabbed a microphone and began singing back. After three minutes of heavy flirting, the two dropped their microphones and laid a kiss on each other that had the Atlanta crowd screaming like hungry citizens at the Roman Colosseum."

After waiting four years for country's first couple to return to Atlanta together, fans went wild when they caught sight of both Tim and Faith on stage at the same time. As the third set of the Soul 2 Soul show 2000 kicked in—to an altered dance track version of a Jim Croce song, *You Don't Mess Around With Tim*—it was more of the same magic they had witnessed in '96, but better because they also got to witness Faith and Tim singing *Let's Make Love* together. Tim McGraw and Faith Hill were back! Together again.

One of the most noted production features posted in fan reviews at various web sites was the content displayed on the jumbo video screens. Female fans loved the Bud Light commercial where "Tim has to bend over twice." Nearly every fan review mentioned the home movie video clip set to the sound track of *My Best Friend* that preceded the third set. As Deanna McKinion of Sevierville, Tennessee, wrote, "That was so sweet! They showed pictures of Tim and Faith when they first went on tour together, at Swampstock, singing *It's Your Love*, the Christmas card with Gracie, several baby pictures of the girls, another was Tim closing one of their coats in Paris. Gracie said, 'I love you Mama Faith!' Faith said, 'I love you Gracie.' Then Maggie said something in her baby talk." An unidentified fan reviewer from Ft. Lauderdale, Florida, wrote, "Faith rose out of the floor standing on the piano. She began the show with *What's In It For Me*, and sang many of her wonderful hits including a very exciting version of *Piece Of My Heart*. *This Kiss* was obviously the crowd favorite—awesome! Faith showed her wonderful vocal talents and her love of singing from the heart. Tim was beyond words, and when they concluded the show together, while singing all their hits, I've never screamed so loud!" Just as fans had done during Faith's This Kiss Tour when they had mentioned her acoustic interlude, during which she had performed cover versions of Cyndi Lauper's *Time After Time* and Rod Stewart's *The First Cut Is The Deepest*, fans often mentioned Faith's rendition of *Love Child* on these Soul 2 Soul shows. They really liked how she and her three backup singers got down and funky and made all the moves the Supremes had made way back when.

Tim's dramatic entrance each night was announced by the throb of a dance mix version of *Indian Outlaw*. He appeared on a catwalk, outlined suddenly by a blare of spotlights. Standing there in his black leather coat and cowboy hat, he began to sing the lyrics to an even catchier song— *Something Like That*. The essence of cool, this guy. By the time he had shed his coat, revealed his bared biceps and his famous "Faith" tatoo, and the Dancehall Doctors had launched into *Down On The Farm*, Tim had paid back the price of admission and a whole lot more.

On July 18th, Tim was back in court in Orchard Park, where his lawyer negotiated a postponement in order for the defense to prepare the case. Then on August 1st at another hearing in Orchard Park, the felony charge against Tim was reduced to a misdemeanor. Now he merely faced a one year maximum if convicted of one or all of the charges. With the most serious sting taken out of the charges, it was expected that an out of court settlement might end the matter, but this would not be the case. "Unfortunately," the prosecutor would later explain to reporters, "sometimes egos get in the way. They both painted themselves in a corner—the defense and the sherriff's office—and now neither can get out of it." As the story was updated regularly in the press, various individual officers and officials continued to put their spin on Tim's actions and his accountability. While Tim maintained that he was innocent, he and his attorneys had decided to pursue their own strategy. Their investigators had turned up some surprising facts about some of the participants, facts that would come out when they faced a prosecutor in a court room, and they were convinced that it was counterproductive to debate the issue in the media.

"It was tough not to come out and clear up misleading statements," Tim told Lisa Young in November 2000, a few weeks before he was scheduled to face the remaining charges in court, "but I thought the best thing we could do is just let the truth work its way through and let the district attorney's office do their job. It's easier for the truth to work when people aren't trying to spin the story, like other people were trying to do. It becomes obvious when people are talking too much and telling too many different stories what they're trying to do is cover their ass."

During these two months of trial and touring, the tabloid writers had a field day, alleging that Tim and Faith's perfect marriage had begun to show cracks, that everything they had built up was about to come tumbling down. As Faith told *Redbook*, "They've said we were divorcing. Then there was also that story that Tim beats me, which was horrible, because he experienced some of that growing up. His mother was in a very bad situation, and so he, of all people, would know that was just really hurtful. But the rest of the stuff, you just have to laugh at it. The people who know us, who are our friends, who are our family, know the truth."

In September, *Playboy* magazine named their Soul 2 Soul Tour 2000 "Country Concert of the Year." When the Soul 2 Soul Tour 2000 finally wrapped up, it was announced that it had grossed some $50 million. An estimated one million people would eventually pay to see Faith and Tim perform.

In Knoxville on September 6th, Kenny Chesney made a surprise appearance during Tim's Soul 2 Soul set at the Thompson Boling-Arena. *Daily Beacon Online* reporter John Tester was amused, but he had higher praise for Faith's performance. "Hill's amazing stage presence and excellent choice of songs," he wrote in his review, "won the admiration of all who attended. She chose songs that not only appealed to die-hard country supporters, but also to pop lovers. Her talents were dramatically revealed when she sang *It Matters To Me*." On September 8th at Penn State College's Bryce Jordan Center, *Collegian.pen.edu* reporter Alexa James was as struck by Faith's attire as she was by her music. But James was most affected by a story that Faith told that night, a story about a certain jeep ride . . . "In tight white pants, countrified with chap-like fringe and a knew-length white jacket," Alexa wrote, "Hill prepped the crowd for an emotionally charged show. 'I'm feeling a little crazy tonight,' she said. 'All of us are past crazy. You *know* my husband's crazy, and I'm crazy about this venue! In this very venue several years ago, Tim and I made the declaration of our love for one another.' She described a legendary jeep ride through the countryside. 'It was an amazing night,' she gushed. 'We decided in this very town that we were going to be together forever.' The couple's passion and musical talents have skyrocketed since that night. In a purple belly-baring baby tee, sequined magenta wristband, giant silver hoops, and towering white stilettos, the golden-locked Hill grooved and swooned through favorites from her four albums." *Countryreview.com* reporter Brooke Adair Abernathy attended one of the September 8th and 9th shows in Columbus, Ohio. He rated the Soul 2 Soul 2000 show as "the best concert I've ever seen."

On September 16th, when their caravan of trucks and buses pulled up to Madison Square Garden in New York City, it was Tim McGraw's turn to be impressed. "We got there that morning and the sign in front said 'Tim McGraw & Faith Hill Soul 2 Soul Tour—Sold Out,' Tim told *CMA Closeup* magazine's Alicia Lee. He had his camera ready for these photo opportunities. As they wandered down the long hallway toward their designated dressing room, he and Faith gawked at the posters and photos of the artists who had come there before them. Presley, Sinatra, Springsteen. "It's amazing," Tim says, "to come out of your dressing room and you're walking by Elvis on the wall, hearing the music and knowing you're going out there to a sold out show." Dave Dunkley was equally awed. "We got to play Madison Square Garden," he says. "That was a dream come true. It was incredible. I walked around three feet off the ground after that. That place was just awesome! As a concert venue or sports venue, I mean . . . that's where Ali and Frasier fought. It just has an incredible aura about it."

Daylight hours during the tour were filled with interviews, but Tim made sure he spent some time working out. McGraw's stage image has changed some over the years, but he still looks like the guy body-molding t-shirts were originally invented for. Beneath the brim of his black, wide-brimmed hat, his eyes regard you a tad more seriously, at times, yet he has not forgotten how to smile. A droopy moustache had come and gone and has now been replaced by a goatee and finely chiselled sideburns. "Image is

SET THIS CIRCUS DOWN

just another thing that you have going on, too," he says, "that you try to match it all up with. It's all about creating and this imaginary thing you have going on in your head. That's what making records boils down to. It's all about creating an emotion and a vibe. You get these little sounds in your head of what you want everything to sound like, so you go in there and try to find songs that you can incorporate these sounds into."

When the time was right both Tim and Faith jogged together. Sometimes he'd shoot baskets and play a little three on three with the Warren Brothers. Tim missed his dogs. He longed to be out riding one of his horses or tearing around his new acreage on an ATV. Or just sitting out on the land. Tim and Faith believed they had found the site for their dream house, for the day when the fans no longer showed up at the arenas, no longer bought millions of albums. If they could wait that long. Gracie would be going to school soon and that would change everything. In his heart, Tim knew that it would soon be time to set their circus down. There would come a day when they could no longer travel this way on a year 'round basis. As Gracie neared school age, that possibility became ever more real. "They'll want to be with their friends," Faith said, "and the time for the touring part of my career will not be as plentiful."

As it was, they had taken their home with them on the road, duplicating everything for the kids. Faith explained how they had done everything they could think of to ensure Gracie and Maggie's road experiences would not jeopardize their feeling of family and home. "I don't lay around the tour bus all day," Faith told Ed Bumgardner, "although there are times when that would be an awfully great thing to do. At this point, my main concern is those girls. I have a nanny to look after them while I'm working, but I'm their mother, and they are my responsibility. Young minds are the most (easily) influenced, so it's important for me to spend time with them. So no matter how dog-tired I might be, I make sure that they always have something to keep their minds occupied." Reading to her children, as Edna had read to her when she was small, would be something that could be done at home or on the road in the back bedroom of their Silver Eagle. Tried and true titles like the Dr. Zeuss books and the Winnie the Pooh books are an important part of the family library.

Faith's magic baby bus had been outfitted with a bunk for their nanny and one for Gracie, and a full-size fridge so that meals could be prepared in much the same manner they would be at home. "We have multiples of everything," Faith told *Star* magazine. "The same car seats, blankets, the same toys, so they don't miss out on their favorite things at home altogether." Journalists had noted this ongoing re-creation of the home environment had included furniture and lamps and other household fixtures. "It's the coolest bus I've ever been on," Tim told *Country Weekly*. "It's very homey. It's got a bedroom, bathroom, a couple of bunks for the girls and toys. Toys everywhere! It even has a trundle bed that comes out from under our bed so Maggie can sleep with us. And it has a sink big enough for the girls to take baths in. They'll have a tent with all their toys. The main thing is making sure they're happy and comfortable out on the road. Gracie's even started sleeping on her own on the bus. She's real excited that she's a big girl now because she can sleep in her own bunk. She has her own tv, and Ricky Martin, Britney Spears and Dixie Chicks posters, too. She's set." Having other children like John and Martina McBride's kids as friends, Gracie and Maggie simply think that everybody lives this way.

Warner Nashville released *Let's Make Love* to radio on October 21st. Halloween was spent at home before the family headed out in November to resume the Soul 2 Soul 2000 Tour. Gracie dressed up as Dorothy. Maggie was the wicked witch. When they did get back on the road, the tour would not end until December 12th in Orlando, Florida.

Faith Hill's first CBS Network Television Special aired on Thanksgiving night, a live concert performed at the Palace of Auburn Hills in Detroit, Michigan, with husband Tim as her special guest. No less than 13 million viewers tuned in to the show. Despite initial opposition to Faith's fourth album, the first year of the new millennium had turned out very well for Faith and Tim. Their music had opened many doors, including television studio doors in both New York and Los Angeles. The music video for *The Way You Love Me* is an incredible mini-movie where Faith plays several roles that she may have wished she could have been when she was very little—a weather reporter, a waitress, a nurse. Each role is explored in scenes that appear to be from a sit-com that was never made. Each scenario zanier than the last. Girls will be girls, and girls *do* love to have fun. Faith had also had fun with a mini-acoustic segment during her shows in 1999 singing Cyndi Lauper's *Time After Time* and other golden oldies including Elton John's *Don't Let The Sun Go Down On Me*, Aretha Franklin's *Chain Of Fools*, and Rod Stewart's *Stay With Me*. And once she felt at ease during photo sessions and video shoots, she revealed the identity of the person who had helped her loosen up. It was not Jim Carrey, or Cledus Judd, or reruns of *I Love Lucy*. "I hated doing photo sessions, period," Faith confessed to *Country Weekly*. "I really didn't enjoy it. But

I've got a new attitude about it now. I just go in and say, 'Hey, this is fun. I really should enjoy myself because it's going to be here forever. Gracie, our oldest daughter, loves it! She comes in and there's tons of shoes, clothes, lipstick and makeup, and she just goes crazy! And to see her having fun, it taught me something. 'Hey, mom, enjoy it!' "

By the time that Faith walked onto the movie set built for *The Grinch That Stole Christmas*, starring Jim Carrey, she had learned this lesson well. Invited to record *Where Are You Christmas*, a song written by Mariah Carey, Will Jennings, and James Horner, for the soundtrack, she needed to make a music video, and the producers of the Hollywood version of the popular Dr. Seuss title had agreed to let her make use of their set. So, it was "welcome to Whoville." As she explained to VH1, "It's a magical video. I've wanted to work with the director, Paul Hunter, for so long and he's really outdone himself on this one. It's really magical. It's like being there in Whoville for real. And they've created the mountain that the Grinch lives on and they are all going to be part of the video. So it's like the story we all grew up knowing and reading, and we're here. I'm here, I'm part of it. It's really exciting." The only downside would be that—with the Soul 2 Soul 2000 Tour not winding down until December 12th—Faith would be hard pressed to take care of all those last minute details for her own family Christmas. "I have to be very organized when planning for Christmas this year," she admitted. "But we will be home, that's the good thing. And we'll have this movie to watch."

As a result of her work with the Faith Hill Family Literacy Project and Colin Powell, Faith was able to donate a check for $50,000 to the Nashville Public Library Fund on behalf of the Project and 7-11 Stores. This project had been inspired, in part, as a response to her father's illiteracy. The money would go toward purchasing books for the children's wing in the new Nashville Public Library. Faith and Tim have worked with several charitable organizations, helping raise money for numerous worthy causes. They have supported Faith's brother who works at the Jackson Zoo with a benefit concert for the facility, and on December 2nd they took time out from their Soul 2 Soul Tour to play a benefit concert to provide support for the families of the 17 American soldiers killed in the bombing of the USS *Cole*.

On November 21st, Curb Records released Tim's "Greatest Hits" package, which debuted once again at the top of the *Billboard* album chart. Faith Hill was still riding high at second with BREATHE. By the time the holiday season rolled around, nearly everybody had forgotten all about the horse incident in Buffalo. On the night of Thursday, December 14th, it would be driven from Tim's mind, too, when he began experiencing severe abdominal pains and Faith drove him to Baptist Hospital in Nashville where surgeons performed an emergency appendectomy. McGraw made a full recovery and was back on his feet in time to accompany his wife to the American Music Awards on Monday, January 8, 2001. Which was fortunate since Faith had a lot of hardware to haul home after winning three major awards, including Favorite Female Vocalist and Favorite Female Country Vocalist. Tim took home the Favorite Male Country Vocalist award. The next morning, newspaper headlines declared, "Country Couple Dominate Music Awards." When asked for the secret of their success, Faith said, "We have a philosophy. We work hard, we have fun and try to be nice."

Then in the early months of 2001, the Recording Industry of America and the National Endowment of the Arts published their choice of the "365 Best Songs of the Century," listing Tim's record of Rodney Crowell and Claudia Church's *Please Remember Me* as the seventh best country song (and record) of the century, coming after *Your Cheatin' Heart, Stand By Your Man, I Walk The Line, On The Road Again,* and *King of the Road*— and just ahead of Garth Brooks' *Friends In Low Places*. Not bad company at all.

But the news item making headlines from *USA Today* to *Country Weekly* was not how many awards the first couple of country music were winning. Rather, it was a fashion story. The afternoon of the People's Choice Awards in LA Faith had done what girls do before going out on the town in Hollywood, visited her hairstylist—in this instance, celebrity hairstylist Peter Savic. "It was the snip seen around the world," Wendy Newcomer reported. "Faith Hill stepped onstage recently to accept her People's Choice Award for Favorite Female Musical Performer, but soon it was her new jagged, bobbed hairstyle—not her hits—that was on everyone's lips." *Country Weekly's* online poll filled up like a big old fish net. "Some raved. Some ranted," Newcomer notes. "Many simply wondered, 'Why would she do a thing like that?'"

"I just did it for a change," Faith explained. "I love it. I've never seen myself like this!" In a letter to her fan club, Faith wrote, "Everybody wants to know why I cut my hair? Well, for one, I was so tired of long hair after being on tour and everything else. I needed a vacation from my hair. However, I must say that one of the great experiences of being a woman is that we have the right to change our hair whenever the mood hits us. It is liberating. Remember it is just hair."

On February 21st, 2001 Faith and Tim won their first Grammy award for Best Collaboration with Vocals for *Let's Make Love*. Faith had her arms full with two more awards for Best Vocal Performance and Best Album for BREATHE.

On April 24th, Curb Records released Tim's SET THIS CIRCUS DOWN. As his seventh album literally flew out the doors of the record marts from coast to coast, it was announced that he had sold more than 25 million albums and singles, charted 21 Top 10 hits, and 13 number one hits. The lead single, *Grown Men Don't Cry*, would soon be used in two promotional radio ads by the National Fatherhood Initiative during their Father's Day Weekend fundraising campaign.

*Arizona Republic* critic Larry Rodgers nailed the spirit of SET THIS CIRCUS DOWN in his review when he wrote, "McGraw gives country rock with just enough twang." Alicia Lee agreed with this assessment. "While *Angry All The Time* is a true country confessional," she observed in *CMA Closeup*, "the rest of 'Circus' deftly blends the energy and attitude of McGraw's beloved '70s rock with country fiddle and vocal twang. The most captivating track on the record is the Mark Collie-penned ballad *Forget About Us*. A stark electric guitar opens the cut in a very Bruce Springsteen-like manner that's heightened by the raw, hovering background vocals. It's almost sounds like Bruce himself is offering Tim some assistance on harmony."

"This whole record," Tim told Lee, "I wanted to be kinda Springsteen, and the harmony I wanted to be that 'off kind of harmony' of a Tom Petty vibe." As Tim has said, country has become more urban, more middle Americana, and his records appeal to people from all walks of life. People who never used to like a fiddle or a pedal steel in the mix, and who might have thought they were too cool to listen to songs like *Grown Men Don't Cry*, were drawn in by Tim's undeniably sincere rendering of the lyrics in the chorus. Everybody could tell whom he had in mind as he sang these words.

> *I'm sitting here with*
> *my kids and my wife*
> *And everything that I*
> *hold dear in my life*
> *We say grace and*
> *thank the Lord*
> *Got so much to be*

*thankful for*
*Then it's up to bed*
*and my little girl*
*Says I haven't had*
*my story yet*
*And everything*
*weighing on*
*my mind my mind disappears*
*just like that*
*When she lifts her head*
*off her pillow and says*
*I love you Dad . . .*

— *Grown Men Don't Cry* (Steve Seskin, Tom Douglas)

The cover illustration, inspired by fantasy author Ray Bradbury's *Something Wicked This Way Comes*, shows dark clouds threatening a striped circus tent. Was this some sort of reference to the legal issues that loomed over his life? Was there some other symbolism intended? Some journalists connected the dots. Brian Mansfield, writing in *USA Today*, noted, "During the past year, the country singer, 33, has seen his share of dark clouds, an altercation with police in Buffalo last June, a dispute with his record company over the time of the album's release, incessant, occasionally vicious, rumors about the status of his marriage to fellow superstar entertainer Faith Hill." Mansfield also suggested that "some tracks share this sense of foreboding."

"I wouldn't say it's dark," Tim told *USA Today*. "There's a serious tone to some of the music. There's some stuff that makes you think a little bit. But I also do stuff that you don't have to think about. I like to hear songs sometimes that are just silly and don't mean anything. Lord knows I've cut enough of them." One of the songs that maybe made you think a little bit was *Things Change*, which Brian Mansfield called Tim's "boldest musical statement of his career." As Tim explained, "There's all this argument going on about traditional country and progressive country and all that. I don't understand that argument. Music is music. If you start making records according to how critics or other people in the industry think you ought to make records, to me, that's what selling out is. When I sing, it's going to be country, and I'll cut tracks any way I want to." He was even more blunt when speaking to other interviewers, telling one journalist:

"The only people who have a problem with country versus pop are those who haven't had success with either."

The chorus to the title track looks forward to that day when Tim McGraw and Faith Hill will settle down. The song seems to be written just for Tim and Faith by Bill Luther and Josh Kear.

*And we go rolling
down this highway
Chasing all our
crazy dreams*

*I've gone your way and
you've gone mine
And everywhere in
between*

*One of these days
we'll find a piece
of ground
Just outside some
sleepy little town
And set this circus
down . . .*

— *Set This Circus Down* (Bill Luther, Josh Kear)

Despite this wish for calm in their lives, May 2000 was another hectic month for Faith, with the *Pearl Harbor* movie premiere in Hawaii and the long flight back to Buffalo, NY, where Tim and Kenny fought the law and won. One story that hadn't been widely reported outside of Nashville before the trial in Buffalo concluded was a prior incident involving Tim McGraw in some fisticuffs during a concert in Jacksonville, Florida. Tim's mother and two sisters had the best seats in the house, of course—in the front row. "This big guy, about six-foot-four, two-eighty," Tim recalls, "he and this girl that was sitting there got into this big fight in the first row. I had just come out for my encore and I look down and this guy takes a big swing, and my sister happens to be sitting in between him and this girl he was fighting with—and he caught my sister square on the mouth." Just as the deputy that had been pulling Kenny Chesney off that horse behind Ralph Wilson Stadium found himself being tackled by Tim McGraw, the big guy in the front row soon learned that he had made a big mistake. "I just dove off the stage out of instinct," Tim explains. "Just dove off the stage and I kept the microphone in my hand and all you could hear over the sound system was 'boom, boom, boom.'" As Jim Croce almost once said, "you don't mess around with Tim." "It turned out it was a big fight," Tim explains, "and the guy ended up going to the medic's tent and he was all bleeding and stuff. I guess my microphone caught him a couple of times. But they invited me back the next year for double the money. So the first thing I asked was, 'Do I have to fight again?'"

As court proceedings in Orchard Park resumed, Tim remained steadfast in his claim he was innocent. "Everybody can read between the lines," Tim said. "Our story hasn't changed. Whose has? Their's has; our hasn't. It was an assault on my character, and I don't take that lightly." As McGraw's attorney, stated, "Tim takes it very seriously because he's very much a pro-law-and-order guy. He has a lot riding on this . . . He has an image he's concerned about . . . I mean, he's Father of the Year." The National Fatherhood Initiative had honored Tim with their "Father of the Year" award in June.

By this time with only the misdemeanor charges against him, there was little chance that he was going to go to jail for months or for the full year that was deemed the maximum. The only thing at issue now was his character, which he intended to defend as skilfully as he and his attorney could. The principal players in the trial were Kenny Chesney, who approached Captain Coyle's daughter Sharlene Turner, who had been standing by the horse, Chico, and asked if he could ride it; deputy sergeant Rokitka and deputy Art Litzinger, who drove a police vehicle into the compound; McGraw and Russo, who came to Chesney's aid; and Captain James Coyle, of the mounted division, whose horse Chico had become the center of attention. Justice Edmund S. Brown presided. The chief prosecutor was assistant DA Michael J. Mchale, who was working with Lou Haremski, also from the DA's office. Tom Eoannou headed up the defense team. They stage the courtroom melodrama in front of an audience that included representatives of the local and national press as well as an increasing number of local families and citizens. McGraw and Hill fans clustered at the exit as Faith and Tim left each day, clamoring for autographs, but Tim waved them off.

With the world outside Orchard Park eager to learn of the daily events in this confrontation, *CourtTV.com* reporter Harriet Ryan painted this picture of the opening day proceedings: "Orchard Park, NY—Tim McGraw looked nervous as he arrived at the Town Court here Monday to face misdemeanor charges that could send him to jail for a year. The country singer, in a conservative navy suit instead of his usual jeans and cowboy hat, wore a sober expression and clutched his wife's hand tightly as they entered the suburban Buffalo courtroom. . . . His superstar wife Faith Hill, exuding wholesomeness from her front row seat, had a stunning smile for him every time he turned around." Women who toted their children into the court encouraged them to "wave at Faith." During jury selection, one potential candidate had "gawked at Hill, who was dressed in a cappucino-colored suit with a cream ribbon in her hair and pearls on her ears and around her neck, and stammered, 'I'll have something to tell my grandchildren.'" The proceedings were somewhat unconventional. "At one point," journalist Leanne Carter noted, "McGraw called Hill over for a cross-the-court kiss. Aside from public displays of affection, there are other aspects of the trial that are not commonplace at a criminal trial in a larger city setting. There have been gum-chewing lawyers and mothers arriving to take in the proceedings with small children in tow. Perhaps the most glaring oddity, one definitely not missed by McGraw's lawyers, is the jurors mingle in the parking lot, bathrooms and hallways with the prosecutors and defendants. Jurors were also in attendance at a press conference held by Sherriff Patrick Gallivan."

Erie County assistant-DA Lou Haremski delivered his opening address to the jury stylishly, alternately stroking then slicing McGraw's high-profile character. At one point in his delivery, he said, "I couldn't conjure up a single evil thought about this individual." Defense attorney Thomas Eoannou also delivered a passionate oration: "McGraw has maintained that he did nothing wrong and that the officers involved overstepped the boundaries of their authority. Tim ran over to help a friend and got blasted with a night stick, that's what happened here. He doesn't want to be treated like a celebrity—look where it got him." Stacked against the grim presence of Sheriff Gallivan, Capt. Coyle of the Mounted Division, Coyle's daughter Sharlene Turner, and an assortment of deputies employed by the Sheriff's department were a throng of spectators who appeared to be one hundred percent Faith Hill and Tim McGraw fans. Judge Brown would have his hands full dealing with the many outbreaks of levity in his courtroom. During testimony by one of the prosecution's witnesses, one senior citizen in the gallery would blurt, "He didn't see anything and he was right there."

The first witness to take the stand was the deputy Tim McGraw was alleged to have assaulted. *CMT.com* reporter Edward Morris described the scene: "Detective Arthur Litzinger testified Tuesday that he suffered a back injury when McGraw seized him around the neck and threw him into a patrol car as he was attempting to pull Chesney from the horse. Litzinger said that deputies ordered Chesney to dismount but admitted under cross-examination that no one asked the singer if he had permission to be on the horse." Sergeant Mark Rokitka was next. As Morris reported: "Sgt. Mark Rokitka of the Erie Country Sheriff's Department testified that Singer Kenny Chesney refused to get off a horse. . . . As Rokitka and his partner, Litzinger, tried to pull Chesney off the horse, McGraw attacked Litzinger. 'All this happened in a split second!' he said. After the alleged attack, Rokitka ran at McGraw. 'I couldn't move him, so I screamed, *You attacked my partner! You attacked my partner!*'" Deputy Rokitka also alleged that the defendant then attacked him. As Morris reports: " 'He was coming at me fast!' Rokitka testified. Rokitka readied his baton and struck McGraw's left thigh just as Litzinger subdued McGraw from behind."

Throughout testimony by all of the prosecution witnesses, defense lawyers pointed out inconsistencies. Tim had been taking notes, too, on a legal pad, passing them to Tom Eoannou. "Tim McGraw doesn't miss a thing," Eaonnuo told *CMT.com* reporter Ron Pasquale. "He catches every inconsistency in the people's proof and he immediately notifies me. He's a very intelligent guy."

When Sharlene Turner took the stand, it became apparent that all three attorneys representing the three defendants had done their homework. Here they had deduced was the Achilles' heel of the prosecutions' case. It would come out that in the time that had elapsed since June 3, 2000, Captain Coyle's daughter had pled guilty to felony credit card fraud charges and was due to be sentenced immediately following the current trial. She had been grooming and minding the horse at the George Strait Festival while her father "met with other deputies." But she clearly didn't have permission to let unauthorized riders clamber aboard or ride off at a steady trot. Doing so had raised her daddy's ire and, likely, initiated the pursuit of Kenny Chesney

"In testimony," Ron DePasquale reported in a story filed at CMT.com, "Turner admitting to stealing personal information to obtain credit cards in other's names. She also pled guilty to a disorderly conduct charge in September. Turner claimed in testimony that she was then mentally ill and now takes anti-depressants and sees a psychiatrist weekly. She repeatedly replied, 'I do not recall' when asked specific questions about her crimes. However, she remembered the entire incident at the Strait Fest.

Turner broke the tension in the courtroom when she said she did not recognize Chesney when he rode by on a golf cart. 'I'm sorry, I'm not a fan of Mr. Chesney's,' she said as the courtroom burst into laughter and the defense playfully objected. But the point became a serious one when defense lawyers grilled Turner, insinuating that she had seen McGraw at a similar festival in West Virginia five years ago and was an awestruck fan trying to schmooze with the stars."

Harriet Ryan noted that "the lawyers for Russo and Chesney hinted that Turner was a groupie who was using the horse to get backstage and meet musicians and the deputies pressed the charges to get at McGraw's deep pockets." DePasquale further noted that when Turner had become frustrated during the hour-long cross-examination by Eoannou, she had said, "I don't know, you've put me through hell and back again." Eoannou's laconic reply, "you should see what you've done to my client," served to point out her self-interest.

The next day, the trial nearly derailed when 66-year-old Justice Brown was wheeled from the courtroom on a stretcher in the throes of a heart attack. A mistrial seemed out of the question and a compromise saw his replacement provided with a weekend in which to bring himself up to speed on the testimony thus far. Before the trial resumed on the following Monday morning, Tim and his co-defendants were served with a writ that contained a civil lawsuit filed by Sergeant Mark Rokitka of the Erie County Sherriff's Department. The subpoena for the writ was dated May 15, 2001, one day prior to his testimony in the case. Thomas Eoannou told the press, "the fact that they would do it right in the middle of the courthouse makes it obvious they're looking for money after they say they weren't."

The trial resumed with Justice John M. Curran presiding. Prosecution called a total of eight witnesses. When several deputies' testimony differed substantially from their statements given at the time of the incident, defense hammered away. Country deejay and Mounted Reserve Division deputy Wayne Wolf added a wrinkle when he failed to identify the defendant Tim McGraw as the main actor in the melee, pointing instead to Russo and identifying him as the person who had taken on both deputies. This point of view was echoed by mounted division deputy James Picowsky, who also identified Russo as the man doing the brawling. More confusion came when defense endeavored to elicit information on exactly who had arrested Tim McGraw and under what circumstances. During cross-examination of Chief Thomas Steabell, the ranking officer on the night of the altercation, the court heard testimony that Steabell had come aboard the artist's bus. He said he had "negotiated" with Tim McGraw. Defense attorney Eoannou in his efforts to disprove charges of resisting arrest, asked why McGraw had not been read his rights, hand-cuffed, and placed in a patrol car. When requested to, McGraw had willingly attended a meeting at the local firehall, but not because he had resisted arrest and was then giving himself up.

Two private security guards called as witnesses both said they saw McGraw "push Litzinger away, but never choke him." One of these witnesses, Timothy Hoch, said, "It was in the manner as a tight end hits a quarterback." Which was a heavy push but not at all like the action described by deputies who had previously testified. Or in the manner described by Sherriff Gallivan in the many statements he had issued. The final witness, Michael Burton, relayed the information that Sharlene Turner had run after deputies Litzinger and Rokitka crying out, "No, it's okay, I let him have the horse."

"Prosecutors wrapped up their evidence with a marathon of eight witnesses," Harriet Ryan reported, "whose testimony about the country singer's backstage fracas with police was so contradictory that one juror even broke into a smile of disbelief. 'I question whether they were even there,' said lawyer Anthony Lama, who represents co-defendant Mark Russo. 'When you look at all the testimony, none of them has matched up.'"

On the final day of testimony, Tim McGraw took the stand. "McGraw charged that sherriff's deputies aggressively assaulted him," Ron DePasquale reported, "rather than vice versa. McGraw conceded that he did push Detective Arthur Litzinger while the deputy was attempting to pull Chesney off a police horse . . . But McGraw denied grabbing Litzinger's neck and attempting to snap it, as the deputy testified. McGraw also denied coming after Litzinger's partner Sgt. Mark Rokitka. McGraw told the jury that Rokitka was the aggressor and that he kept yelling, 'I'll kill you! You touched my partner!' Litzinger, McGraw said, urged Rokitka to back off, saying, 'Mark, calm down. We made a mistake.'"

Key to understanding what had motivated deputies Litzinger and Rokitka to pursue Chesney was an incident that had taken place at the fire hall command post where Tim was taken into custody. As Ron Pasquale reported, "At the fire hall, McGraw said he heard Capt. James Coyle tell his daughter Sharlene Turner—who according to Chesney, had given the singer permission to ride the horse—to lie. 'He said, *You'd better not tell them you gave him permission to ride that horse. You'd better lie, or they'll sue our asses off.'* " Pasquale also identified Tim's key line of testimony: "McGraw said, 'I knew then what this was about. I couldn't believe it, that he said that right in front of me, then stared me down.' "

In defense of his actions, Tim's legal team had found a precedent that stated, "New York state law says that when a police officer is using excessive force, physical force can be used to repel that. A police officer cannot randomly use force against a citizen." Tom Eoannou also told jurors, "Because you put on a badge and a blue suit does not mean that you can hit people." Eoannou delivered a convincing summation, calling the trial a "joke," and charging that "the sherriff of all Erie County had put aside the county's business to assassinate Tim McGraw." Eoannou concluded with a line provided to him by his client when he stared the jury down and said, "In about a minute, I'm going to ask you to 'set this circus down.' That's the name of Tim McGraw's latest album. It was written about this case."

During his closing argument, prosecutor Lou Haremski attempted to spin his previous "nice guy" depiction of Tim by saying, "he's a performer, he thinks he can sell you." But his case had been weakened and then irreparably damaged by failure of prosecution witnesses to deliver convincing evidence. While the jury retired to decide a final outcome, the media began to focus on what was deemed to be a likely victory for the defendants. Now the story had been shortened to include mostly Kenny and Tim's sworn testimony. Chesney had testified that Sergeant Mark Rokitka had struck him in the ribs with a billy club and pulled him from the horse. Tim had testified that he jumped in because he feared that Kenny might go "face first into the concrete." He had been grabbed by the neck and struck with a night-stick, despite telling police that his wife and daughters were standing nearby.

The jury exonerated Tim McGraw, as Harriet Ryan reported for *CourtTV.com*. "As the forewoman repeated 'not guilty' 12 times, the courtroom packed with country fans broke into applause and McGraw's superstar wife Faith Hill cried joyously in the front row. McGraw's eyes were red, too, but his jaw was set in anger. Throughout the reading of the verdict, he glowered at the local sheriff who he believes exploited the June incident for political gain."

"McGraw wrapped Chesney in a bear hug," Ron Pasquale told his readers. "McGraw hugged his lawyer next, and, as his camp continued to celebrate, he stared down Erie County Sheriff Patrick Gallivan. Calmly and cooly, McGraw took a laminated copy of a *People* magazine article in which the sheriff had commented about the star and walked toward Galli-van. He tossed the article onto the lap of the sherriff, who sat in the front row."

"It's yours now," Tim said. He turned to Faith who was speaking with their daughters on her cell phone and walked out the door with his wife and lawyer. Outside the courtroom amidst a throng of clamoring fans, he told reporters, "We've been waiting 11 months to have our day in court. We didn't want a plea deal; we didn't want anything. We wanted to tell our story, to tell the truth. The justice system works. The people of Buffalo have been wonderful to us—we'll be back and we'll play music here. I had complete faith in the justice system."

As this circus set down, Tim and Faith turned attention to their grow-ing family. Soul to soul, heart to heart, Faith and Tim had by now pretty well done it all, but there will be new music ringing through their home. In June 2001, they announced that Faith was pregnant, once again. "For Tim McGraw and Faith Hill," *Country Weekly* reported, "the sweetest sound in the world is not a hit song or a cheering audience—it's the pitter patter of little feet. And come next January, the happy couple will add another pair of baby booties to their growing family." As Tim and Faith said in a joint press release, "All four of us are beyond excited. . . . Gracie and Maggie can't understand why they have to wait until January to see the baby." Gracie and Maggie had one less month to wait to see their sister Audrey Caroline, who was born on December 6, 2001, an early Christmas gift from Tim and Faith.

Back in 1997, Faith had confessed, "Tim and I plan to have a million children. Really, we plan to have a very big family." A tad old fashioned, maybe, but then again maybe not, for the woman who sings with her daughters and her husband while doing chores in the family home is also the artist from Star, Mississippi who has given the world all her passion on songs like *This Kiss* and *Breathe*. She has never let her family down; she has never let her fans down. Faith has bought out the Elvis in all of us, dreamed of her heart having wings, believed fiercely in family values. Faith's vision of perpetual bliss.

Since the day they married, Tim has maintained that family comes first. "We get asked a lot how we balance family and career," he has com-mented. "Well, it's not hard to balance . . . The family comes first." Yet this is the guy from Start, Louisiana people pay to see and hear play rau-cous, rowdy, and loud on songs like *I Like, I Love It*, then power-down and rip their hearts from their chests on hits like *Don't Take The Girl*.

The artist who was named the Country Music Association 'Entertainer of the Year' for 2001. And the artist who joined George Strait, Alan Jackson, Marina McBride, and Sara Evans onstage for the "Country Freedom Concert" to raise funds for the Salvation Army Relief Fund in support of the families who lost loved ones in the World Trade Center disaster on September 11th in New York. When suicidal terrorists took the lives of thousands of innocent victims in that towering inferno, they inadvertently renewed the American faith in personal freedom and family values. As Tim McGraw commented, "I love going home and playing with those kids. I pick them up, turn them upside down, shake them and they laugh constantly. I'm a lucky man." And he is right.

# DISCOGRAPHY

## Tim McGraw

### Tim McGraw
(1993 Curb Records D2-77603)

*Welcome to the Club*  (Steve Seskin/Andre Pesis)
*Two Steppin' Mind*  (Buddy Brock/John Northrup)
*You Can Take It With You*  (When You Go)  (Frank Dycus/Kerry Kurt)
*Ain't No Angels*  (Billy Montana/Brad Davis)
*Memory Lane*  (Joe Diffie/Lonnie Wilson)
*Tears In The Rain*  (Joe Diffie/Lonnis Wilson/Wayne Perry)
*What She Left Behind*  (Kenny Beard/Earl Clark/Paul Nelson)
*What Room Was The Holiday In*  (Jim Vest/Joyce Shoaf/Arti Portilla)
*I Keep It Under My Hat*  (Kent Anderson/Kerry Kurt Phillips/Michael Higgins)

### Not a Moment Too Soon
(1994 Curb Records)

*It Doesn't Get Any Countrier Than This*  (Jerry Vandiver/Randy Archer)
*Give It To Me Strait*  (Reese Wilson/Stephen Gruberger)
*Wouldn't Want It Any Other Way*  (Ed Hill/David Frasier)
*Down On The Farm*  (Jerry Laseter/Kerry Kurt Phillips)
*Not A Moment Too Soon*  (Wayne Perry/Joe Barnhill)
*Indian Outlaw*  (Tommy Barnes/Gene Simmons/John D. Loudermilk)
*Refried Dreams*  (Jim Foster/Mark Peterson)
*Don't Take The Girl*  (Craig Martin/Larry W. Johnson)
*40 Days And 40 Nights*  (Tommy Barnes)
*Ain't That Just Like A Dream*  (Tony Mullins/Stan Muncey Jr.)

## All I Want
(1995 Curb Records)

*All I Want Is A Life*  (Tony Mullins/Stan Munsey/Don Pfrimmer)
*She Never Lets It Go To Her Heart*  (Tom Shapiro/Chris Waters)
*Can't Really Be Gone*  (Gary Burr)
*Maybe We Should Just Sleep On It*  (Jerry Laseter/Kerry Kurt Phillips)
*I Didn't Ask And She Didn't Say*  (Reese Wilson/Van Stephenson/Tony Martin)
*Renegade*  (Jeff Stevens/Steve Bogard)
*I Like It, I Love It*  (Steve Dukes/Jeb Stuart Anderson/Mark Hall)
*The Great Divide*  (Brett Beavers)
*You Got The Wrong Man*  (Wayne Perry/Joe Barnhill)
*Don't Mention Memphis*  (Billy LaBounty/Rand Bishop)
*When She Wakes Up*  (And Finds Me Gone)  (Tommy Barnes)
*That's Just Me*  (Deryl Dodd)

## Everywhere
(1997 Curb Records D2-77886)

*Where The Green Grass Grows*  (Jess Leary/Craig Wiseman)
*For A Little While*  (Phil Vassar/Steve Mandile/Jerry Vandiver)
*It's Your Love*  (With Faith Hill)  (Stephony Smith)
*Ain't That The Way It Always Ends*  (Don Sampson/Skip Ewing)
*I Do But I Don't*  (Mark Nesler/Tony Martin)
*One Of These Days*  (Kip Raines/Monty Powell/Marcus Hummon)
*Hard On The Ticker*  (Craig Wiseman/Gary Lloyd)
*Everywhere*  (Craig Wiseman/Mike Reid)
*Just To See You Smile*  (Mark Nesler/Tony Martin)
*You Just Get Better All The Time*  (Tony Joe White/Johnny Christopher)
*You Turn Me On*  (Billy Lawson)

# A Place in the Sun
(1999 Curb Records)

*The Trouble With Never*  (Tony Martin/Mark Nelser)
*Seventeen*  (Aimee Mayo/Bill Luther/Chris Lindsey)
*She'll Have You Back*  (Deryl Dodd/ Blake Allen Chancey)
*Somebody Must Be Prayin' For Me*  (Frank Vinci/Kris Bergnes/Bob Moulds)
*My Best Friend*  (Aimee Mayo/Bill Luther)
*Senorita Margarita*  (Bob DiPiero/George Teren)
*Some Things Never Change*  (Brad Crisler/Walt Aldridge)
*You Don't Love Me Anymore*  (Greg Barnhill/Kim Carnes)
*Something Like That*  (Rick Ferrell/Keith Follese)
*Please Remember Me*  (Rodney Crowell/Will Jennings)
*Carry On*  (Even Stevens/Hillary Kanter/Mark Collie)
*My Next Thirty Years*  (Phil Vassar)
*Eyes Of A Woman*  (Steve Mandile/Rory Michael Bourke)
*A Place In The Sun*  (Steve Dukes/Chris Lindsey)

# Tim McGraw Greatest Hits
(2000 Curb Records D2-77978)

*Indian Outlaw*
*Don't Take The Girl*
*She Never Lets It Go To Her Heart*
*I Like I, I Love It*
*Just To See You Smile*
*It's Your Love*  (With Faith Hill)
*Where The Green Grass Grows*
*For A Little While*

*Please Remember Me*
*Something Like That*
*My Best Friend*
*Maybe We Should Just Sleep On It*
*Down ON The Farm*
*My Next Thirty Years*
*Let's Make Love*  (With Faith Hill)

# Set This Circus Down
(2001 Curb Records D2-78711)

*The Cowboy In Me*   (Craig Wiseman/Jeffrey Steele/Al Anderson)
*Tellerude*   (Troy Verges/Brett James)
*Things Change*   (Aimee Mayo/Bill Luther/Chris Lindsey/Marv Green)
*Angel Boy*   (Danny Orton)
*Forget About Us*   (Mark Collie)
*Take Me Away From Here*   (Steve Bogard/Jeff Stevens)
*Smilin'*   (Bill Luther/Aimee Mayo/Chris Lindsey/Marv Green)
*Set This Circus Down*   (Bill Luther/Josh Lear)
*Angry All The Time*   (Bruce Robison)
*Let Me Love You*   (Aimee Mayo/Bill Luther/Chris Lindsey/Marv Green)
*Grown Me Don't Cry*   (Steve Seskin/Tom Douglas)
*Why We Said Goodbye*   (Billy Kirsch/Tom Douglas)

# Faith Hill

## Take Me As I Am
(1993 Warner Bros. Records CDW 45389)

*Take Me As I Am*   (Bob DiPiero/Karen Staley)
*Wild One*   (Jamie Kyle/Pat Bunch/Will Rambeaux)
*Just About Now*   (Gary Burr/Jon Vezner)
*Piece Of My Heart*   (Bert Berns/Jerry Ragavoy)
*I've Got This Friend*   (With Larry Stewart)   (Faith Hill/Bruce Burch/Vern Dant)
*Life's Too Short To Love Like That*   (Sandy Ramos)
*But I Will*   (Troy Seals/Eddie Setser/Larry Stewart)
*Just Around The Eyes*   (Gary Burr)
*Go The Distance*   (Trey Bruce/Thom McHugh/Faith Hill)
*I Would Be Stronger Than That*   (Gary Burr)

## It Matters to Me
(1995 Warner Bros. Records CDW 45872)

*Someone Else's Dreams*   (Craig Wiseman/Trey Bruce)
*Let's Go To Las Vegas*   (Karen Staley)
*It Matters To Me*   (Mark D. Sanders/Ed Hill)
*Bed Of Roses*   (Will Rambeaux/Jaime Kyle)
*A Man's Home Is His Castle*   (Ariel Caten)
*You Can't Lose Me*   (Trey Bruce/Thom McHugh)
*I Can't Do That Anymore*   (Alan Jackson)
*A Room In My Heart*   (Sunny Russ)
*You Will Be Mine*   (Rob Honey)
*Keep Walkin' On*   (Karen Staley/Tricia Walker)

## Faith
(1997 Warner Bros. Records CDW 46790)

*This Kiss* (Robin Lerner/Annie Roboff/ Beth Nielsen Chapman)
*You Give Me Love* (Matraca Berg/Jim Photoglo/Harry Stinson)
*Let Me Let Go* (Steve Diamond/Dennis Morgan)
*Love Ain't Like That* (Tim Gaetano/A.J. Masters)
*Better Days* (Bekka Bramlett/Billy Burnett/Annie Roboff)
*My Wild Frontier* (Franne Golde/Robin Lerner/Marsha Malamet)
*The Secret Of Life* (Gretchen Peters)
*Just To Hear You Say That You Love Me* (With Tim McGraw) (Diane Warren)
*Me* (Aimee Mayo/Marv Green)
*I Love You* (Aldo Nova)
*The Hard Way* (Keith Brown/Donna Douglas)
*Somebody Stand By Me* (Sheryl Crow, Todd Wolfe)

## Breathe
(1999 Warner Bros. Records CDW 47373)

*What's In It For Me* (Billy Burnette/Bekka Bramlett/Annie Roboff)
*I Got My Baby* (Bob DiPietro/Annie Roboff)
*Love Is A Sweet Thing* (Brett James/Troy Verges)
*Breathe* (Holly Lamar/Stephanie Bentley)
*Let's Make Love* (With Tim McGraw) (Chris Lindsey/Marv Green/Bill Luther/
    Aimee Mayo)
*It Will Be Me* (Gordon Kennedy/Wayne Kirkpatrick)
*The Way You Love Me* (Keith Follese/Michael Delaney)
*If I'm Not In Love* (Constant Change)
*Bringing Out The Elvis* (Leif Larsson/Louise Hoffstern)
*If My Heart Had Wings* (Aime Roboff/Fred Knobloch)
*If I Should Fall Behind* (Bruce Springsteen)
*That's How Love Moves* (Jennifer Kimball/Fitzgerald Scott/Ty Lacy)
*There Will Come A Day* (Bill Luther/Aimee Mayo/Chris Lindsey)

# REFERENCES

## Books

Bowen, Jimmy (with Jim Jerome). *Rough Mix*. New York, NY: Simon & Schuster, 1997.

Dickerson, James. *Women on Top*. New York, NY: Billboard Books, 1998.

Gray, Scott. *Perfect Harmony*. New York, NY: Ballantine Books, 1999.

Jones, George (with Tom Carter). *I Lived To Tell It All*. New York, NY: Random House, 1996.

Jones, Nancy & Tom Carter. *Nashville Wives*. New York, NY: Cliff Street Books/ Harper Collins, 1998.

Tritt, Travis, with Michael Bane. *10 Feet Tall and Bulletproof*. New York, NY: Warner Books, 1994.

Whitburn, Joel. *The Billboard Book of Top 40 Albums*. New York, NY: Billboard Books, 1995.

Whitburn, Joel. *The Billboard Book of Top 40 Country Albums*. New York, NY: Billboard Books, 1996.

Whitburn, Joel. *The Billboard Book of Top 40 Country Hits*. New York, NY: Billboard Books, 1996.

Whitburn, Joel. *The Billboard Book of Top 40 Hits*. New York, NY: Billboard Books, 1995.

## Newspaper & Magazine Articles

Abowitz, Richard. "Perfect Harmony: Faith Hill & Tim McGraw Find Family & Success Together." *Showbiz Weekly*, July 23, 2000.

Anonymous. "I Know How Lucky I Am." *McCalls*, November 2000.

Anonymous. "The 50 Most Beautiful People in the World 2000." *People*.

Anonymous. "Faith Accompli." *People*, July 1999.

Anonymous. "Making Music a Family Affair." *The Costco Connection*, June 2001.

Anonymous. "A Conversation with Faith." *Warner Brothers Media Kit* 1998.

Anonymnous. "Country's Hill & McGraw Wed." *Associated Press*, Oct. 8, 1996.

Anonymous. "Country Couple Dominate American Music Awards." *A.P.*, Jan 9 2001.

Anonymous. "Country Singers Claim Cop Fracas Left Lasting Damage." *Sun Wire Services*.

Anonymous. "Next Big Country Diva." *Country Weekly*, February 1994.

Anonymous. "About Faith." *Entertainment Weekly*, December 10, 1999.

Anonymous. "Power of Faith." *Housekeeping*, N/A.

Anonymous. "Leap of Faith." *US Weekly*, May 15, 2000.

Anonymous. "Country Stars in Horse Dust Up." *U.S. Weekly*, June 19, 2000.

Anonymous. "On the Cover: Artist Profile." *Music Row*, November 8, 1999.

Anonymous. "On the Cover: Artist Profile." *Music Row*, February 23, 1998.

Anonymous. "Interview with Tim McGraw." *CMA Closeup*, February 1995.

Anonymous. "Interview with Tim McGraw." *CMA Closeup*, April 1999.

Anonymous. "McGraw Keeping Secret." *Associated Press*, September 23, 1996.

Anonymous. "McGraw Found Not Guilty." *Ottawa Sun*, May 25 2001.

Anonymous. "Mister McGraw: An Exclusive Interview." *Music City News*, May 1999.

Anonymous. "Hill and McGraw Expecting Child." *Associated Press*, December 5, 1996.

Anonymous. "Faith Hill." *People*, July 12, 1999.

Anonymous. "Faith Conquers Musical Hill." *Country Weekly*, February 22, 2000.

Anonymous. "Sexiest Country Star: Tim McGraw. *People*, November 15, 1999.

Anonymous. "Life Under the Big Top." *Country Music*, May, 2001.

Anonymous. "Neither Kenny or I Did Anything Wrong." *countryyahoo.com*.

Anonymous. "Tim McGraw Gets Cooking."

Anonymous. "Stormy Weather Hits Country Show." *Country Weekly*, June 25, 1996.

Anonymous. "Tests of Faith." *Tennessean*, February 19, 2001. Posted *mcgraws.com*.

Anonymous. "Top 25 Sexiest Stars." *Country Weekly*, May 30, 2000.

Anonymous. "The Stories Behind FAITH." *Warner Brothers Media Kit*, 1998.

Anonymous. "Tim Sued for Wreck." *Country Weekly*, April 23, 1996.

Anonymous. "Workaholic Tim McGraw." *Country Weekly* March 19, 1999.

Arnold, Mary. "New First Couple of Country." *Country Music & More*, November 2000.

Benson, Ray. "Strait Back Then." *Knix Magazine*, February 1999.

Brooks, Nancy. "Tim McGraw: Keep the Faith." *Country Song Roundup*, July 2000.

Caligiuri, Jim. "You Gotta Have Faith." *Glamour*, January 2000.

Cater, Leanne. "McGraw Refuses To Plea Bargain." *Ottawa Sun*, May 20, 2001.

Cooper, Peter. "McGraw May Face Prison in Assault Case." *Tennessean*, June 6, 2000.

Delaney, Larry. "Faith Hill: Country's Record Breaker." *Country Music News*, February 1994.

Durcholz, Daniel. "Soul 2 Soul Tour Hits St. Louis." *Post Dispatch*, September 27, 2000.

Farley, Christopher. "Tennessee Two-Step Tim McGraw Is on a Roll. And His Better Half Isn't Doing Badly Either." *Time*, June 6, 1998.

Flippo, Chet. "Hill's *Breathe* Benefits from CMAs." *Billboard*, October 1999.

Flippo, Chet. "Hill's 'Breathe' Blows Out of The Stores & Into The Number One Slot on *Billboard's* Top 200 & Country Album Charts." *Billboard*, December 2000.

Ford, Don. "Faith in the Future." *Country Music People*, August 1994.

Graff, Gary. "Faith Hill Maximum Overdrive." *Country Song Roundup*, January 2000.

Griwkowsky, Fish. "Grassroots Recordings." *Edmonton Sun*, June 2, 1997.

Griwkowsky, Fish. "Tim Dandy." *Edmonton Sun*, August 1, 1997.

Griwkowsky, Fish. "The Real McGraw." *Edmonton Sun*, February 1, 1998.

Halbersberg, Elianne. "Bringing Tim's Circus to Town." *Mix*, July 1, 2001.

Harris, Beth. "Lifetime Paints Intimate Portrait of Faith Hill." *Associated Press Newswire - Seattle Post Intelligencer*, February 19, 2000.

Hunter, James. "Quick Draw McGraw." *Entertainment Weekly*, November 10, 1995.

Hunter, James. "There's a New Sheriff in Town." *Blender*, June/July 2001.

Jerome, Jim & Beverly Keel, Zelie Pollon, Mary Green, Michael Fleeman. "Faith Hill's Tough Road To True Love." *People*, August 21, 2000.

Joyce, Mike. "At RFK, Giving Everything for Their Country." *Washington Post*, May 17, 1999.

Keel, Beverly. "Horseplay! Chesney & McGraw: What Really Happened." *Nashville Scene*, June 19, 2000.

Kennedy, Paul. "Concert Rev: Jackson & Hill." *Country Music News*, June 1994.

King, Susan. "Faith's Country." *Los Angeles Times*, November 19, 2000.

Krewen, Nick. "A Little Luck, a Lot of Talent, and a Secret Formula Keep Tim McGraw on Top of the Charts." *Country Weekly*, October 10, 1995.

Krewen, Nick. "Tim & Faith Have a Ball on Their Wedding Day." *Country Weekly*, October 29, 1996.

Krewen, Nick. "Tim McGraw Knows Where The Green Green Grass Grows." *Country Weekly*, February 1997.

Krewen, Nick. "New Life Begins at 30 for McGraw." *Country Weekly*, June 3/97.

Lee, Alicia. "McGraw Takes His Circus on the Road." *CMA Closeup*, March 2001.

Lewis, Randy. "Grammys: Nods to New and Tradition." *LA Times*, February 22, 2001.

Lovejoy, Sandy. "Baby Talk: New Daddy McGraw Overwhelmed." *Knix*, December 1997.

Lovejoy, Sandy. "McGraw Interview: A Rambling Conversation." *Knix*, May 1999.

Mansfield, Brian. "Faith Finds Perfect Balance." *USA Today*. ND.

Mitchell, Rick. "Faith Hill Belts Out Soul in Country Dress." *Houston Chronicle*.

Morris, Edward. "Love Reigns: Country Crowns Its Newest Supercouple." *Country Weekly*, October 5, 1999.

Munson, Kyle. "Big Draw McGraw Sticks To His Guns." *Des Moines Register*, April 28, 1999.

Nash, Alanna. "Review: ALL I WANT." *Entertainment Weekly*. ND.

Neal, Chris. "Tim On Trial." *Country Weekly*, July 10, 2001.

Neill, Logan. "Now Teammates, McGraws in Harmony." *St. Petersburg Times* March 28, 1998.

Newcomer, Wendy. "Room to Breathe." *Country Weekly*, November 11, 1999.

Newcomer, Wendy. "It's Tim Time." *Country Weekly*, February 22, 2000.

Newcomer, Wendy. "Baring Souls." *Country Weekly*, July 11, 2000.

Newcomer, Wendy. "Hair Today, Where Tomorrow?" *Country Weekly*, March 6, 2001.

Newcomer, Wendy. "Things Change for the Better." *Country Weekly*, February 6, 2001.

Newcomer, Wendy. "Baby on Board." *Country Weekly*, July 10, 2001.

Overall, Rick. "Big Country Tours Set To Arrive." *Ottawa Sun*, December 2, 1997.

Overall, Rick. "Strait Talking." *Ottawa Sun*, June 28, 1998.

Paxman, Bob. "Pony Prank Puts Pair in Pokey." *Country Weekly*, July 11, 2000.

Phillips, Scott. "Tim's Day in Court Delayed." *Calgary Sun*, July 26, 2000.

Pond, Neil. "Baby Talk with Tim McGraw." *Country Music*, March 1998.

Ploetz, Elmer. "Strait Puts Classic Finish on Jamboree." *Buffalo News*.

Ploetz, Elmer. "McGraw Trial Begins—Jury Election." *Buffalo News*, May 5, 2001.

Rodgers, Larry. "McGraw & Hill Concert Struggles to Live Up to the Hype." *Arizona Republic*, August 6, 2000.

Rodgers, Larry. "McGraw Gives Country-Rock with just Enough Twang." *Arizona Republic*, June 23, 2001.

Rodgers, Larry. "Just a Family Man: Tim McGraw's Priorities Are Faith and Kids." *Arizona Republic*, July 5, 2001.

Russell, Kristin. "Star Stats—Tim McGraw." *Country Weekly*, March 6, 2001.

Standen, Karyn. "Wal-Mart Stores Pipe in Faith Hill." *Ottawa Citizen*, November 9, 1999.

Spinelli, Nic. "Day of Country Music Pleases Crowd." *Jacksonville Times Union*. N/A.

Sytnick, Patrick. "McGraw in Major Leagues." *Edmonton Sun*, July 30, 1997.

Tarradell, Mario. "Faith Hill Moves Away from Country." *Dallas Morning News*.

Tester, John. "Hill, McGraw Concert Full of Soul." *Knoxville Daily Beacon*, September 8, 2000.

Tianen, Dave. "Country Sweetheart Hill Takes on Illiteracy." *Milwaukee Journal Sentinel*, April 9, 1999.

Van Wyk, Anika. "Gotta Have Faith." *Calgary Sun*, January 21, 1998.

Van Wyk, Anika. "Life's Good: McGraw Says His Family Could Be The Waltons." *Calgary Sun*, August 2, 1997.

Van Wyk, Anika. "McGraw Feared for Kids." *Calgary Sun*, June 17, 2000.

Wilker, Deborah. "Faith Hill Kissed by Success." *Knight Ridder Newspapers*.

Williams, Janet E. "Secrets of Her Success." *Country Song Roundup*, 1998.

Wolfe, Jean. "Keeping the Faith." *Redbook*, June 2000.

Yarborough, Chuck. "All Stars, All Country, Is All Right in Stadium." *Cleveland Plain Dealer*. ND.

Young, Lisa. "Tim McGraw Faith, Family & Fame. *Country Music Today*, December 2000.

## Other Sources

Anonymous. "Tim and Faith Soul 2 Soul: Technical Rider." *thesmokinggun.com*.

Anonymous. "All the Right Moves." *loveequine.com*.

Anonymous. "Faith Hill News & Past Faith Hill News." *country.tzo.com*.

Anonymous. "Country-Radio.Net Music News item 7/21/2000: Erie County Sheriff's Department Statement by Sheriff Patrick Gallivan." *southeastcountry.com*.

Anonymous. "Concert Review: Atlanta Soul 2 Soul Tour." *country.tzo.com*.

Anonymous. "Duets Redux." *mcgraws.com*.

Anonymous. "Rev: *Tim McGraw: A Mother's Story* by Betty Trimble." *amazon.com*.

Anonymous. "Faith Hill Band Members." *faithhill.com*.

Anonymous. "Faith and Tim in Paris." *mcgraws.com*.

Anonymous. "Dancehall Doctors—Band Members." *timmcgraw.com*.

Anonymous. "Faith Prevails." *mcgraws.com*.

Anonymous. "Latest Tim & Faith News." *country.tzo.com/public*.

Anonymous. "Dunbar Man Is in The Band: Drummer Returns Home with McGraw-Hill Tour. *mcgraws.com*.

Anonymous. "Tim McGraw News." *timmgraw.com*.

Anonymous. "Tim McGraw Takes Stardom in Stride." *mcgraws.com.*

Anonymous. "Things Change—But Questions Keep Coming." *mcgraws.com.*

Anonymous. Various promotional paragraphs including quotes made by Jo Dee Messina at *jodeemessina.com.*

Anonymous. "Media release: Faith Hill Literacy Project." *Faithhill.com.*

Anonymous. "Tim/Faith Latest News." *country.tzo.com.*

Anonymous. "Two for the Road: Messina and McGraw Are More than Alright." *bostonherald.com* and *McGraws.com.*

Anonymous. "Tim McGraw Celebrates Chart Topper 14." *McGraws.com*

Anonymous. "Faith Hill Milestones." *Faithhill.com.*

Anonymous. "Faith Hill Puts on Best Country Concert to Date." *mcgraws.com.*

Anonymous. "News & Reviews." *Faithhill.com.*

Anonymous. "Move Over Shania." *mcgraws.com.*

Anonymous. "A Country of Their Own: Tim and Faith Have Carved Out a Place in the Sun." *mcgraws.com.*

Anonymous. "Married Couple to Bring Their Soul 2 Soul Tour to Where Else? AllTel Arena." Review of Sept 26, 2000 show in Little Rock. *mcgraws.com.*

Anonymous. "Let's Make Music: Interview with Tim & Faith." *mcgraws.com*

Anonymous. "Faith & Determination." *mcgraws.com.*

Anonymous. "Faith Hill Breathe Bio." *wbr.com.*

Anonymous. "McGraw, Hill Kiss in the New Year." *mcgraws.com.*

Anonymous. "Not Guilty Verdict in the McGraw Trial." *mcgraws.com.*

Anonymous. "Whoville VH1 Interview with Faith Hill." *mcgraws.com.*

Anonymous. "Work Never Ends Behind Scenes of Tour." *mcgraws.com.*

Anonymous. "Tim McGraw Discography with R.I.A.A. Certified Stats." *countrymusic.about.com.*

Anonymous. "Top-selling Country Singer Tim McGraw Is a Reluctant Outlaw." *mcgraws.com.*

Anonymous. "Tug McGraw: The Early Years." *aol.com/densekelly.*

Anonymous. "A Selection of Tug McGraw Baseball Cards." *aol.com/densekelly.*

Anonymous. "A Duo of Desire: Tim McGraw and Faith Hill." *mcgraws.com.*

Anonymous. "Country Singers Claim Cop Fracas Left Lasting Damage." Sun wire services.

Anonymous. "As Faith Would Have It." *mcgraws.com.*

Anonymous. "McGraw Up and Around." *countrystars.com.*

Anonymous. "McGraw Undergoes Emergency Appendectomy." *countrystars.com.*

Anonymous. "Media Biography: Set This Circus Down." *timmcgraw.com.*

Anonymous. "Faith Hill: Down Home Diva." *mcgraws.com.*

Anonymous. "Faith Hill: Smile, Smile, Smile." *mcgraws.com.*

Anonymous. "Soul 2 Soul Tour 2000." July, August Newsletter." *faithhill.com.*

Anonymous. "Soul 2 Soul Tour 200 Fan Concert Reviews." *faithhill.com.*

Anonymous. "A Fan's Perspective." Oct/Nov/Dec 2000 Newsletter. *faithhill.com.*

Anonymous. "Faith's Sexy Three Day Rule." *Star Magazine* article posted at *loveequine.com.*

Anonymous. "Hill Wins Dispute with CMA." *mcgraws.com.*

Anonymous. "McGraw Officials Speak Out on Arrest." *mcgraws.com.*

Anonymous. "Soul 2 Soul Set Sail." *geocities.com.*

Anonymous. "Story Behind the Song: The Way You Love Me." *mcgraws.com.*

Anonymous. "Story Behind the Song: Breathe." *mcgraws.com.*

Anonymous. "Singing Sensation Faith Hill Is Cover Girl's Newest Face." PRNewswire, April 7, 1999.

Abernathy, Brooke Adaire. "Soul 2 Soul Tour Stamps Out all Competition— Nationwide Arena, Columbus, Ohio." *countryreview.com.*

Bumgardner, Ed. "Faith Hill Delivers." *loveequine.com.*

Bumgardner, Ed. "Act of Faith." *loveequine.com.*

DiLonardo, Mary Jo. "McGraw's Former Novelty Buys Place in the Sun." *CNN.com.*

DiLonardo, Mary Jo. "Two Stars, One Glow: Concert Review/Atlanta." *CNN.com.*

Dickinson, Chris. "On the Road with Tim McGraw, Faith Hill and Their Two Kids." *cmt.com.*

Evans, Rob. "Tim McGraw, Faith Hill to Follow Tour with Swampstock." *live daily Online@citysearch.com.*

Evans, Rob. "McGraw, Hill to Perform at Benefit for USS Cole Survivors." *live daily Online@citysearch.com.*

Evans, Bob. "New Dates, Seats Added to Faith Hill, Tim McGraw Co-bill." *livedaily@citysearch.com.*

Fan quotes found at *McGraws.com.*

Flippo, Chet. "McGraw Charged with Assaulting Police Officer. *cmt.com.*

Flippo, Chet. "McGraw Denies Assaulting Officer." *cmt.com.*

Flippo, Chet. "Felony Charge Dropped." *cmt.com.*

Flippo, Chet. "Tim McGraw Hits Number One." *cmt.com.*

Flippo, Chet. "Tim McGraw's Circus Is a True Big Top." *cmt.com.*

Flippo, Chet. "Tim McGraw's Circus Holds Top Album Spot." *cmt.com.*

Flippo, Chet. "McGraw, Hill Keep It in Family." *cmt.com.*

Flippo, Chet. "McGraw on Top of Country World." *cmt.com.*

Flippo, Chet. "McGraw Circus Under Big Tent." *cmt.com.*

Flippo, Chet. "Tim McGraw, Kenny Chesney Court Date Delayed. *Cmt.com.*

Hill, Faith. "Jan/Feb 2001 Newsletter to Fans." *Faithhill.com.*

Hill, Faith. "Oct/Nov/Dec 2000 Newsletter to Fans. *Faithhill.com.*

Hill, Faith. "Breathe cut by cut." *Faithhill.com.*

James, Alexa. "Hill, McGraw Renew Vows at Center." *collegian.psu.edu.*

Ladd, M.E. "Diana Ross & the Divas of Doom." *apeculture.com.*

McGraw, Tim. "Tim McGraw Chat May 8th, 2001 by AOL." *aol.com.*

McGraw, Tim. "Tim McGraw Chat August 20, 2000 by Bud Light and Excite." *mcgraws.com.*

McGraw, Tim. "Tim McGraw Chats before the 1999 ACM Awards." *mcgraws.com*.

McKenna, Dave. "Faith Hill's Contagious Joy." *loveequine.com*.

McKinion, Deanna. "Fan review Soul 2 Soul 2000." *goecities.com*.

Morris, Edward. "McGraw Assault Trial Gets Under Way." *cmt.com*.

O'Connell, Molly. "Country Croonin' McGraw." *Sesameworkshop.org*.

O'Connor, Christopher. "Tim McGraw Beats Back Phantom Menace." *cmt.com*.

Pasquale, Ron. "Deputy Describes McGraw's Alleged Attack." *cmt.com*.

Pasquale, Ron. "McGraw Trial Delayed by Judge's Heart Attack." *cmt.com*.

Pasquale, Ron. "McGraw's Legal Troubles Increase With Civil Suit." *cmt.com*.

Pasquale, Ron. "McGraw Testifies Deputies Assaulted Him." *cmt.com*.

Pasquale, Ron. "McGraw, Chesney Proud, Defiant in Court Win." *cmt.com*.

Ryan, Harriet. "McGraw's Trial Off and Running." *CourtTV.com*.

Reid, Dixie. "Top of the Hill." *loveequine.com*.

Roboff, Annie. "The Stories Behind The Hits." *geocities.com/aroboff/stories*.

Roboff, Annie. "Annie's Attic." *geocities.com/aroboff/annies_attic*.

Ryan, Harriet. "The Singers, the Deputies and a Horse." *CourtTV.com*.

Ryan, Harriet. "Presecution Rests on Weak, Contradictory Evidence against McGraw." *CokurtTV.com*.

Ryan, Harriet. "Horse Pilfering, Star Seeking, Songwriting: Another Day in the McGraw Trial." *CourtTV.com*.

Ryan, Harriet. "Country Stars' Horse Trial Is Big Deal in Small Town." *CourtTV.com*.

Ryan, Harriet. "Judge's Heart Attack Delays McGraw Case." *CourtTV.com*.

Ryan, Harriet. "Free to Roam: McGraw & Chesney Acquitted." *CourtTV.com*.

Sculps, Dave. "Interview with Faith Hill." *CountryNow.com*.

Silverman, Steven M. "McGraw Faces Music." *People.com*.

Silverman, Steven M. "McGraw Loses Appendix." *People.com*.

Silverman, Steven M. "McGraw, Chesney at Trial." *People.com*.

Wix, Kimmy. "Tim McGraw: Working Hard to Rest Easy." *country.com*, April 29 1999.

Zalaway, Jon. "McGraw & Chesney Arrested." *livedaily.com*, June 2000.

Zalaway, Jon. "McGraw & Hill Add Six New Tour Dates." *livedaily.com*.

# ACKNOWLEDGEMENTS

## Lyrics

*This Kiss.* By Beth Nielsen Chapman, Robin Lerner, Annie Roboff. Copyright 1997 Puckalesia Songs/Nomad=Noman Music/Warner Tamerlane Corp. (BMI)/ Alamo Music Corp./Anwa Music/BNC Songs (ASCAP).

*Down On The Farm.* By Kerry Kurt Phillips, Jerry Laseter. Copyright 1993 EMI Full Keel Music/Dreamworks Songs (ASCAP)/Songs of Dreamworks (BMI).

*Indian Outlaw.* By Tommy Barnes, Gene Simmons, John D. Loudermilk. Copyright Edge O' Woods Music/Taguchi Music(ASCAP)/Great Cumberland Music(BMI)/Acuff-Rose Music Inc. (BMI).

*Don't Take The Girl.* By Larry Johnson, Craig Martin. Copyright 1992 Sony/ATV Songs LLC dba Tree Publishing Company (BMI)/Warner-Tamerlane Publishing Corp. (BMI).

*Wild One.* By Jamie Kyle, Pat Bunch, Will Rambeaux. Copyright 1993 Warner Brothers Music Corp./Daniel The Dog Songs (ASCAP)/Warner Tamerlane Publishing Corp./Pat Bunch Publishing/ Reynsong Publishing Corp. (BMI).

*I Like It, I Love It.* By Steve Dukes, Jeb Stuart Anderson, Markus Hall. Copyright 1995 EMI Full Keel Music (BMI)/ Dreamworks Songs (ASCAP)/Lehsem Music LLC/Publishing Two's Music (ASCAP).

*All I Want Is A Life.* By Stan Munsey, Don Pfrimmer. G.I.D. Music Inc. (ASCAP), Royalhaven Music Inc., (BMI) 1995.

*Renegade.* By Jeff Stevens, Steve Bogard. Copyright 1995 Warner-Tamerlane Publishing Corp. (BMI)/Rancho Belita Music (BMI)/Jeff Stevens Music (BMI).

*It's Your Love.* By Stephony Smith. Copyright 1996 EMI Blackwood Music Inc. (ASCAP).

*Everywhere.* By Mike Reid, Craig Wiseman. Copyright 1997 Almo Music Corp./Daddy Rabbit Music/Brio Bros. Music (ASCAP).

*Where The Green Grass Grows.* By Jess Leary, Craig Wiseman. Copyright 1997 Song Matters Inc./Famous Music Corporation (ASCAP)/Almo Music Corp./ Daddy Rabbit Music (ASCAP).

*Please Remember Me.* By Rodney Crowell, Will Jennings. Copyright 1995 Sony/ATV Tunes LLC (ASCAP)/Blue Rider Songs (BMI).

*Something Like That.* By Rick Ferrell, Keith Follese. Copyright Mr Noise Music/We Make Music (BMI)/Music Of Windswept/ Follazoo Music (ASCAP).

*Let's Make Love.* By William Luther, Aimee Mayo, Marv Green, Chris Lindsey. Copyright 1999 Careers Music Publishing Inc. (BMI)/ Silverkiss Music Publishing (BMI)/Warner-Tamerlane Publishing Corp. (BMI)/Songs of Nashville Dreamworks (BMI).

*What's In It For Me.* By Billy Burnette, Bekka Bramlett, Annie Roboff. Copyright 1999 Irving Music Inc./Beau Billy Songs/ Miss Ivy Music (BMI)/Almo Music Corp./ Anwa Music (ASCAP).

*Love Is A Sweet Thing.* By Brett James, Troy Verges. Copyright 1999 Sony ATV Songs LLC dba Tree Publishing Co./Songs of Terrace/Songs of Universal, Inc. (ASCAP).

*Breathe.* By Holly Lamar, Stephanie Bentley. Copyright 1999 Cal IV Songs (ASCAP)/Universal Songs of Polygram International Inc./Hope Chest Music (BMI).

*Bringing Out The Elvis*. By Leif Larsson, Louise Hoffsten. Copyright 1997 BMG Music Publishing Scandanavia AB/Larson Music (ASCAP).

*If My Heart Had Wings*. By Annie Roboff, J. Fred Knobloch. Copyright 1999 Almo Music Inc./Anwa Music/J.Fred Knobloch Music (ASCAP).

*The Cowboy In Me*. By Craig Wiseman, Jeffrey Steele, Al Anderson. Copyright 2001 BMG Songs Inc./Mrs Lumpkins Noodle (ASCAP)/Songs of Windswept Music/Stairway to Bittners Music (BMI).

*Things Change*. By Amiee Mayo, Bill Luther, Chris Lindsey, Marv Green. Copyright 2001 Careers BMG Music Publishing Inc./Silverkiss Music Publishers (BMI)/Monkey Feel Music/Nashville Dreamworks Songs (ASCAP).

*Set This Circus Down*. By Bill Luther, Josh Kear. Copyright 2001 BMG Songs Inc./ Tennessee Ridgerunner (ASCAP)/Careers BMG Publishing (BMI).

*Grown Men Don't Cry*. By Steve Seskin, Tom Douglas. Copyright 2001 Larga Vista Music/Scarlet Rain Music (ASCAP)/ SONY ATV Songs LLC.

## Photos

p. 2:   Ron Galella/Corbis Sygma/Magma

p. 6:   Frank Trapper/Corbis Sygma/ Magma

**Color Insert:**

p. 73:  Fred Prouser, Reuters NewMedia Inc/Corbis/Magma

p. 74:  Neal Preston/Corbis/Magma

p. 75:  Matthew Mendolsohn/Corbis/ Magma

p. 76:  Rose Prouser,/Reuters NewMedia Inc/Corbis/Magma

p. 77:  Tami Chappell/Reuters NewMedia Inc/Corbis/Magma

p. 78:  Ethan Miller/Reuters NewMedia Inc/Corbis/Magma

p. 79:  Tami Chappell/Reuters NewMedia Inc/Corbis/Magma

p. 80:  Sam Mircovich/Reuters NewMedia Inc/Corbis/Magma